Barb Wagner

Blue River Press
Indianapolis

*Longhorn Lingo* © 2008 Barb Wagner

All rights reserved under International and Pan-American Copyright Conventions

No part of this book may be reproduced, stored in a database or other retrieval system, or transmitted in any form, by any means, including mechanical, photocopy, recording or otherwise, without the prior written permission of the publisher.

Cover designed by Phil Velikan
Author photo taken by Vicki Seal
 www.sealthemoment.com
Cartoon illustrations by Harold A. Duckett
www.cartoonmonster.tv
Packaged by Wish Publishing
Research Assistant: Kent A. Wagner

Printed in the United States of America
10 9 8 7 6 5 4 3 2 1

Distributed in the United States by
Cardinal Publishers Group
www.cardinalpub.com

*To Kent, my husband and best friend, for sharing your passion, dedication and love.*

*To Dylan and Austin, my two very special sons, for giving me the space, the love and the reason to do this.*

To Sandy!

"Hookem Horns"!

LingoLady.com

# Table of CONTENTS

| | |
|---|---|
| Acknowledgements | 7 |
| Preface | 11 |
| Introduction | 15 |
| Important Message | 17 |
| chapter 1. The History of American Football | 19 |
| chapter 2. Football: The Game | 21 |
| chapter 3. Players and Positions | 25 |
| chapter 4. Longhorn Lingo | 29 |
| chapter 5. Longhorn Season Stats, 1997-2007 | 95 |
| chapter 6. Memorable Longhorns | 107 |
| chapter 7. The Football Lingo Trivia Quiz | 115 |
| chapter 8. House & Tailgate Party Suggestions | 121 |
| chapter 9. Jokes | 145 |
| About the Author | 153 |

# Acknowledgements

**This book began** as a question: "What the heck did that mean?" The question would not be in play if my two sons, Dylan and Austin, never played the wonderful sport of hockey.

A special thanks goes to my spectacular and most incredible husband, Kent Wagner, who has played sports his entire life and has helped me become a loyal fan. Although you thoroughly enjoy conducting stats and research for all of my books, I cannot thank you enough for taking vacation time from your work to help me with this book. This book wouldn't be so complete if it weren't for you. Thank you for being that sport guru that I complained about 18 years ago when I met you!

I also would like to thank my two remarkable boys, Dylan and Austin for their remarkable support and patience. Thank you for being so understanding when there were times I had to let you down. That was a major contribution that you both made on your own accord. Mommy will make it up to you one day.

Mom (Bev MacLean), thank you for encouraging me to always follow my dreams. Also thank you for telling me, on more than a few occasions during my life, how proud you were of me.

Brooks Wagner, my caring nephew, I would like to thank you for taking time out of your busy schedule to help me make my dreams come true.

I would like to thank Luis Goncalves, my life coach, for inspiring me to become a leader within myself. Luis, thank you for believing whole- heartedly in me. I saw it many times in your eyes and on your face; I heard it many times in your voice and through your words. Those moments will last a lifetime within me. Thank you from the bottom of my heart.

Bob Groza, thank you for being a special and devoted friend. You were the only person to ever inspire me to become an author. Thank you, thank you, thank you!!

Steve Shaw, thank you for being a magnificent hockey coach to my son Dylan. I don't know if this book would ever be in play if it weren't for your asking my son to "pick up the puck" that particular day.

Rob McKnight, thank you for being a wonderful friend who sat many times in the kitchen throwing different terms at me to add to my books.

Julie Couture, thank you for being one of my best friends for over 18 years. Your constant praise along with your inspiring words kept me grounded and eager to obtain my goal.

Thank you Scott Wagner, my wonderful brother-in-law and mentor. Thank you for keeping me grounded and for being there when I needed some sound advice.

Thank you Lise Wagner, my special sister-in-law whom I cherish like a sister, for extending your shoulder to me when I, at times, felt a little overwhelmed.

Thank you Frank Sicoli, a loyal friend who always made sure I was on the right track. Thank you for the many laughs you gave me. Honestly, I don't think I ever laughed so much in my life.

A huge thank you goes out to Laura Canada and her beautiful family. I can't thank you enough for welcoming us to Texas the way you have. The Southern hospitality from you and your families has been more than appreciated. Thank you for making Texas feel like home.

Thank you Harold Duckett, my dedicated cartoonist, for being able to put humor and fun into learning the lingo associated with the game and for being flexible with my last-minute requests.

I would like to thank Tom Bast for referring me to Tom Doherty. And a heart-warming thanks goes to Tom Doherty, my publisher, for believing in my projects and having a vision when 118 other publishers didn't. You truly are the best!!

I would like to thank you, the dedicated fan, for reading this book. If it weren't for you, this book wouldn't even be thought of. (Big Hug.)

In truth, so many people have contributed extensively to this book, considering that somewhere, and somehow, they have created the lingo that will stay with us even as more unique sayings are created as time goes by.

Finally, I am most grateful and thankful to my only father, the Lord, my God. I had 118 good reasons to give up and quit but He put a dream in my heart and a promise inside of it. That's what kept me going. Joel Osteen, thank you for sharing this with me.

was quite funny. He in fact 'picked up the puck' with his hand and gave it to me." I replied with, "I noticed he was a little slow because he had his gloves on. Hopefully next time he'll take them off sooner when he picks up the puck." Coach Steve's smile slowly left his face, he nodded slowly and said, "Sure."

Once I got home, I emailed Kent explaining what had occurred during practice. I conveyed to him how baffled I was. Kent immediately responded with, "Please don't speak to anyone else about hockey until I come home!"

That lone experience was just the beginning of my being taken back by the game of hockey and its lingo. While sitting in the stands listening to the spectators yelling, "Hey…look out for the cherry picker over there," I wasted far too much time actually looking for one. The broadcasters, if the truth be told, really played a number on me with comments like, "Beat him like Grandma does an old throw rug" as well as "He put it on the top shelf where Grandma keeps the peanut butter." What the heck did that mean? I frequently found myself coming across more colorful language associated with all sports, not just hockey.

Once the hockey season ended and we started playing golf again, it happened again. It was 'ladies night' at St. Mary's Golf and Country Club, and I was playing with one of the course managers, Karen. Karen hit her tee shot on the first hole and hit the ball far to the left. She turned to me and asked, "Would you mind if I had a mulligan?" She then stated, "If you'd like, we can both have one." I replied, "Sure, it's hot outside today and I could really go for one right about now," not really knowing what a mulligan was. We finished all 18 holes, and I wondered to myself why I never did get that 'mulligan' that Karen had talked about.

When I arrived home later that evening, I told Kent what a good time I had but was a little disappointed that I didn't get to try the special drink that Karen was talking about. He asked what kind of drink I was referring to. I told him it was called a 'mulligan.' I added that we should order one next time we played golf, seeing as other people were talking about it as well. Kent's head went down in what I expected to be disgust. I knew I was in for another lesson, and it was time to get out my pen and paper.

Our family moved from Ontario, Canada, to Cypress, Texas, and in no time learned that football was a very popular sport in Texas, almost like hockey was to Canadians. Our neighbors, who are die-hard fans for the 'other Texas team,' have their 5-year-old son Ryan playing football. One night, Kent and I were outside talking to Ryan before his first big game, when Kent unexpectedly said, "Hey, Ryan, did your coach teach you how to do a clothes line?" I commented, "Why would a coach teach five-year-old boys to hang their own uniforms on the clothesline?" Once again, I got the look from Kent and thought to myself, Barb, better go get the pen and paper.

I had additional moments when my youngest son, Austin, played baseball for one of the most amazing baseball coaches around, Tom Valcke, who is the president/CEO for Canada's Baseball Hall of Fame.

I now realize that I'm not alone in misunderstanding what some of these terms mean. Whether you're a pro of a particular sport or a dedicated fan, we all started off as newbies and at one time or another, we've all thought to ourselves, What the heck did that mean?

As you can well imagine, some of my greatest memories as a devoted wife and parent were learning about the game. The truth of the matter is, sports lingo and jargon have always been around and will always be a part of each game, even in the years to come.

Knowledge is power, and I am so grateful to have found a way to share my knowledge in a fun and enjoyable way. My goal is to pass on to all beginners of a sport, *"the power,"* by understanding the colorful language associated with each sport that they decide to be a part of.

Cheers to the game!
*Barb Wagner*

# Introduction

**After moving from** Toronto, Ontario, Canada, to beautiful Cypress, Texas, in June 2007, within a very short time one thing became very apparent to my family and me: the pride Longhorns fans have for their team.

When Coach Brown hired Oscar Giles to be his assistant coach/defensive ends in 2005, on Oscar's first day on the job, he made a list of goals. Number one was to help Texas win a national championship. Number two was to help kids graduate from the university. Number three, he wanted kids to be better sons and better fathers. Oscar's duty was to teach kids the pride and tradition of this program, not only while they were there but once they left. I have since learned that Oscar was not alone with these goals. Mack Brown and Darrell Royal, along with many other spectacular coaches and teachers, all wanted the same, if not more for their students.

*What it Means to be a Longhorn* is a book I recently read that was full of personal memories of 70 or so former Longhorn football players. Each story is its own, yet I discovered that everyone associated with the game or with the university had one thing in common, and that was pride.

Though their stories differ from one to another, Ricky Williams, Longhorns star running back in 1995-1998 truly summed it up when he quoted in the book, "It's about pride. It's about taking pride in what you do, pride in who you are, and taking pride in how you handle yourself. It is something that I will always cherish, and something that no one can take away from me."

something that I will always cherish, and something that no one can take away from me."

After completing my research, I wasn't the least bit surprised to find out why all former players, along with current players and students of U of T, were all full of pride. Since my research, I now have a sense of pride to be living in Texas, one of Americas largest, most beautiful and successful states. I take pride associating myself with so many incredible, dedicated and loyal Longhorns fans. I am very excited and proud to be writing this Longhorn Lingo book, which will be the first of many books to be written for my sports lingo series. This book comes at a perfect time for Texas because Longhorn football has never been more popular.

Part of what makes college football such an entertaining sport is the colorful language associated with the game. I wrote this book for those who are new to the sport and for those dedicated Longhorn fans who want to gain knowledge or be entertained. Whether you want to learn about the commonly used lingo/jargon used in the game, plan a football or tailgate party, test your friends or your own knowledge with some great trivia quizzes and Longhorn stats, this book is loaded with valuable, informative information that is simple and easy to understand for everyone.

College football, especially when you're watching the Longhorns, is an exciting time for all. But let's be honest: Being a football fan is fun but at times maybe a little difficult to understand. We all started off with "what the heck did that mean?" at one time or another, but as you start understanding the terms associated with the game, you soon begin to create an appreciation for the sport. I certainly did!

Hookem Horns!

## IMPORTANT MESSAGE

Kerry Shook, an incredible minister in the Woodlands area said during his "Live Boldly" lesson, "There are two types of people in the world: givers and takers. No one ever remembers what they take out of life; we're only remembered for what we give back in life."

My contribution is to give a generous donation to the schools that allow me to do a book signing for them. This contribution can go toward their reading and/or sports program.

Together, we can make a difference!
www.lingolady.com

duced it to the North Americans. The game later evolved into two separate leagues: the American Football League and the Canadian Football League.

The ball used back in the 1800s was nothing more than a pig's bladder. Yuk! I can't even imagine fighting over that ball…ooohhh wait a minute... is that why they called it a pigskin? Now that makes sense! Fortunately, today most footballs are made of cattle hides or synthetic materials.

The design of the football has changed over the years. Its current oval shape is geared to make the ball difficult to catch and hold. The shape also creates an unpredictable bounce, which adds more challenge to the game. Gripping the ball was once an issue, so white laces were sewn on the ball's surface. It seems that there have been many attempts to alter the football's design; for example, dimples on footballs have been attempted, but there was a tendency for dirt and mud to get caught in them.

In the early days, football was known as a "mob game." There was an unlimited number of players on the field, and the rules were fairly vague. In 1905, 19 fatalities nationwide were reported. That's when President Theodore Roosevelt threatened to shut the game down unless drastic changes were made.

Changes were made, and the less-violent version of the sport has certainly flourished in North America and the world. As an example, the NFL's championship game, the "Super Bowl," broadcasts to more than 150 countries! And no where is the sport quite as popular as the great state of Texas.

The University of Texas has an absolutely amazing stadium which holds approximately 83,000 spectators. It is in the process of being renovated, and when the renovations are completed the stadium will hold over 95,000. That kind of crowd was a bit of a shock to me — I grew up in Canada about 20 minutes away from Hamilton, Ontario. I once attended a CFL Hamilton TigerCats football game at the Ivor Wynne Stadium, which seats about 34,000 fans. That's right…34,000. For one second try and imagine my face when I saw a full crowd at the UT. Ya….

# Chapter 2
# FOOTBALL: THE GAME

If you're someone like me who did not grow up watching football, then you'll probably find it to be a very complicated sport. Between strategies, positions, plays and penalties, I'm not surprised anyone finds it confusing!

Fortunately, my husband sat me down and went over "Football Basics 101" when we first moved to Texas, and now I can help you too! Here are a few questions (and answers) that will help you understand the basics of this great sport.

> Before any game, regardless the sport, my husband would always test me in the car ride there. I don't know if it would have anything to do with me blurting out, "Hey... where are the goalies?" at our first football game or... "Why the heck did that umpire throw a flag on the field?"

**Q: What is the object of the game?**
**A:** Two teams compete to score points by moving a ball into the end zones of their opponents.

**Q: How is this done?**
**A:** This can be done by passing the ball from one player outside the end zone to another player who's inside, running the ball from the playing field into the end zone or sometimes kicking the ball through an end zone's goal posts.

Longhorn Lingo

Q: How many players are on each team?
A: Each team has 11 players on the field. If you're playing for fun, you can play with eight or fewer participants.

Q: What is the name of the team that has the ball?
A: The team with the ball at any given time is called the offense. The other team, which has to try to stop the offensive advance and "defend" its end zone, is called the defense.

Q: How are points scored?
A: Points are scored in the following manner:
1) touchdown (ball is run into the end zone) = 6 points
2) field goal (ball is kicked between the goal posts) = 3 points
3) safety (ball is run into the end zone after a touch down) = 2 points
4) point(s) after touchdown (ball is kicked between the goal posts after a touchdown) = 1 point

Q: Who throws the ball?
A: The quarterback passes the ball. The person who catches the ball is the receiver. When the ball is caught, the receiver tries to run toward the end zone. The receiver will run until he is tackled or forced out of bounds.

Q: What happens when the receiver is tackled or forced out of bounds?
A: When this happens, it is called the new line of scrimmage and is the starting point for the next play. If the ball has traveled 10 yards from the last line of scrimmage, a first down has occurred.

**Q:** What are a "down" and a "first down"?

**A:** The players only have four attempts to move the ball 10 yards. Each of these four attempts is called a down. If they don't make it to the mark on the first try, then they have a 2nd down (they might call it "2nd and 10," meaning it's the 2nd down and they have 10 yards to go before they reach the next mark). If they don't make it on the 2nd down, then they go to a 3rd down, etc. If it gets to a 4th down and they still don't make it to the mark, then the ball is turned over to the other team's possession. If they successfully move the ball 10 yards or more, they get to go back to first down.

**Q:** Why is a first down so important?

**A:** Because the team now is entitled to have four more attempts (downs) to get another first down. As long as they keep getting first downs, they stay in possession of the ball and advance the ball toward the other team's end zone in an attempt to score.

**Q:** What is an interception?

**A:** An interception occurs when the quarterback passes the ball toward his receiver and is caught by the other team. The team that "intercepted" the ball will then gain possession of the ball.

**Q:** What is a touchdown?

**A:** A touchdown occurs when the ball is caught by a player in the end zone or run into the end zone by a player. Six points are scored.

**Q:** Is there an extra point after a touchdown?

**A:** Yes, one extra point can be scored if the kicker can kick the ball through the goal posts. Two points can be scored if the offensive team runs or throws the ball (and it is caught) into the end zone.

Longhorn Lingo

**Q: Why are penalties so bad?**
**A:** In football, the goal is to achieve yards toward the opponent's end zone. Penalties punish teams by taking away yards that they earned. If the penalty is against the defense, the offensive team can be rewarded with additional yards.

**Q: What is a field goal?**
**A:** A field goal earns three points for the offensive team and is scored when the kicker kicks the ball through the goal posts. This is not in conjunction with a touchdown. What happens is that, in many cases, the team is close to the opponent's end zone but is having trouble getting a first down. Rather than risking losing the ball to the opposition (since they are having difficulty obtaining a first down), they make a field goal attempt. They may be 30, 40 or even more yards away from the goal posts when they attempt a field goal.

**Q: Why do teams punt?**
**A:** If a team is having difficulty obtaining a first down, and they are too far from the goal posts to kick a field goal, they will punt the ball toward the opponent's end zone. They have to give possession to the opposing team, but they do not want the other team to have good field position. By punting the ball, it forces the other team to travel farther in their attempt to score a touchdown.

Understanding the basics of football is the first step toward a life-long appreciation for the sport (and toward being allowed to stay in the room during the game...).

# Chapter Three
# PLAYERS AND POSITIONS

The players and positions can be very confusing, so what I've decided to do is practice the K.I.S.S. (Keeping It Simple for the Student) format. We all know that there are exceptions to almost every rule, but when it comes to football, there are a ton– far too many to mention in this short book– so this chapter will cover only the bare basics for you. Good luck!

> If I was ever to play football, I would want to be the running back. As soon as I saw those big goons coming after me, I'd be "running back" to the bench; unless it was Jesse James Palmer. That is one tackle I would definitely take for the team!!!!

The first thing you need to know is that each team has 11 players on the field at one time. The team that has the ball is considered to be the offensive team, and the other team is considered to be the defensive team.

## The Offensive Team

The offensive team is the team that begins a play from scrimmage and has possession of the ball.

Center (C) — This offensive lineman hikes or snaps (or in my term, throws the ball through his legs) to the quarterback at the start of each play. After snapping the football, the center must be ready to block the defensive linemen.

Offensive guard (OG) — The two guards are the offensive linemen directly on either side of the center and inside the tackles.

Offensive tackle (OT) — The offensive tackles play on the outside of the guards.

Tight end (TE) — Tight ends play on either side of, and roughly next to, the tackles.

Wide receiver (WR) — The wide receivers are speedy pass-catching specialists. Their main job is to run pass routes and get open for a pass.

Fullback (FB) — A fullback is positioned behind the middle of the line. They may do some running, some blocking, and some short receiving.

Running back (RB) — The running back carries the ball on most running plays and is also frequently used as a short-yardage receiver.

Tailback (TB) — This running back is positioned behind the middle of the line and deepest of all backs.

Slotback (SB) — A player positioned just outside the outermost offensive lineman, the slotback is slightly offset from the line of scrimmage which designates the position as a slotback rather than a tight end.

H-back (HB) — An H-back (halfback) lines up similarly to a slotback, but in a deeper position and not as wide, and frequently serves as a blocker for a more deeply positioned back.

Wingback (WB) — This player is positioned just outside the outermost tight end. The wingback is slightly offset from the line of scrimmage which designates the position as wingback rather than tight end.

Quarterback (QB) — Typically the quarterback is positioned to take a snap handed between the center's legs. The quarterback also calls the plays and runs the team's offense from the field.

## Defense

The defensive team or defense is the team that begins a play from scrimmage not in possession of the ball. The object of the defensive team is to prevent the other team from scoring.

- Defensive end (DE) — The two defensive ends play on opposite outside edges of the defensive line.
- Defensive tackle (DT) — Sometimes called a defensive guard. The defensive tackles are side-by-side linemen who are between the defensive ends.
- Linebacker (LB) — This player lines up behind the defensive linemen and in front of the defensive backfield. The linebackers are a team's second line of defense.
- Cornerback (CB) — Typically these two players primarily cover the wide receivers. Cornerbacks, also known as defensive backs, will attempt to prevent successful quarterback passes by either swatting the airborne ball away from the receiver or by catching the pass themselves.
- Safety (FS or SS) — The safeties are the last line of defense (farthest from the line of scrimmage) and usually help the corners with deep-pass coverage.

  The free safety (FS) is usually the smaller and faster of the two, providing variable and extra pass coverage.

  The strong safety (SS) is usually the larger and stronger of the two, providing extra protection against run plays by standing somewhere between the free safety and the line of scrimmage.
- Defensive back — It is not a specific position; however, it is any position besides the line, including cornerbacks, safeties, etc., that is behind the line of scrimmage.
- Nickelback and Dimeback — Teams normally use four defensive backs. When adding a fifth defensive

back to the game, he is called a nickelback. When adding a sixth defensive back to the game, he is referred to as the dimeback.

Not that I want to complicate things any more than they already might be, but a team also has the following:

## Special teams

The units of players who handle kicking plays are known as special teams. Three important special-team players are:

1) The punter, who handles punts.
2) The place-kicker or kicker, who kicks off and attempts field goals and extra points
3) The long snapper, usually the center, who snaps the ball for punts and field goal attempts.

Also included on special teams are the returners. These players return punts or kickoffs and try to get in good field position.

*Hook'em Horns!*

# Chapter Four
# LONGHORN LINGO

There is nothing more frustrating than being with someone who throws around football lingo that you don't understand and that makes you think, "What the heck did that mean?" So I've provided this handy dictionary for your use. To make things simple, I've alphabetized the lingo for your easy referral.

## –A–

### Air Raid

An offensive philosophy where the offensive team's running game is nearly non-existent. The offense will run a series of short passes, medium passes and long passes and will bombard the defense with a variety of pass plays.

### Artificial Turf

A synthetic surface that is used in place of grass on some

If you are reading a definition for a particular word, and another word pops up that doesn't make sense, do a quick search in this directory for the other unknown word. Putting all of the words and definitions together will make it easier for you to understand. If you still don't understand what you are reading — because I know some of the lingo definitions can be somewhat confusing — try and get someone to break it down in more simple terms for you. Or you could do what I do: just pretend that you understand. It always works for me!

football and baseball fields. It is also known as Astroturf. Darrell K. Royal-Texas Memorial Stadium is currently a grass stadium and does not have artificial turf.

## Astroturf

See Artificial Turf.

## Assistant Coach

This is a specialized coach who is directly under the supervision of the head coach. They are also known as co-ordinators. Each college football team generally has assistant coaches for offense and defense, as well as for more specialized areas like quarterbacks and linebackers. For example Greg Davis is the offensive coordinator/quarterbacks coach and Mac McWhorter is the associate head coach for the offensive line at UT.

## Auction

Used in place of a draft in leagues that have a salary cap. Instead of taking turns drafting players, teams bid on players. The highest bidder gets the rights to that player.

## Audible

This is a play that is called by the quarterback at the line of scrimmage to make a change from the play that was called in the huddle. When you hear the quarterback shout from side to side, this is so he can be certain that all the players hear the change. My husband indicated that I am quite audible at times...whatever that means.

## Automatic

This is changing a play by calling out a predetermined set of signals, usually done by the quarterback when he doesn't like the play at the line of scrimmage. Same as "audible."

## Automatic First Down

This is awarded to a team after a specific penalty is called against its opponent. Personal fouls such as roughing the kicker or flagrant face masking penalties will result in an automatic first down.

# –B–

## Back

This is a position that is behind the offensive and defensive linemen. Offensively, the back is used primarily for running plays: running back, tailback, quarterbacks, halfback, fullbacks and wingback. Defensively, the backs are generally faster players with some or all responsibility to cover receivers: linebackers, cornerbacks and safeties. Ricky Williams was a record-setting running back while at the University of Texas. Ricky set the NCAA record for career rushing yards during his time at Texas. He also won the Heisman Trophy in 1998 as the most outstanding player in collegiate football.

## Back Judge

The official who sets up 20 yards deep in the defensive backfield on the wide receiver side of the field. His duties vary from watching clipping on kick returns to standing under the goalpost to ruling on whether a kick is good or not.

## Backfield

The group of players on offense who are lined up behind the line of scrimmage. The term is also used to refer to the area of the field behind the linemen. Note: The quarterback and the running backs line up in the backfield.

## Backup

This person is a second-string player who does not start the game. They are used primarily to relieve a starter.

## Balanced Line

An arrangement that consists of an equal number of linemen on either side of the center. A common arrangement would be end-guard-tackle-center-tackle-guard-end.

### Ball

Well, obviously, by "ball" we mean the football that is used in the game. However, there are regulations about the size and shape of the ball. It must weigh no more than 14 to 15 ounces and be a natural tan color. It also must be inflated to a pressure of between 12½ to 13½ pounds per square inch.

### Ball Carrier

The player who attempts to advance the ball during a rushing play. It can be any player who has possession of the ball. Vince Young (UT, 2003-2005) was an exhilarating ball carrier as a quarterback and finished as "runner-up" to the Heisman Trophy winner in 2005, the year the Longhorns won the national championship.

### Ball Security

During a play, the player maintains control over the football while avoiding a fumble.

### Beat

Whether you have the football or not, you beat a player if you get past the opponent who is attempting to tackle you. Getting beat on a constant basis could cost the player in the starting lineup his job.

### Bench Players

The players that are not in the team's starting lineup. These players are referred to as second-string players.

### Bird Cage

The facemask that is worn by football players.

### Blackout

When a game is not sold out, the regional television network is forbidden from showing a local game on TV.

## Blind Side

If the quarterback is only looking to the right, he will be blindsided from the left side, which means he couldn't see the defender approaching. This can be a very dangerous play for the quarterback.

## Blitz

The blitz is a defensive plot in which one or more linebackers or defensive backs charge into the opponent's backfield. Normally these guys remain behind the line of scrimmage.

## Block

When a player pushes or obstructs an opponent in an attempt to keep him from getting to a specific part of the field or to a player. Fans also talk about blocking, which is when a player uses his body to obstruct another player's path. Examples of this include: cut block, zone block, trap block, pull block, screen block, pass block, double-team block.

## Bomb

When a deep and long pass is thrown to a receiver who is running down the field. This can also be referred to as "going deep." Roy Williams (UT, 2000-2003), now a member of the NFL's Detroit Lions, was the recipient of many "bombs" in his day as a wide receiver with the Longhorns.

## Bootleg

An offensive play which implies misdirection. The quarterback pretends to hand the ball to another player and then carries the ball in the opposite direction of the supposed ball carrier with the intent of either passing or running.

## Bowl Game

This is a college football game which is played after the regular season. The game is played in late December or early January between two successful teams. The term

Longhorn Lingo

"bowl" originated from the Rose Bowl Stadium. In college football, bowl games are played instead of using a playoff system like the NFL. The Longhorns rank second in NCAA bowl appearances with 47 and have an overall record of 24-21-2. Only Alabama has more appearances at 54.

## Bump-and-Run

A play where the pass defender will hit the defender within five yards (one yard in college) of the line of scrimmage. This is done to slow him down and hopefully to prevent the player from catching a pass. In order to slow the receiver coming off the line of scrimmage, the cornerbacks will often use bump-and-run coverage.

## Bust

This refers to a player whose team has very high expectations of them, but the player never lives up to his potential.

## Buttonhook

The buttonhook route is when a receiver runs a certain distance straight down the field, stops hard and runs straight back toward the quarterback. It can also be called a hook route or a dig route.

–C–

## Carry

A statistic referring to the number of times a rushing player (in any position) attempts to advance the ball during an offensive play.

## Call a Play

Instruct any player to carry out a pre-planned play from a coach. This is usually done by the head coach (Mack Brown) or the offensive coordinator (Greg Davis). It is known that some quarterbacks in the NFL call their own plays.

## Center

An offensive player position. The center generally snaps the football. After snapping the football, he has to be ready to block the defensive linemen. Dallas Griffin was an outstanding center for UT and claimed the coveted Draddy Trophy in 2007. The trophy, often referred to as the Academic Heisman, recognizes an individual as the absolute best in the country for his academic success, football performance and exemplary community leadership.

## Checkdown

A checkdown pass is when the quarterback is required to complete a short pass to a running back or tight end. This is a desperation pass to avoid a sack.

## Chop Block

This is a block below the knees, which can be dangerous and cause career-ending knee injuries. Many offensive linemen frequently try to cut defensive linemen down by using chop blocks.

## Clipping

This is an illegal block in which a player hits an opponent from behind, below the waist, typically at leg level. Clipping is a foul that results in a 15-yard penalty.

## Clothesline

An illegal and dangerous play in which a player strikes an opponent across the face or neck with an extended arm. The penalty for a clothesline is 15 yards.

Clothesline

## Coffin Corner

The corner of the field of play where the sideline and goal line meet. A punter often tries to kick the ball out of bounds near a cof-

Longhorn Lingo

fin corner to stop the other team from returning the ball and to pin them back near their goal line.

### Coin Toss

Before a game, the team captains meet in the middle of the field to flip a coin. The team that wins the coin toss has the choice of kicking off or receiving the kick. The losing team chooses which goal they would like to defend.

### Complete Pass

When the receiver catches the ball before it hits the ground. The receiver must have full control of the ball in order for it to be considered a complete pass. A quarterback is rated by the number of complete passes he has thrown against his number of attempted passes.

### Completion

Refers to a complete pass which is caught by an eligible receiver on the offensive team. In the NFL, the receiver has to have possession and control of the football with both feet inbounds. In college football, the receiver has to have only one foot inbounds.

### Conferences

Groupings into which the teams are divided. The NFL is divided into National and American Conferences. The Texas Longhorns compete in the Big 12 conference along with Baylor, Colorado, Iowa State, Kansas, Kansas State, Missouri, Nebraska, Oklahoma, Oklahoma State, Texas A&M and Texas Tech. College football has a number of conferences.

### Controlling the Game Clock

The offensive team uses this strategy to either save or use up time on the game clock, which often dictates its choice of plays. Controlling the clock is especially significant during the end of the half or the end of the game.

## Cornerback

This is a defensive back who lines up near the line of scrimmage and across from a wide receiver. They are also referred to as a "corner" or "defensive back." Nathan Vasher (UT, 2000-2003) was an explosive cornerback who was drafted in the fourth round of the NFL draft by the Chicago Bears and played in Superbowl XLI against the Indianapolis Colts.

## Count

This refers to the numbers that a quarterback will shout loudly on the line of scrimmage while waiting for the ball to be snapped. This is also referred to as the "snap count." The quarterback uses a long count every now and then in the hope of drawing the defense offside. Should this happen, it will result in a five-yard penalty.

## Counter

A play in which most blockers move in one direction while the running back with the ball moves in the opposite direction.

## Cover

Refers to defending a position, player or location on the field. Each defender, on each play, is assigned to guard a player or area of the field.

## Coverage

The type of play a team uses to prevent the opposing team from advancing the football. The individual type of coverage can be called out in the defensive huddle before each play. Some coverage options are man to man, others are zone-type plays. My husband says that his only concern is how much long-distance coverage I have for calling my friends.

## Crackback Block

An illegal block delivered below the opponent's waist by an offensive player who had left the area of close line play and then returned to it, or was not within it at the snap. The term is also used to describe a legal block (delivered from the front or from the side with the offensive player's helmet in front of the blocked player) by a wide receiver.

## Curl

A receiver runs downfield and quickly turns back to run toward the original line of scrimmage. This is a hard route to defend.

## Cut

This is when a running player makes a sharp change of direction.

## Cut Blocking

A type of blocking that offensive linemen, and on occasion other blockers, use legally below the waist in an attempt to bring the defenders to the ground. Cut blocking is, to some extent, controversial, as it runs the risk of major leg injuries to the blocked defenders.

# –D–

## Dead Ball

When the ball is not in play.

## Defensive Team

The team not in possession of the ball when they begin at the line of scrimmage. Their job is to keep the opposition out of their end zone.

## Defensive Back

A cornerback or safety position on the defensive team; commonly defends against wide receivers on passing plays.

Generally there are four defensive backs playing at a time. A good group of defensive backs can shut down an opponent's passing game and force them to run the ball more. Quentin Jammer (UT, 1997-2001) has quietly become one of the NFL's shutdown cornerbacks. Quentin signed a six-year deal with the San Diego Chargers in 2002 after graduating.

## Defensive Backfield

This is the area of the field behind the defensive linemen that is defended by the defensive backs.

## Defensive End

This is a defensive player position that lines up on the outside of the defensive line. Their job is to deliver pressure to the quarterback. Tim Crowder (UT, 2003-2006) had a brilliant college career recording 190 tackles, 19 sacks, 76 pressures, 14 PBD, two INT's, eight forced fumbles and two fumble recoveries in 51 career games with the Longhorns. Crowder is now a member of the NFL's Denver Broncos.

## Defensive Holding

This is when a player uses his hands to stop an offensive player from catching the ball during a passing play or obstructs the player past the first yard from the line of scrimmage. This is also known as "Illegal Use of the Hands." Defensive holding will result in a five-yard penalty on the offending team and an automatic first down.

## Defensive Line

These are the defensive players who line up on the line of scrimmage opposite the offensive linemen. I'm sure you've noticed that the defensive lines are usually made up of the biggest defensive players, including defensive ends and tackles. The Longhorns defensive line played an integral part in their 2007 Holiday Bowl win over Arizona State by allowing only 22 net yards rushing the entire game.

## Defensive Linemen

These are the defensive players who line up on the line of scrimmage. They are responsible for stopping the ball carriers and tackling the quarterbacks.

## Defensive Tackle

The defensive tackle is positioned on the inside of the defensive line. His main function is to contain the run. A defensive tackle who lines up directly across from the center is known as a nose tackle. Nose tackles are quite often the heaviest player on the defense. When a defensive tackle lines up between the offensive guard and offensive tackle he is known as a three-gap technique tackle. Rodrique Wright (UT, 2002-2005) is now playing for the Miami Dolphins of the NFL and has developed into one of the nation's top tackles.

## Delay of Game

This is a foul which takes place when the offensive team does not put the ball in play before the clock runs out. This will result in a five-yard penalty.

## Depth Chart

A team's roster that lists all players with rankings from starter to second- and third-string players. The depth of a team is particularly important when players are sidelined due to injury.

## Dimeback

The dimeback is referred to as the sixth defensive back. Most teams will play defense with four defensive backs. The fifth defensive back is known as the nickelback and the sixth is the dime back.

## Dime Coverage

Defensive pass coverage used when the offensive team is in an obvious passing play situation. When this occurs, the defensive squad will play with six defensive backs to cover the pass, thereby calling it dime coverage.

## Dime Package

See Dime Coverage

## Direct Snap

This is a play when the ball is passed directly to the ball carrier by the center.

## Division

The subdivision of teams into conferences, such as the East, North, South and West Divisions. There is also a grouping of teams in college football, with Division I having the most competitive teams and Division III having the least.

## Double Coverage

When two defensive players cover one receiver. Usually a team's best receiver will face double coverage during particular plays. The reason for this play is to prevent a long yardage gain due to the receiver's talent.

## Double Foul

When both teams commit a foul during the same play. A double foul usually results in the penalties cancelling each other out.

## Double Team

See Double Coverage.

## Down

One of four chances an offensive team has to gain 10 yards. A unit of the game that starts with a legal snap or legal free kick after the ball is ready for play and ends when the ball becomes dead.

## Down and In

When the receiver runs downfield and then suddenly cuts sharply toward the middle of the field.

### Down and Out

A pass pattern where the receiver runs down the field, and then he suddenly cuts toward the sideline. You will see a play like this when the team is trying to save the time on the clock.

### Down Box

A field official holds a rod with a box attached to the top which contains four cards numbered one to four. This is used to keep an eye on the number of the down being played. After each play, the holder will change the numbers to indicate what down is currently being played.

### Down Lineman

When a player stationed in front of his line of scrimmage has either one (three-point stance) or two (four-point stance) hands on the ground.

### Down the Field

To play in an offensive position toward the direction of the opponent's goal line.

### Draft

A procedure where the managers of NFL teams take turns picking the best college players to fill out their playing roster. This is also known as the NFL draft. My husband claims that he sometimes feels a very cold draft when he's around me.

### Draft Choice

A player who is chosen to play for a specific team. The order in which an NFL team makes its draft choices is determined by the previous year's record. Vince Young (UT, 2003-2005) was selected in the first round (third overall) by the Tennessee Titans in the 2006 NFL draft.

### Draw Play

The quarterback drops back as if he were going to pass the ball, but instead he hands it off to a running back or runs with the ball himself.

## Drive

A series of plays that occurs from the time an offense takes possession of the ball until they either score or turn the ball over to the other team.

## Drop Back

When a quarterback takes several steps backward into an area called the pocket after taking the snap from the center. Most quarterbacks drop back a certain number of steps before attempting to make a pass.

## Drop Kick

This is when a player drops the ball and kicks it right after it hits the ground. This is considered to be a free kick.

# −E−

## Eligible Receiver

Any offensive player who can legally touch a forward pass.

## Encroachment

An illegal action by a player who crosses the line of scrimmage and makes contact with an opponent before the ball is snapped. This is a foul and is punishable by a five-yard penalty.

## End

This refers to a player position on offense or defense. The end on the right side of an offense is referred to as a tight end. The end on the opposite side is called a wide receiver. David Thomas (tight end at UT, 2002-2005) now with the New England Patriots, and Cory Redding (defensive end at UT, 1999-2002), now with the Detroit Lions, are two examples of Longhorn ends currently playing in the NFL.

## End Line

The boundary line that runs the width of the field along each end. You will see end lines at the very back of the end zone on both sides of the field.

## End Zone

This is the area bounded by the sidelines that is between the end line — or deadline in Canadian amateur football — and the goal line. A touchdown is given to the team who has possession of the football and crosses the goal line and enters the end zone.

## Extra Point

A single point awarded to a team for kicking the ball through the upright after scoring a touchdown.

# –F–

## Face Mask

This is the protective grill that forms part of the football helmet. This term can also be applied to the foul or penalty awarded for a player grabbing an opponent's face mask. There are two possible levels to a penalty that results from face masking. The first is when there is incidental contact to a minor degree. This penalty would result in a five-yard loss. The second penalty or foul would be flagrant and could possibly result in injury. This foul would result in a personal foul of 15 yards.

## Fair Catch

The player receiving a football punt or kickoff has the opportunity to catch the ball and return it or call a fair catch. If the player chooses a fair catch, he must raise one hand and wave it, then catch the football. His team will then take possession of the football from that spot on the field. If the player drops the football, it is a live ball and either team can recover it.

## Fair Catch Interference

A penalty called when a player interferes with the person attempting to catch the ball. No person can interfere with the player's attempt to field the ball once the player signals it to be a fair catch. The penalty for fair catch interference against the offending team is 15 yards.

## Faking a Roughing

An illegal act where a quarterback, punter or kicker pretends to be injured in an attempt to gain a foul against the opposing team. This foul results in a 15-yard penalty against the offending team.

## False Start

A sudden movement made by the offense in the hopes of drawing the defense offside. A false start results in a five-yard penalty against the offending team.

## Field Goal

A scoring play worth three points and made by place- or drop-kicking the ball through the opponent's goal other than via a kickoff or free kick following a safety. A missed field goal can be returned as a punt, if recovered inbounds by the defending team. Ryan Bailey (UT, 2005-present) was the Longhorn's go-to guy for place kicking during the 2007 season. Ryan made 18 of 22 field goal attempts in 2007, including eight of 10 from 40 yards or more.

## Field Judge

This is the official who lines up 25 yards deep in the defensive backfield on the tight-end side of the field. His job includes keeping track of the play clock, calling a delay of game if the clock expires, and watching for illegal use of hands by the receivers and defensive backs.

## Field of Play

This is the area between both the goal lines and the sidelines. The field of play is 360 feet long and 160 feet wide. This includes the two 10-yard end zones.

## Field Position
A relative measure of how many yards a team must travel in order to score: "Good field position" means the offense has less distance to cover.

## First and Ten
When an offensive team has a first down with ten yards to go to get another first down.

## First Down
The first of a set of four downs.

## Flag Football
This is similar to most other forms of football, with any number of players. Tackling is not permitted. There is a flag attached to each side of the player's belt. Once a flag is pulled off, this is considered a tackle and the end of a play.

## Flanker
This is a wide receiver that is on the offensive team and lines up in the backfield outside of another receiver.

## Flat
This is an area on the field which lies between the line of scrimmage and 10 yards into the defensive backfield. It is also within 15 yards of the sideline.

## Flood
This is when offensive coordinators send more players to a particular area of the field than the opposition can effectively cover.

## Formation
A formation refers to the line-up of players before the start of a down. There are both offensive and defensive formations. There are also many — and I mean many — formations in both categories.

## Forward Pass

A pass that touches a person, an object, or the ground that is closer to the opponent's end line than when it was released.

## Forward Progress

The farthest location downfield that the football is marked after the receiver catches the ball. It is marked at that point even if the receiver is pushed back by the defense after catching it.

## Foul

A violation of a playing rule. There are many possible fouls or penalties in the game of football.

## Four-Point Stance

A down lineman's stance with four points on the ground. This means he has his two feet and his two hands on the ground.

## Fourth-Down Conversion

The act of making a first down on a fourth-down play. Most teams will punt the ball on fourth down unless they are trailing in the football game and need to keep possession of the ball. A fourth- down conversion will also be attempted when the offense has a very short yardage situation in order to get their first down.

## Franchise

Term often used to refer to the team or the entire management and players that make up the operations. Note: In the NFL, there are 32 different franchises (teams).

## Franchise Player

1. This is a tag given to a star player by his team, management or fans to keep him from leaving via free agency. Franchise players are not often referred to in college.

2. A term that is used to refer to the star or best player on the team. The Houston Oilers made Earl Campbell (UT, 1974-1977) the first overall pick in the 1978 NFL Draft because they felt he had the ability to be a franchise player. He didn't disappoint during his first year in the NFL. He earned the Rookie of the Year, MVP and Offensive Player of the Year awards.

## Free Agent

When a player's contract expires with his most recent team, and he is in search of offers from other teams to pay him the highest price. A lot of players change teams during free agency in order to earn the most money from the highest-bidding team.

## Free Kick

A kickoff or safety kick. It may be a placekick, dropkick, or punt. A punt, however, may not be used on a kickoff following a touchdown or a successful field goal.

## Free Safety

This refers to a specific player's position on defense. Free safeties will typically play deep on the field and assist other defensive backs in covering their zone for deep pass plays by the offensive team. Defensive backs will be assigned a specific player to cover, while free safeties play a zone defense and help the other defensive backs cover their receivers.

## Freeze

The offensive team will attempt to keep control of the ball to prevent the other team from scoring. As the end of a game approaches, the team with the lead may attempt to freeze the football. This is also referred to as "controlling the game clock." I've seen my husband freeze after telling him that I just had an idea about something.

## Front Four

The front four consists of linemen in a formation that includes two ends and two tackles. This is also referred to as the defensive line.

## Fullback

This refers to an offensive player's position. Fullbacks are lined up deep behind the quarterback in the T-formation. In modern formations this position may be varied, and this player has more blocking responsibilities than the halfback or tailback. Ahmard Hall (UT, 2003-2005) took over the starting Longhorns fullback position in 2005 and celebrated a national championship at the end of the season. Ahmard signed with the Tennessee Titans of the NFL as a rookie free agent in July 2006.

## Fumble

A ball that a player accidentally lost possession of; in Canadian football the term includes muffs.

# –G–

## Game Ball

The ball used in the actual game. Quite often game balls are given to a player who accomplishes a milestone, such as a first touchdown or pass or a record-setting game.

## Gap

The spaces between the players lined up at the line of scrimmage. I sometimes feel a gap between my husband and me when it comes to shopping.

## Goal

The end zone, which is 10 yards deep and 160 feet wide.

## Goal line

The front line of the end zone.

### Goal-Line Stand

The act of the defense stopping the opposition at or near the goal line on several attempts.

### Goalpost

A tall metal structure that stands at the back of each end zone. Teams attempt to kick the ball through the posts for field goals.

### Going for It

When a team facing a fourth down tries for a new first down instead of punting or kicking a field goal. If the team fails in the attempt, it then loses possession of the ball to the opposing team.

### Gridiron

The football field.

### Grounding

This is when the quarterback throws the ball down on the field to avoid a sack. This can also be referred to as intentional grounding, which can result in a penalty.

### Guard

This refers to a player position on offense. A good offensive guard is key to a potent running game. Kasey Studdard (UT, 2003-2006) started his last 38 games in the left guard position for the Texas Longhorns. He was signed by the NFL Houston Texans on July 23, 2007.

### Gunslinger

This term is used for a quarterback who acts in an aggressive and decisive manner by consistently throwing risky passes in the hope of a higher reward.

# –H–

## Hail Mary

A long pass play, thrown toward a group of receivers near the end zone in hope of a touchdown. Used by a team as a last resort as time is running out in either of the two halves and usually by a team trailing in the second half. One of the most memorable college football Hail Mary passes was thrown by Doug Flutie from Boston College in October 1999. Flutie completed a 48-yard Hail Mary to Gerard Phelan with no time left on the score clock to upset the Miami Hurricanes 47-45 in the nationally televised Orange Bowl game in Miami, Florida.

## Halfback

An offensive player who lines up in the backfield behind the quarterback and is usually responsible for carrying the ball on run plays.

## Hand-off

When a player hands a live ball to another player.

## Hang Time

The length of time a punt is in the air. The longer the ball "hangs" in the air during a punt, the more time the defense has to run down field and cover the kick returner.

Hang Time

## Hash Marks

These are the lines between which the ball begins each play. The lines are parallel to and equal distance apart from the side lines and are marked on the field as broken lines. If a play is stopped while the ball is between the hash marks, the ball is spotted where it was stopped for the following play. If the play ends outside the hash marks, the ball is spotted at the closest hash mark.

## Head Coach

The member of the coaching staff who is responsible for all aspects of the team and is in charge of all other coaches. Longhorns head coach Mack Brown has served in that capacity since 1998. He has compiled a winning record of 103-25 and has the best winning percentage (.805) of any coach in Longhorn history.

## Head Linesman

The head linesman is the official who sets up straddling the line of scrimmage on the sideline designated by the referee. His job duties vary from keeping tabs on the chain crew to watching for illegal motion, illegal shifts, illegal use of hands and illegal men downfield.

## Heisman Trophy

This award is presented each year to the best college football player in the country. The Heisman Trophy is named in honor of John W. Heisman, the first athletic director of the Downtown Athletic Club. Earl Campbell (1977) and Ricky Williams (1998) are the only two Longhorn players to win this award.

## Helping the Runner

No player is permitted to assist a teammate by either pulling or pushing him in an attempt to gain yardage. The penalty for helping the runner is 10 yards against the offending team.

## Hike

Synonym of "snap." The handoff or pass from the center that begins as a play from the line of scrimmage.

## Hitch and Go

This refers to a pass pattern by a receiver who runs downfield and makes a quick hitch to the inside or outside and then continues downfield for a deeper pass.

## Holder

This is the player who holds the ball upright for a place kick. Quite often backup quarterbacks are used for their excellent ball-handling ability. Punters are also used for their ability to catch long snaps.

## Holding

An illegal action where one player keeps another from advancing by holding his uniform or body. Offensive holding is a 10-yard penalty. My husband has committed this action by preventing me from going into a T.J. Maxx store.

## Hole Number

A number assigned to a gap between the offensive linemen and the tight end.

## Home Field Advantage

The benefit a team gets by playing games in its own stadium. The benefits are fan support, knowledge of the field and not having to travel to another stadium. The Longhorns enjoy the home field advantage of playing at Darrell K. Royal-Texas Memorial Stadium.

## Home Game

A game played in a team's own stadium.

## Hook and Lateral

A trick play in which a receiver, usually a wide receiver, runs a hook pattern moving toward the line of scrimmage to make a catch and then laterals the ball to a second player going in a different direction. The hook and ladder is not commonly used.

## Hot Dog

A player who shows off his talent and showboats in a way that is not respectful to his team, his opponents or the sport of football.

## Huddle

An on-field gathering of members of a team in order to secretly communicate instructions for the upcoming play. Quarterback Colt McCoy (UT, 2006-present) called the signals in the Longhorns offensive huddles in 2007.

## Hurry-up Offense

An offensive strategy intended to gain as much yardage as possible while running little time off the clock. Teams who use it often make plays without a huddle. This technique is sometimes used to keep the defensive team off balance. This strategy is most often used when there is little time left on the clock.

# –I–

## I-Formation

This is a formation that includes a fullback and tailback lined up with the fullback directly in front of the tailback. If a third back is in line, this is referred to as a Full House I or Maryland I. If the third back is lined up alongside the fullback, it is referred to as a Power I.

## Illegal Formation

On offense, the players must be lined up on the line of scrimmage for at least one count before the ball is snapped. If not, then it is an illegal formation. Failure to do so is a five-yard penalty against the offending team.

## Illegal Motion

When two players from the offense are in motion at the same time. Illegal motion results in a five-yard penalty against the offending team.

## Illegal Procedure

A penalty resulting from a player moving along the line of scrimmage prior to the snap of the football. The penalty for illegal procedure is five yards against the offending team.

## Illegal Shift

This penalty generally refers to the offensive linemen failing to reset for one second after two players have shifted position at the same time. The penalty for an illegal shift is five yards against the offending team.

## Inbounds

The area within the playing field. The area that is inbounds includes anything inside the sidelines and end lines.

## Inbound Lines

This term refers to the hash marks on the field.

## Incomplete Pass

A forward pass of the ball that touches the ground before being caught. In the NFL, the time clock will stop after an incomplete pass is made.

## Ineligible Receiver

There are certain players on the offense who are not allowed to catch passes. For example, in most situations offensive linemen cannot be receivers. If an offensive lineman catches the ball, he may cause his team to be penalized. The exception to this rule occurs when the ball has already been tipped by a different player.

## Injury Report

A listing of players' injuries along with their projected status for the next game.

## Intentional Grounding

A type of illegal forward pass, when the quarterback throws the ball without an intended receiver with no chance of completion to any offensive player, for the sole purpose of conserving time or loss of yardage. The quarterback may purposely throw the ball out of bounds or into the ground to avoid taking a sack. This foul costs the offense a loss of down and 10 yards. My kids have experi-

# Longhorn Lingo

enced a different type of intentional grounding on more than a few occassions.

## Interception
The legal catching of a forward pass thrown by an opposing player. Five players hold the Longhorn's single season record for interceptions with seven. They include Nathan Vasher (2001), Jerry Gray (1984), William Graham (1981), Jack Crain (1940) and Noble Doss (1940).

## Interference
To illegally hamper a player's opportunity to catch a pass or to block for another player carrying the football. This will result in a penalty. My husband has, on many occasions, interfered with my spending.

# –J–

## Jack
The interior linebacker (ILB) of the 3-4 formation that plays in the weak side of the formation. Also known as Mo.

## Jumbo
This is an offensive package which includes two tight ends, a fullback and a halfback. This is similar to heavy jumbo, where either the halfback or the fullback is replaced by another tight end.

# –K–

## Key
A specific identified player on field formation or a shift in formation that would alert players about the play the opposition is going to run. Putting the tight end in motion, for example, could alert the defense that the offensive team may be planning for a play in that direction.

## Kick

To strike the ball deliberately with the foot.

## Kicker

A player who specializes in placekicking (i.e., field goals and kickoffs). The Longhorns single-season record for points scored by a place-kicker is held by David Pino with 113 points during the 2005 season. A close second is held by Ryan Bailey with 112 points during the 2007 season.

## Kicking an Opponent

A penalty which is the result of a player kneeing or kicking an opponent. Kicking an opponent results in a 15-yard personal foul penalty against the offending team, and the guilty player can be disqualified from the game if the foul is ruled to be flagrant.

## Kicking Game

The part of a team's game that involves punting, field goals, kickoffs, free kicks and extra points.

## Kickoff

A free kick that starts each half or overtime, or restarts the game following a touchdown or field goal.

## Kick Returner

A player on the receiving team who specializes in fielding kicks and running them back. A kick returner is often a reserve wide receiver who is usually one of the faster players on the team. The Longhorns all-time longest kickoff return was accomplished by Johnny Lam Jones in 1978 for a touchdown against Southern Methodist University.

# –L–

## Lateral

A backward pass to a teammate behind the line of scrimmage. This pass can also be parallel to the line of scrimmage.

### Linebacker

A defensive player position. The linebackers (LB) typically play one to six yards behind the defensive linemen. They are the most versatile players on the field because they can defend both run and pass defense. There are two types of linebacker: middle linebacker (MLB) and outside linebackers (OLB). Derrick Johnson (UT, 2001-2004) became the first Longhorns linebacker since 1966 to be selected in the first round of the NFL draft when he was selected by the Kansas City Chiefs.

### Line Judge

The official who lines up on the opposite side of the field from the head linesman. His duties vary from assisting the head linesman in making illegal motion, illegal shifts, offside and encroachment calls to supervising the timing of the game.

### Lineman

An offensive or defensive position on the line of scrimmage. A lineman can be a tackle, guard, or center on offense, or a tackle or end on defense.

### Line of Scrimmage

An imaginary line that stretches the width of the field and separates the two teams prior to the snap of the ball.

### Line to Gain

A term that indicates the distance that is required for first-down yardage.

### Live Ball

A term that is used for any ball in play. It doesn't matter whether the ball is in a player's possession or not.

### Long Snapper

A center that specializes in the long snaps required for punts and field goal attempts. Most teams employ a specialist long snapper instead of requiring the normal center to perform this duty.

### Loose ball

This term is used for a ball that is in play and not in a player's possession. This term includes a ball in flight during a pass.

## −M−

### Man Coverage

See man-to-man coverage.

### Man in Motion

The guys that you see running behind the line of scrimmage while the quarterback calls out the signals.

### Man-to-Man Coverage

Linebackers and defensive backs are each assigned to cover a particular receiver. I've seen some of my husband's friends do a man-to-man coverage when their wives are looking for them.

### Margin of Victory

The total difference in points in a game, arrived at by subtracting the losing team's score from the winning team's score. For example, UT wins 14-7. Their margin of victory is seven points.

### Middle Guard

The defensive tackle who lines up directly opposite the offensive center on the line of scrimmage. This player is also referred to as a nose guard or nose tackle. A middle guard is generally big and strong enough to take on double teams on a consistent basis. Casey Hampton (UT, 1996-2000) started in 37 consecutive games for the Longhorns and became the first defensive lineman to lead the team in tackles two consecutive seasons (1999-2000). Casey is now a member of the Pittsburgh Steelers of the NFL.

## Midfield

The 50-yard line, which divides the length of the field in half.

## Motion

This is when an offensive player begins to move laterally and parallel to the line of scrimmage before the ball is snapped. An offense will often try to confuse the defense by sending a receiver or running back in motion. This is also referred to as "man in motion." The man in motion cannot cross the line of scrimmage until the ball is snapped.

## Multiple Offense

A team's offensive strategy that utilizes a number of different formations. Multiple offenses are used as an attempt to confuse the defense and keep them guessing.

# –N–

## NCAA

National Collegiate Athletic Association. Principal governing body of college sports, including college football.

## Necessary Line

This refers to the imaginary line that the offense must reach to obtain a first down. When a team gets a first down, the new necessary line is exactly ten yards away.

## Neutral Zone

This is the area between the lines of scrimmage or between the free kick restraining lines stretching from sideline to sideline.

## Nickelback

An extra defensive back who is used for certain passing situations. Also one of my favorite Canadian rock bands. GO CHAD GO!!!

## Nickel Defense

When the defense brings in a fifth defensive back to increase coverage in the backfield. Teams will often switch to a nickel defense when the opposing team's offense is in an obvious passing situation. This will allow the defense better coverage downfield.

## No Good

To be unsuccessful. This term is often used to describe an unsuccessful field-goal attempt. My kids also say this about my cooking.

## No-Huddle Offense

This is a play or series of plays where the offensive team quickly returns to the line of scrimmage without huddling to call in a play. Also called a hurry-up offense. Most teams use this strategy in the last two minutes of the half in order to get the ball down the field in a short amount of time, but it can be used throughout the game. When used during the game, this strategy can be confusing to defensive units, as they have no time to prepare for the next play.

## Nose Guard

See Nose Tackle.

## Nose Tackle

A defensive player who lines up "opposite the center's nose." Shawn Rogers (UT, 1997-2000) recorded 199 tackles during his Longhorns career before he was drafted in the second round of the NFL draft by the Detroit Lions.

## –O–

## Odds

A gambling term relating to the return on your money from a bet on a game, which is based on the likely outcome of the game as determined by an odds maker.

### Odds maker
A person who establishes the odds for sports betting.

### Offending Team
The team (defensive or offensive) that committed a foul or penalty.

### Offense
The team that has possession of the football while attempting to score points. The purpose of playing offense is to score points against the other team by either running or passing the football for yards. The offense plays against the other team's defense. The Longhorns produced their most proficient offensive game in their history in 1998, when they obtained 692 yards (total offense) against Rice University.

### Offensive Backfield
This can mean one of two things:
- The area of the playing field.
- The players usually consisting of a quarterback and a running back; however, receivers may also be in the backfield.

### Offensive Holding
A penalty called against an offensive player who uses his hands against a defensive player attempting to tackle the ball carrier or advance forward. Offensive holding results in a 10-yard penalty against the offending team.

### Offensive Line
These are the five offensive players who line up on the line of scrimmage. Their job is to block for the quarterback and ball carriers.

### Offensive Linemen
The offensive linemen are the five players who line up together at the line of scrimmage and block the defense attempting to tackle the quarterback or running back. Of-

fensive linemen include centers, guards and tackles. Justin Blalock (UT, 2003-2006) is a graduated Longhorn offensive lineman who is currently playing in the NFL for the Atlanta Falcons.

## Offensive Pass Interference

This is a foul or penalty which is called against an offensive player who significantly obstructs a defensive player's chance to intercept a forward pass or pushes off of the defender to give himself an advantage. Offensive pass interference results in a 10-yard penalty on the offending team and is the coach's worst nightmare. These penalties quite often stall an offensive team's drive.

## Offensive Team

This is the team which has possession of the football and is attempting to score against the defense.

## Officials

The men in the striped jerseys who officiate or referee the game.

## Off-Season

The time of the year when the football season ends and the next season has yet to begin. It's when no football is played.

## Offside

This is a penalty that occurs after the ball is snapped and any part of the defender's body is beyond his line of scrimmage. This type of infraction results in a five-yard penalty against the offending team.

## On Downs

Term used to describe an offensives team's position of losing possession of the ball after it failed to obtain a first down on its fourth attempt. The Longhorns regained possession of the ball due to their opposition losing the ball "on downs."

# Longhorn Lingo

## Onside Kick

This is a play in which the kicking team tries to recover the kicked ball. The ball must travel at least ten yards before the kicking team can recover it. This play is generally attempted when time on the clock is an issue, or to catch the other team by surprise.

## Open Receiver

A receiver who is wide open with no one covering him.

## Open Up Hole

To push or force the opposition aside in order to make room in their defense for a running back to run with the ball. Offensive linemen try to "open up holes" in the defensive line for the running backs to get through. Longhorn backs like Ricky Williams (UT, 1999) took advantage of linemen opening up holes for good yardage gains.

## Option

A type of play in which the quarterback has the choice of handing off, keeping, or laterally passing to one or more backs. This works well when you have a quarterback as talented as the Longhorn's Vince Young.

## Out of Bounds

The part of the field outside the perimeter of the playing field. As soon as a ball carrier or the ball itself touches out of bounds, the play is over.

## Out of Bounds at Snap

No player can re-enter the playing field once the ball is snapped, if out of bounds. The penalty for being out of bounds at the snap is five yards against the offending team.

## Outside

A general term used to describe the outer area of the field near the sidelines. A running back will turn the outside corner in order to cut along the sidelines to gain more yardage.

## Overtime

An extra period of the game which is added when there is a tie score at the end of regulation. In the NFL, overtime ends as soon as either team scores in any way. This is referred to as sudden death overtime. The NCAA college football overtime rules are quite in-depth and are very controversial. For more information, refer to rule 3 in the NCAA rule book, section 1.

# –P–

## Pancake

Term used when a player is seen lying flat on the field after receiving a hard block.

## Pass

When a ball is thrown forward from the line of scrimmage and is caught by an eligible receiver before it hits the ground. The Longhorns single-season record for pass completions was 290 in 13 games during the 1999 season when the Longhorns had a win/loss record of 9-5.

## Pass Defender

A defensive player who attempts to prevent the receiver from catching a pass.

## Pass Interference

This is when a player illegally hinders an eligible receiver's opportunity to catch a forward pass. Offensive pass interference results in a 10-yard penalty against the offense.

## Pass Pattern

A predetermined path which is run by the receiver in order to get open for a pass from the quarterback. This is also known as a pass route.

## Pass Protection

A blocking scheme is used by the offensive line and backs to keep the defense from getting to the quarterback on passing plays and allows the quarterback time and space to throw the ball.

## Pass Route

See Pass Pattern.

## Pass Rush

A determined effort by the defensive line to rush the quarterback in order to prevent the pass. The Longhorns defense in 1956 had a UT record-breaking season by allowing only 91 pass attempts in 10 games. This represents a powerful pass rush defense.

## Passing Game

A team that has an offensive plan to pass more than it runs. A team with a good passing game can generally move down the field more quickly than a team who prefers to run the football. During the national championship season in 2005, the Longhorns passing game produced 26 touchdown passes. This was the second-most in Longhorns history.

## PAT

This refers to the extra point awarded after a touchdown for kicking the ball through the uprights. On an attempted PAT the ball is placed on the three-yard line in college or high school football. The Longhorn's David Pino holds the current single-season record for PAT's with 77 during the national championship season in 2005.

## Penalty

What the players receive when they've been very naughty by breaking the rules of the game. A penalty generally results in some sort of yardage loss or gain; however, it may also result in a loss of down as well.

## Personal Foul

A penalty that might cause injury which results in a 15-yard penalty against the offending team.

## Pick

A fantasy owner's draft position. This is the order in which the players are chosen.

## Picked Off

Intercepted. This is when the defense catches a pass that was intended for the receiver. Nathan Vasher (UT, 2000-2003) and Noble Doss (UT, 1939-1941) share the all-time Longhorns record for career interceptions with 17.

## Pigskin

A slang term for the football.

## Piling On

An illegal play where players continue to jump on the tackled player after he is on the ground. OUCH!! This is also known as dog piling or a late hit. Piling on results in a 15-yard penalty against the offending team.

## Pistol Formation

This is a hybrid version of the shotgun in which the quarterback lines up roughly three yards behind the center and the running back lines up directly behind the quarterback.

## Pitch

An underhand toss of the ball from the quarterback to the running back who is moving laterally away from him. Also known as a pitch out. An offense often uses a pitch, instead of a hand-off, to give the running back a running start toward the outside.

## Pitch Out

See Pitch.

## Place Kick

When the ball is kicked while it is being held in place by another player or on a tee.

## Place Kicker

A kicker who specializes in kickoffs or field goals. Graduate Longhorn Phil Dawson (UT, 1994-1997) holds 13 UT kicking records and currently plays for the Cleveland Browns in the NFL.

## Play

Plan of action the offensive team has following a snap or kickoff.

## Play-Action Pass

A tactic in which the quarterback fakes either a handoff or a throw in order to draw the defense away from the intended offensive method generally resulting in a pass.

## Playbook

A book issued to all team members which includes all of the plays run by the offense and defense. Team members must memorize all plays in the playbook.

## Play Clock

A clock which is displayed above each end zone. The timer is used to increase the pace of the game between plays. The offensive team must snap the ball before the time expires, and if they fail to do so, they will receive a five-yard delay of game foul.

## Playmaker

Refers to both offensive or defensive players of any position. These are the players who step up and create opportunities or make big plays when the team needs them. When the team is down three points with less than a minute left to play, the quarterbacks, running backs and receivers are quite often the play- makers.

## Pocket

This is an area of protection that is given to a quarterback during passing plays by his offensive line.

## Point-After-Touchdown

See PAT.

## Point Spread

A gambling term given by odds makers that indicates the difference in points by which one team will/should beat the other. There are many determining factors in these odds.

## Pooch Kick

A punt or kickoff that is deliberately kicked with less than full force. This low, line drive kickoff often bounces around before it is fielded by the kick returner. This is also referred to as a squib kick.

## Possession

To be in control of the football.

## Post

A pass thrown by the quarterback downfield in the direction of the goalpost. The receiver will run downfield and angle toward the post to receive the pass. This is also referred to as a post pattern.

## Postseason

This refers to the time after the regular season when the better teams play in a tournament style format to determine the champion.

## Power Sweep

This is a running play where two or more offensive linemen pull out of their stance after the snap and run toward one side, leading the running back in that direction. This can also be referred to as a sweep.

## Preseason

The period of time before the regular season, during which teams play exhibition games and check out new players. These games do not count toward the regular-season standings.

## Prevent Defense

A defensive strategy that utilizes deep zone coverage in order to prevent a big pass play from happening downfield, usually at the expense of giving up yards at shorter distances.

## Previous Spot

This refers to the exact spot on the field where the previous play started. Penalties called during a play are often enforced from the previous spot on the football field.

## Primary Receiver

This is the receiver who is supposed to be the first option for the quarterback to throw to. Each individual play will be designed to throw to a primary receiver. If the receiver is covered, the quarterback will look for his second and third options. This is when it is advantageous for the quarterback to have more time in the pocket to throw the football.

## Pulling

The action of an offensive lineman who leaves one area of the field and instead of blocking the player in front of him, steps back and moves down the line ("pulls") to block another player. I've been known for pulling my husband out of golf stores and Best Buy.

## Pump Fake

When the quarterback, in an attempt to fool the defensive team, fakes a pass and keeps the ball in his hand.

## Punt

A kick in which the ball is dropped by the punter, and he kicks it before it reaches the ground.

## Punter

This is a kicker who specializes in punting as opposed to place kicking. Longhorn Al Lowry kicked a record 82-yard punt during a game in 1972 against Baylor. This record still stands today.

## Punt Return

When a punt is fielded by the receiving team and advanced for better field position. The punt returner generally attempts to move the ball as far up the field as possible. The all-time longest punt return record in Longhorn history is held by Bohn Hilliard in 1932. The return was for 95 yards and a touchdown against Oklahoma.

## Pylon

A short orange marker at each of the end zone's four corners.

–Q–

## Quarter

There are four periods, or quarters, of play in the standard game. Each quarter is fifteen game clock minutes but generally takes much longer since the clock is not continually running.

## Quarterback

An offensive player who lines up behind the center, from whom he takes the snap. He is the leader on the field and calls the plays in the huddle. Major Applewhite (UT, 1998-2001) holds several Texas quarterback records and was the leader of a potent offense during his career.

## Quarterback Controversy

A public outcry from fans or the media when a starting quarterback is not playing well and the back-up quarterback is playing better than he is.

## Quarterback Rating

A numeric value used to calculate the performance of quarterbacks.

## Quarterback Sneak

When the quarterback quickly snaps the ball and runs and jumps forward.

## Quarter Defense

A defensive formation with seven defensive backs, three down linemen and one linebacker.

## Quick Count

An offensive strategy used by the quarterback to call plays quickly on the line of scrimmage to pull the defense offside.

## Quick Kick

An unexpected punt. The offense lines up to make a play and surprises the defense by kicking the ball instead.

# –R–

## Reading the Defense

The ability of the quarterback to read the defensive formation while calling the plays on the line of scrimmage. The quarterback will sometimes call an audible play change if he can tell what the defense is going to do before the play. A quarterback who can read the defense is extremely valuable to a team.

## Ready List

A list of players who are prepared for specific games or plays that is made by the coaches. The coach will have a ready list of players who may play in certain situations or against specific teams.

## Receiver

A player on the offensive squad who will catch passes. Roy Williams (UT, 2000-2003) holds numerous Longhorn records as a receiver. The most notable record is for most career receptions, with 241.

## Reception

When a player catches the ball.

## Recovery

When a player takes control of the football after a fumble.

## Red Dog

Refers to a defensive play where a linebacker or defensive back will vacate his normal duties to put pressure on the quarterback. This is also referred to as a blitz.

## Red Flag

When a coach throws a weighted red marker onto the field. This indicates that the coach is telling the officials that he wants a certain play reviewed. This is also referred to as a challenge flag.

## Red Shirt

A college player who did not play any games in a season due to a coach's choice. This player is allowed to practice with the game squad and will be given an additional year of eligibility. These players are given extra time to mature and then become "red shirt freshmen" in their second or sophomore year of college.

## Red Zone

The area between the 20-yard line and the goal of the defensive team.

## Referee

The official who directs the other six officials on the field. He is the only official who wears a white hat, while the others all wear black hats.

## Runback

When the football is run back up the field by a player after a kickoff, punt or interception. Any time there is a change of possession, the yardage gained from the place where the player caught the ball to the location he was tackled is classified as the runback. This can also be referred to as a punt return or kickoff return.

## Running Back

This player is lined up in the backfield behind the quarterback and will have the ball handed to him after the snap to gain yardage on the ground. Jamaal Charles (UT, 2005-2007) is the most recent Longhorn running back to be drafted into the NFL. He was recently drafted in the 2008 NFL draft by the Kansas City Chiefs. Jamaal is the only running back in UT history to post a run of at least 80 yards and a reception of at least 70 yards.

## Running into the Kicker

This penalty is incurred when a player runs into the kicker and makes incidental contact. This will result in a 5-yard penalty.

## Running out the Clock

A game strategy that is commonly used by the leading team at the end of the game. It involves repeatedly executing simple plays that allow the game clock to continue running in an effort to bring the game to a quicker end.

## Running Play

A play where the offense attempts to advance the ball without a forward pass.

## Rush

A running play. This can also be known as a pass rush.

## Rushing

Carrying the football on the ground by either the running back, quarterback or receiver, after catching the ball.

My husband says that I don't do enough of this when trying to get ready for a social event. That's why we're usually late.

# –S–

## Sack
When the quarterback gets tackled behind the line of scrimmage.

## Safety
1. A player's position on defense.
2. A method of scoring two points by the defense when one of its players tackles an opponent in possession of the ball in his own end zone.

## Safety Blitz
A defensive play which allows one or both safeties to rush the quarterback. A safety blitz can either be designed to sack the quarterback or to force him into throwing the ball in a hurry.

## Safety Valve
A short pass is thrown to a running back when the quarterback cannot find an open receiver before the pass rush closes in.

## Scatback
A running back that is generally very fast and good at making defenders miss him, as opposed to running them over on purpose like a 'power' back.

## Scramble
A tactic when the quarterback runs from the pocket in an attempt to avoid being sacked, giving the receivers more time to get open.

# Longhorn Lingo

## Scrambler

A quarterback who has the ability to run around, giving his receivers time to find open area to catch a pass. Vince Young (UT, 2006) was a dangerous scrambler and rusher of the football.

## Scrambling

Quick and evasive movements by a quarterback attempting to avoid being sacked or tackled.

## Screen Pass

A short pass made to a receiver in the flat who then runs with the ball behind a wall of blockers downfield.

## Scoring System

The formula for calculating how teams will gain points in a fantasy football league. This is usually determined by the participants prior to beginning a season.

## Scrimmage

This refers to a simulated game between two teams during practice. During training camp, teams often scrimmage with other teams or amongst themselves as a means of getting ready for the regular season.

## Secondary

Defensive players, specifically the safeties and the cornerbacks, who line up behind the linebackers and basically defend the pass.

## Second Forward Pass

An illegal pass where a player receives a forward pass behind the line of scrimmage and then in turn throws a second forward pass to another receiver downfield. A second forward pass results in a five-yard penalty against the offending team.

## Serpentine Draft

A style of draft where the player selection process changes. The team to pick last in the first round will choose first in the second round. This is used in fantasy football leagues.

## Series

The group of four downs a team has to advance 10 yards.

## Shield Punt

When seven men line up on the line of scrimmage and immediately start to cover the punt while three offensive players stay to guard the punter.

## Shift

When one or more offensive players move at the same time before the snap. All players who move in a shift must come to a complete stop prior to the snap.

## Shotgun Formation

The quarterback in this formation receives the snap five-eight yards behind the center.

## Side Judge

An official who lines up about 20 yards behind the players in the backfield before the play. His duties are generally the same as the back judge.

## Sideline

The boundary line on the side of the field of play.

## Signal Caller

This refers to the player, usually the quarterback, who will call the plays in the huddle or at the line of scrimmage.

## Signals

The codes or phrases that players call when running a play on the field or before a play on the line of scrimmage. My husband has mastered my signals to him.

## Single Elimination

A tournament where each team is eliminated after only one loss.

## Single-Wing Formation

A seldom-used offensive formation which was created by legendary coach Glen Scobey "Pop" Warner. It used three backfield teammates to block for the player carrying the ball.

## Slant

When the ball carrier is running across the field at an angle instead of running straight toward the end zone.

## Sleeper

A player who did not perform well the previous season, but who is expected to outperform his expectations the following season. This would make him a sleeper pick in a football draft.

## Slobber-Knocker

A brutal or gruesome tackle or hit.

## Slot

The area between a split end and the offensive line.

## Snap

When the ball is thrown or handed by the center to the quarterback, to the punter or to the holder on a kick attempt. However, it can also mean to speak sharply. For example, my husband says that I snap at him when he chooses to watch college football on TV on Saturday afternoons.

## Snap Count
This is the "hut" sound that the quarterback yells to signal for the snap to be made.

## Sneak
An offensive play where the quarterback, immediately on receiving the snap, runs forward with the ball. I've been known to sneak some of my shopping bags into the house: "This old thing? I've had it for months."

## Snoozer
A player who is expected to perform at lower standards than previous years. This would make him a poor choice if drafted, based on his previous performance.

## Spearing
A player using the crown of his helmet to hit another player. Spearing is illegal and results in a 15-yard penalty against the offending team.

## Special Teams
The group of players who participate in kicking plays. Special team's kickoff returner Eric Metcalf set a Longhorn single-game record in 1987 by returning seven kickoffs in one game in Houston.

## Spike
When a player slams the football to the ground. You normally would see this type of celebration after scoring a touchdown.

## Spiral
A ball passed or kicked with a spin which propels it farther with more accuracy; the ball points in the same direction throughout its flight and rotates very smoothly.

## Split End
When I first heard the term "split end" being used, the first thing I thought about was my hair. Apparently this is

not the case in football. Split end instead refers to a receiver who lines up on the line of scrimmage but splits to the outside of the formation.

## Spot

A mark on the field which shows where the ball will be placed. This is usually determined by the forward progress of the football.

## Square In

A pass pattern run by a receiver. The receiver will run straight downfield and will make a sharp turn to the inside of the field.

## Square Out

A pass pattern run by a receiver. The receiver will run straight downfield and will make a sharp turn to the outside sidelines of the field.

## Squib Kick

A low, line-drive kickoff in which the ball is intentionally kicked low to the ground, often bouncing on the ground before being picked up.

## Stance

The position a player will stand in prior to the snap of the football. You will see most linemen get down in a three-point stance. This means they will have one hand on the ground and both feet planted when the ball is snapped. The only time I've ever been in that position is before the door's open when Coach is having a major sale.

## Starter

The player, regardless of his position, who is the first to play his position within a given game or season. Now it all depends on the position and the game situation, but this player may be replaced or have to share time with one or more players later in the game.

## Stiff Arm or Straight Arm

When a ball carrier uses a hand and straight arm at the opponent's head or chest area to ward off a would-be tackler. This is generally used to keep the tackler at a distance from his body.

## Striking an Official

This is a major mistake! Players get a big "time-out" for this one. A player may never strike, intentionally bump or push an official or referee. Committing such an act will result in a 15-yard penalty, and the guilty player is automatically removed from the game. Depending on the severity, the player may also face further suspension.

## Striking an Opponent

When a player hits another player with his fist. To strike another player is illegal in football. This is considered to be a personal foul and can result in a 15-yard penalty. The offending player can also be removed from the game.

## Strong-I

This is a formation where the tailback is lined up directly behind the quarterback, and the fullback is lined up offset to the strong side of the formation.

## Strong Safety

A defensive player who usually lines up in the secondary to assist in stopping the pass, but usually aligns close to the line of scrimmage in order to help stop the run.

## Strong Side

I'll try and keep this one simple. Depending on the formations of the teams, the side of the field (left or right) that has the most players is considered the strong side. The strong side is the side of the field with the most offensive players on or just behind the line of scrimmage. My husband says I have a very strong side. I'm not too sure what side that is yet.

## Stunt

A tactic used by defensive linemen. They switch roles in an attempt to get past the blockers. Usually you will see a defensive lineman crossing behind another in hopes of either going unblocked or gaining an advantage on his blocker.

## Substitution

To replace one player with another. Substitutions can be used to give certain players a rest or to relay a play into the huddle from the coaches on the sidelines.

## Subway Alumni

Fans who follow a college football team but did not graduate from that school. The term subway alumni was first used to describe the many New York City fans that followed the Notre Dame Fighting Irish Football Club.

## Succeeding Spot

This refers to where the next play would start from if there was no penalty called on the play.

## Suicide Squad

The player on Special Teams who is on the field during punts and kicks who then must race down the field to tackle the player returning the football.

## Super Bowl

The championship game of the NFL, played between the champions of the AFC and NFC at a neutral site each January or early February. This game is the final game of the NFL playoffs. The last Longhorn to play on a winning Super Bowl team was Casey Hampton, DT, who was a member of the champion Pittsburgh Steelers. The Steelers beat the Seattle Seahawks 21-10 in 2006 to disappoint two other UT alumni on the losing squad. Those two players were Marcus Tubbs, DT, and D.D. Lewis, DT.

## Sweep

A running play in which several blockers lead a running back on a designed play to the outside. Depending on the design of the play and the number of blockers, this is sometimes referred to as a power sweep.

# –T–

## T-Formation

A classic offensive formation with the quarterback directly behind the center and three running backs behind the quarterback. Their positioning is in the shape of a T.

## Tackle

This term is used in 2 areas.
1. To bring the ball carrier to the ground.
2. A player position on the line, either an offensive tackle (T) or a defensive tackle (DT). All-time UT great Jerry Sisemore played in the Pro Bowl on two occasions (1980, 1982) while a member of the Philadelphia Eagles of the NFL.

## Tackling

Physically grabbing the opposition and bringing him to the ground.

## Tailback

Player position on offense that is farthest (deepest) back, except in kicking formations. Also often referred to as the running back, particularly in a one-back offense.

## Take a Knee

When the ball carrier ends the play by deliberately touching a knee to the ground. The only other time you would most likely see this is when your sweetie is ready to propose to you.

## Longhorn Lingo

### Takeaway
When the defense takes the ball away from the offense by either a fumble recovery or interception. One of the variables used to measure the quality of a defense is the number of takeaways they have recorded. My husband has threatened to take away my credit cards. Why? I just don't know.

### TD
The abbreviation for touchdown.

### Territory
The area of the field that a team protects. The defense prevents the offense from entering their territory.

### Third and Long
When the offense faces a third-down situation and is more than a short play away from a first down. Third down with 10 yards to go is classified as third and long.

### Three and Out
This is when an offensive team fails to gain a first down on the first three plays of a drive. They are forced to punt on the fourth down.

### Three-Point Stance
This is the starting position many linemen take at the line of scrimmage before the football is snapped. In other words, his two feet and one of his hands are on the ground.

### Tight End
An offensive player position—often known as Y receiver—who lines up on the line of scrimmage, next to the offensive tackle. Tight ends are used as blockers during running plays, and either run a route or stay in to block during passing plays. Jermichael Finley (UT, 2006-2007) is the most recent UT tight end to be drafted by an NFL team. Jermichael was drafted in the third round of the 2008 NFL draft by the Green Bay Packers.

## Time of Possession

This means the amount of time one team has the ball in its possession relative to the other team.

## Time-Out

A stoppage in play called by one of the teams in order to discuss their upcoming strategies. Each team receives three time-outs during each half.

## Too Many Men

The maximum number of men per team allowed on the field is 11. Having more than 11 men on the field for any given play is illegal. If a team has too many men on the field, a delay of game is called, resulting in a five-yard penalty.

## Total Offense

A statistic that combines yards rushing and yards passing.

## Touchback

A play when the ball is ruled dead on or behind a team's own goal line which generally happens after a kickoff, punt, interception or fumble.

## Touchdown

This is a scoring play that is worth six points. A scoring play is when any part of the ball, while legally in the possession of a player who is inbounds, crosses the plane of the opponent's goal line.

## Trade

This means to switch players between teams. Trading occurs quite often in professional sports.

## Trap

Considered to be a basic blocking pattern in which a defensive lineman is permitted past the line of scrimmage, only to be blocked by a "pulling" lineman.

## Longhorn Lingo

### Trap Block
A blocking strategy where a defensive player is allowed to penetrate the line of scrimmage, only to be blocked by another player behind the line. This can also be referred to as a mousetrap.

### Trenches
The area immediately around the line of scrimmage, where the offensive and defensive linemen do battle. This is where all the hard hitting and physical battles occur.

### Trick Play
A variety of plays that use deception to catch the other team off guard. Some of the famous trick plays would include: the fake punt (kick), "Statue of Liberty," flea-flicker, center-eligible, surprise onside kick and halfback pass plays. My favorite trick play at home is when my husband asks what I've spent after shopping, and I tell him to focus on what I've saved.

### Tripping
When a leg or foot is used to illegally trip another player. This will result in a 10-yard penalty against the offending team.

### Trips
A formation in which three wide receivers are lined up on the same side of the field. I personally would like to take a trip to Hawaii.

### True Freshman
A college player who is one year out of high school. This contrasts with a redshirt freshman who has practiced with the team for one year, but who has not played yet in any games.

### Turn In
A receiver's pass route where he runs downfield and turns in sharply toward the inside of the field.

## Turn Out

A receiver's pass route where he runs downfield and turns out sharply toward the sidelines.

## Turnover

The loss of the ball by one team to the other team. This is usually the result of a fumble or an interception. In 1982, the Longhorn defense created 27 turnovers by fumbles. This record still stands in the UT record book for most turnovers (by fumble) in a season.

## Turn the Ball Over on Downs

This is when a team uses all four of their downs without either scoring or making a first down. They have to then relinquish the ball to the other team.

## Tweener

The gifted player who does not possess enough size for one position or enough quickness for another.

## Two-Level Defense

A defense with only two levels of defensive organization instead of the usual three. This is considered to be a much more aggressive defense than normal.

## Two-Minute Warning

A stoppage of the clock at the two-minute mark of the second and fourth quarters. The two-minute warning often serves as an extra timeout for a trailing team that manages the clock properly.

## Two-Point Conversion

A scoring play worth two points, immediately after a touchdown by running or passing the ball into the end zone on one play starting from the opponent's two-yard line.

# – U –

## Umpire

He is the official who lines up on the defensive side of the ball approximately five yards from the line of scrimmage. His responsibilities vary from making sure the offense has no more than 11 players on the field to wiping the ball dry between plays on rainy days.

## Unbalanced Line

An offensive formation which does not have an equal number of linemen on each side of the ball.

## Under Center

This refers to the quarterback lining up directly behind the center to take the snap.

## Unnecessary Roughness

An illegal action where the official believes the player used excessive force during a play. Unnecessary roughness is a personal foul and results in a 15-yard penalty against the offending team.

## Unsportsmanlike Conduct

A penalty where the official feels a player acted in a manner which was inappropriate to another player. A call for unsportsmanlike conduct is considered a personal foul and results in a 15-yard penalty against the offending team.

## Upman

Every player on the return team during a kickoff is called an upman, with the exception of the one or two designated kickoff returners who stand farthest away from the starting point of the kicking team.

## Uprights

The two vertical posts that project upward from the crossbar on the goal post. A field goal must pasts between the uprights to count as three points.

# −V−

## Veer
A quick-hitting run where the ball is handed to a running back whose routes are determined by the slant of the defensive linemen.

# −W−

## Waive
Releasing a player from a team roster. This generally refers to players in the National Football League.

## Walk-on
A player who is not receiving a college scholarship to play football.

## Weak Side
The offense opposite the side on which the tight end lines up. My husband says I actually have two weak sides; shopping and traveling.

## West Coast Offense
An offensive philosophy that uses short, high-percentage passes as the core of a ball-control offense.

## Wheel Route
A pass route in which the receiver, usually the running back, takes off up the field and travels parallel along the line of scrimmage.

## Wide
A term which relates to the outer areas of the field, when a receiver runs his play route "wide" to the sidelines. This can also relate to a place-kick which has gone "wide" right and missed the uprights for a field goal.

## Wideout

A receiver who lines up far to the outside at the line of scrimmage. His primary job is to catch passes from the quarterback. He is also known as receiver, wide receiver, split end or flanker.

## Wide Receiver

An offensive player position that lines up on or near the line of scrimmage, but splits to the outside. His main job is to catch passes from the quarterback.

## Wing Back

See Wide Reciever.

## Win-Loss

This is the ratio of wins to losses. For example, 6-1 means six wins and one loss.

## Winning Percentage

The percentage of wins that a team has completed which is based on the following formula: Winning Percentage = (#wins + #ties/2)/(#games played). UT's Mack Brown is the NCAA's winningest coach over the past 11 seasons, with a winning percentage of .819. His win/loss record is (113-25).

## Wishbone Formation

A football formation which involves three running backs lined up behind the quarterback in the shape of a Y, similar to the shape of a wishbone.

## –X–

## X-Receiver

A term used in play calling that usually refers to the split end or to the wide receiver that lines up on the line of scrimmage.

### X's & O's

This refers to the diagrams of plays used by coaches on paper, a chalkboard, or sometimes even computers. Coaches generally use X's and O's to differentiate between the defensive and offensive players in a diagram.

X's & O's

# —Y—

### YAC

Short for "Yards After Catch." This relates to the amount of yardage a receiver gains after catching the football for a reception.

### Yard

The unit of measure on the football field. A team is required to gain 10 yards for a first down. The football field is 120 yards in length.

### Yardage

The number of yards gained or lost during a play, game, season or career.

### Yards from Scrimmage

The number of yards gained by the offensive team advancing the ball from the line of scrimmage.

### Yellow Flag

The weighted yellow marker that is thrown onto the field by the officials which signifies that a foul has been committed by either the offensive or defensive team. This can also be referred to as a "flag."

## Y-Receiver

The term usually used in offensive play calling which refers to the tight end.

# –Z–

## Z-Receiver

This is a term that is used in offensive play calling that generally refers to the flanker, or the wide receiver that lines up off the line of scrimmage.

## Zebra

No, not the one you would see at the zoo! I got caught looking for one when I heard "here come the zebras." I later found out it's a colloquial term for an official, referring to their black-and-white- striped uniform.

## Zone Blitz

A defensive package combining a blitz with zone pass coverage. This play allows the defense to choose the blitzer after the offense shows formation and pass coverage requirements, and features unpredictable blitzes from different linebackers and defensive backs.

## Zone Defense

A defense in which players who are in pass coverage cover zones of the field, instead of individual players. Pure zone packages are seldom used; most defenses employ some combination of zone and man coverage.

## Zone Read

This is a type of "option offense" where the quarterback and tail back line up approximately side by side. Once the quarterback receives the snap, the two players will then cross paths and go through the motions of a hand-off. Depending on the defensive reaction, the quarterback either completes the handoff, or he will pull the ball out and run with it himself.

# Chapter 5
# LONGHORN SEASON STATS 1997-2007

## 2007 Season

**Coach:** Mack Brown
**Season:** 10-3-0
**Big 12:** 5-3-0

**Final Statistics:**

| Date | National Rank | Opponent | Results |
|---|---|---|---|
| Sept. 1 | (#4) | Arkansas State | W 21-13 |
| Sept. 8 | (#7) | #19 TCU | W 34-13 |
| Sept. 15 | (#6) | @ Central Florida | W 35-32 |
| Sept. 22 | (#7) | Rice | W 58-14 |
| Sept. 29 | (#7) | Kansas State | L 21-41 |
| Oct. 6 | (#19) | #10 Oklahoma | L 21-28 |
| Oct. 13 | (#23) | @ Iowa State | W 56-3 |
| Oct. 20 | (#19) | @ Baylor | W 31-10 |
| Oct. 27 | (#19) | Nebraska | W 28-25 |
| Nov. 3 | (#14) | @ Oklahoma State | W 38-35 |
| Nov. 10 | (#14) | Texas Tech | W 59-43 |
| Nov. 23 | (#14) | Texas A&M | L 30-38 |
| Dec. 27 | (#17) | #12 Arizona State | W 52-34* |

*Holiday Bowl*

Longhorn Lingo

## 2006 Season

**Coach:** Mack Brown
**Season:** 10-3-0
**Big 12:** 6-2-0
**Final Ranking:** #13 AP; #13 Coaches

**Final Statistics:**

| Date | National Rank | Opponent | Results |
| --- | --- | --- | --- |
| Sept. 2 | (#2) | North Texas | W  56-7 |
| Sept. 9 | (#2) | #1 Ohio State | L  7-24 |
| Sept. 16 | (#8) | Rice | W  52-7 |
| Sept. 23 | (#7) | Iowa State | W  37-14 |
| Sept. 30 | (#7) | Sam Houston State | W  56-3 |
| Oct. 7 | (#7) | #14 Oklahoma | W  28-10 |
| Oct. 14 | (#6) | Baylor | W  63-31 |
| Oct. 21 | (#5) | @ #17 Nebraska | W  22-20 |
| Oct. 28 | (#5) | @ Texas Tech | W  35-31 |
| Nov. 4 | (#4) | Oklahoma State | W  36-10 |
| Nov. 11 | (#4) | @ Kansas State | L  42-45 |
| Nov. 24 | (#11) | Texas A&M | L  7-12 |
| Dec. 30 | (#18) | Iowa | W  26-24* |

*\* Alamo Bowl*

Barb Wagner

2005 Season: NATIONAL CHAMPIONS

**Coach:** Mack Brown
**Season:** 13-0-0
**Big 12:** 8-0-0
**Final Ranking:** 1st AP; 1st USA Today/ESPN

**Final Statistics:**

| Date | National Rank | Opponent | Results |
|---|---|---|---|
| Sept. 3 | (#2) | Louisiana-Lafayette | W 60-3 |
| Sept. 10 | (#2) | @ #4 Ohio State | W 25-22 |
| Sept. 17 | (#2) | Rice | W 51-10 |
| Oct. 1 | (#2) | @ Missouri | W 51-20 |
| Oct. 8 | (#2) | Oklahoma | W 45-12 |
| Oct. 15 | (#2) | #24 Colorado | W 42-17 |
| Oct. 22 | (#2) | #10 Texas Tech | W 52-17 |
| Oct. 29 | (#2) | @ Oklahoma State | W 47-28 |
| Nov. 5 | (#2) | @ Baylor | W 62-0 |
| Nov. 12 | (#2) | Kansas | W 66-14 |
| Nov. 25 | (#2) | @ Texas A&M | W 40-29 |
| Dec. 3 | (#2) | Colorado | W 70-3* |
| Jan. 4 | (#2) | #1 USC | W 41-38** |

*Big 12 Championship*
*\*\* Rose Bowl*

Longhorn Lingo

### 2004 Season

**Coach:** Mack Brown
**Season:** 11-1-0
**Big 12:** 7-1
**Final Ranking:** 5th AP; 4th USA Today/ESPN

**Final Statistics:**

| Date | National Rank | Opponent | Results |
|---|---|---|---|
| Sept. 4 | (#7) | North Texas | W 65-0 |
| Sept. 11 | (#7) | @ Arkansas | W 22-20 |
| Sept. 25 | (#5) | Rice | W 35-13 |
| Oct. 2 | (#5) | Baylor | W 44-14 |
| Oct. 9 | (#5) | #2 Oklahoma | L 0-12 |
| Oct. 16 | (#9) | #24 Missouri | W 28-20 |
| Oct. 23 | (#8) | @ #24 Texas Tech | W 51-21 |
| Oct. 30 | (#8) | @ Colorado | W 31-7 |
| Nov. 6 | (#6) | #19 Oklahoma St. | W 56-35 |
| Nov. 13 | (#6) | @ Kansas | W 27-23 |
| Nov. 26 | (#5) | #22 Texas A&M | W 26-13 |
| Jan. 1 | (#6) | #12 Michigan | W 38-37* |

*Rose Bowl*

## 2003 Season

**Coach:** Mack Brown
**Season:** 10-3-0
**Big 12:** 7-1-0
**Final Ranking:** 12th AP; 11th USA Today/ESPN

**Final Statistics:**

| Date | National Rank | Opponent | Results |
|---|---|---|---|
| Aug. 31 | (#5) | New Mexico State | W 66-7 |
| Sept. 13 | (#6) | Arkansas | L 28-38 |
| Sept. 20 | (#13) | @ Rice | W 48-7 |
| Sept. 27 | (#13) | Tulane | W 63-18 |
| Oct. 4 | (#13) | #16 Kansas State | W 24-20 |
| Oct. 11 | (#11) | #1 Oklahoma | L 13-65 |
| Oct. 18 | (#20) | @ Iowa State | W 40-19 |
| Oct. 25 | (#19) | @ Baylor | W 56-0 |
| Nov. 1 | (#16) | #12 Nebraska | W 31-7 |
| Nov. 8 | (#11) | @ #21 Oklahoma St. | W 55-16 |
| Nov. 15 | (#6) | Texas Tech | W 43-40 |
| Nov. 28 | (#6) | @ Texas A&M | W 46-15 |
| Dec. 30 | (#5) | #15 Washington St. | L 20-28* |

*Holiday Bowl*

Longhorn Lingo

2002 Season

**Coach:** Mack Brown
**Season:** 11-2-0
**Big 12:** 6-2-0
**Final Ranking:** 6th AP; 7th USA Today/ESPN

**Final Statistics:**

| Date | National Rank | Opponent | Results |
| --- | --- | --- | --- |
| Aug. 31 | (#3) | North Texas | W 27-0 |
| Sept. 14 | (#3) | @ North Carolina | W 52-21 |
| Sept. 21 | (#3) | Houston | W 41-11 |
| Sept. 28 | (#3) | @ Tulane | W 49-0 |
| Oct. 5 | (#2) | Oklahoma State | W 17-15 |
| Oct. 12 | (#3) | #2 Oklahoma | L 24-35 |
| Oct. 19 | (#8) | @ #17 Kansas State | W 17-14 |
| Oct. 26 | (#7) | #17 Iowa State | W 21-10 |
| Nov. 2 | (#7) | @ Nebraska | W 27-24 |
| Nov. 9 | (#4) | Baylor | W 41-0 |
| Nov. 16 | (#4) | @ Texas Tech | L 38-42 |
| Nov. 29 | (#10) | Texas A&M | W 50-20 |
| Jan. 1 | (#9) | LSU | W 35-20* |

*Cotton Bowl*

## 2001 Season

**Coach:** Mack Brown
**Season:** 11-2-0
**Big 12:** 7-1-0
**Final Ranking:** 5th AP; 5th USA Today/ESPN

**Final statistics:**

| Date | National Rank | Opponent | Results |
|---|---|---|---|
| Sept. 1 | (#5) | New Mexico State | W 41-7 |
| Sept. 8 | (#4) | North Carolina | W 44-14 |
| Sept. 22 | (#5) | @ Houston | W 53-26 |
| Sept. 29 | (#5) | Texas Tech | W 42-7 |
| Oct. 6 | (#5) | #3 Oklahoma | L 3-14 |
| Oct. 13 | (#11) | @ Oklahoma State | W 45-17 |
| Oct. 20 | (#9) | #14 Colorado | W 41-7 |
| Oct. 27 | (#7) | @ Missouri | W 35-16 |
| Nov. 3 | (#5) | @ Baylor | W 49-10 |
| Nov. 10 | (#5) | Kansas | W 59-0 |
| Nov. 23 | (#5) | @ Texas A&M | W 21-7 |
| Dec. 1 | (#3) | #9 Colorado | L 37-39* |
| Dec. 28 | (#9) | #21 Washington | W 47-43** |

*Big 12 Championship*
**Holiday Bowl*

Longhorn Lingo

2000 Season

**Coach:** Mack Brown
**Season:** 9-3
**Big 12:** 7-1 (2nd, South Division)
**Final Ranking:** 12th AP; 12th USA Today/ESPN

**Final Statistics:**

| Date | National Rank | Opponent | Results |
|---|---|---|---|
| Sept. 9 | (#6) | Louisiana-Lafayette | W 52-10 |
| Sept. 16 | (#5) | @ Stanford | L 24-27 |
| Sept. 23 | (#15) | Houston | W 48-0 |
| Sept. 30 | (#13) | Oklahoma State | W 42-7 |
| Oct. 7 | (#11) | #10 Oklahoma | L 14-63 |
| Oct. 14 | (#25) | @ Colorado | W 28-14 |
| Oct. 21 | | Missouri | W 46-12 |
| Oct. 28 | (#22) | Baylor | W 48-14 |
| Nov. 4 | (#20) | @ Texas Tech | W 29-17 |
| Nov. 11 | (#19) | @ Kansas | W 51-16 |
| Nov. 24 | (#12) | #22 Texas A&M | W 43-17 |
| Dec. 29 | (#12) | #8 Oregon | L 30-35* |

*Holiday Bowl*

## 1999 Season

**Coach:** Mack Brown
**Season:** 9-5
**Big 12:** 6-2 (1st, South Division)
**Final Ranking:** 21st AP; 23rd USA Today/ESPN

**Final Statistics:**

| Date | National Rank | Opponent | Results |
| --- | --- | --- | --- |
| Aug. 28 | (#17) | N. Carolina St. | L 20-23 |
| Sept. 4 | | Stanford | W 69-17 |
| Sept. 11 | | @ Rutgers | W 38-21 |
| Sept. 18 | | Rice | W 18-13 |
| Sept. 25 | (#22) | @ Baylor | W 62-0 |
| Oct. 2 | (#15) | #13 Kansas State | L 17-35 |
| Oct. 9 | (#23) | Oklahoma | W 38-28 |
| Oct. 23 | (#18) | #3 Nebraska | W 24-20 |
| Oct. 30 | (#12) | @ Iowa State | W 44-41 |
| Nov. 6 | (#11) | @ Oklahoma State | W 34-21 |
| Nov. 13 | (#10) | Texas Tech | W 58-7 |
| Nov. 26 | (#7) | @ #24 Texas A&M | L 16-20 |
| Dec. 4 | (#12) | #3 Nebraska | L 6-22* |
| Jan. 1 | (#14) | #24 Arkansas | L 6-27** |

*Big 12 Championship*
**Cotton Bowl*

# Longhorn Lingo

## 1998 Season

**Coach:** Mack Brown
**Season:** 9-3
**Big 12:** 6-2 (2nd, South Division)
**Final Ranking:** 15th AP; 16th USA Today/ESPN

## Final Statistics:

| Date | National Rank | Opponent | Results |
| --- | --- | --- | --- |
| Sept. 5 | | New Mexico State | W 66-36 |
| Sept. 12 | (#23) | @ #6 UCLA | L 31-49 |
| Sept. 19 | | @ #5 Kansas State | L 7-48 |
| Sept. 26 | | Rice | W 59-21 |
| Oct. 3 | | Iowa State | W 54-33 |
| Oct. 10 | | Oklahoma | W 34-3 |
| Oct. 24 | | Baylor | W 30-20 |
| Oct. 31 | | @ #7 Nebraska | W 20-16 |
| Nov. 7 | (#20) | Oklahoma State | W 37-34 |
| Nov. 14 | (#18) | @ Texas Tech | L 35-42 |
| Nov. 27 | | #6 Texas A&M | W 26-24 |
| Jan. 1 | (#20) | #25 Mississississippi St. | W 38-11 |

Longhorns Bowl Game Appearances

*Cotton Bowl — 22:* 1943, 1944, 1946, 1951, 1953, 1960, 1962, 1963, 1964, 1969, 1970, 1971, 1972, 1973, 1974, 1978, 1982, 1984, 1991, 1999, 2000, 2003
*Bluebonnet Bowl — 6:* 1960, 1966, 1975, 1980, 1985, 1987
*Sun Bowl — 4:* 1978, 1979, 1982, 1994
*Sugar Bowl — 3:* 1948, 1958, 1995
*Holiday Bowl — 4:* 2000, 2001, 2003, 2007
*Orange Bowl — 2:* 1949, 1965
*Rose Bowl — 2:* 2005, 2006
*Alamo Bowl — 1:* 2006
*Fiesta Bowl — 1:* 1997
*Freedom Bowl — 1:* 1984
*Gator Bowl — 1:* 1974

Bowl Game Results

**1943 Cotton Bowl:** #11 Texas 14, #5 Georgia Tech 7
**1944 Cotton Bowl:** #14 Texas 7, Randolph Field 7
**1946 Cotton Bowl:** #10 Texas 40, Missouri 27
**1948 Sugar Bowl:** #5 Texas 27, #6 Alabama 7
**1949 Orange Bowl:** Texas 41, #8 Georgia 28
**1951 Cotton Bowl:** #4 Tennessee 20, #3 Texas 14
**1953 Cotton Bowl:** #10 Texas 16, #8 Tennessee 0
**1958 Sugar Bowl:** #7 Mississippi 39, #11 Texas 7
**1960 Cotton Bowl:** #1 Syracuse 23, #4 Texas 14
**1960 Bluebonnet Bowl:** Texas 3, #9 Alabama 3
**1962 Cotton Bowl:** #3 Texas 12, #5 Mississippi 7
**1963 Cotton Bowl:** #7 LSU 13, #4 Texas 0
**1964 Cotton Bowl:** #1 Texas 28, #2 Navy 6
**1965 Orange Bowl:** #5 Texas 21, #1 Alabama 17
**1966 Bluebonnet Bowl:** Texas 19, Mississippi 0
**1969 Cotton Bowl:** #5 Texas 36, #8 Tennessee 13
**1970 Cotton Bowl:** #1 Texas 21, #9 Notre Dame 17
**1971 Cotton Bowl:** #6 Notre Dame 24, #1 Texas 11
**1972 Cotton Bowl:** #10 Penn State 30, #12 Texas 6
**1973 Cotton Bowl:** #7 Texas 17, #4 Alabama 13

## Longhorn Lingo

**1974 Cotton Bowl:** #12 Nebraska 19, #8 Texas 3
**1974 Gator Bowl:** #6 Auburn 27, #11 Texas 3
**1975 Bluebonnet Bowl:** #9 Texas 38, #10 Colorado 21
**1978 Cotton Bowl:** #5 Notre Dame 38, #1 Texas 10
**1978 Sun Bowl:** #14 Texas 42, #13 Maryland 0
**1979 Sun Bowl:** #13 Washington 14, #11 Texas 7
**1980 Bluebonnet Bowl:** #13 North Carolina 16, Texas 7
**1982 Cotton Bowl:** #6 Texas 14, #3 Alabama 12
**1982 Sun Bowl:** North Carolina 26, #8 Texas 10
**1984 Cotton Bowl:** #7 Georgia 10, #2 Texas 9
**1984 Freedom Bowl:** Iowa 55, #19 Texas 17
**1985 Bluebonnet Bowl:** #11 Air Force 24, Texas 16
**1987 Bluebonnet Bowl:** Texas 32, Pittsburgh 27
**1991 Cotton Bowl:** #4 Miami, 46, #3 Texas 3
**1994 Sun Bowl:** Texas 35, #19 North Carolina 31
**1995 Sugar Bowl:** #13 Virginia Tech 28, #9 Texas 10
**1997 Fiesta Bowl:** #7 Penn State 38, #20 Texas 15
**1999 Cotton Bowl:** #20 Texas 38, #25 Mississippi St. 11
**2000 Cotton Bowl:** #24 Arkansas 27, #14 Texas 6
**2000 Holiday Bowl:** #8 Oregon 35, #12 Texas 30
**2001 Holiday Bowl:** #9 Texas 47, #21 Washington 43
**2003 Cotton Bowl:** #9 Texas 35, LSU 20
**2003 Holiday Bowl:** #15 Washington St. 28, #5 Texas 20
**2005 Rose Bowl:** #6 Texas 38, #13 Michigan 37
**2006 Rose Bowl:** #2 Texas 41, #1 USC 38
**2006 Alamo Bowl:** #18 Texas 26, Iowa 24
**2007 Holiday Bowl:** #17 Texas 52, #12 Arizona State 34

# Chapter 6
# MEMORABLE LONGHORNS

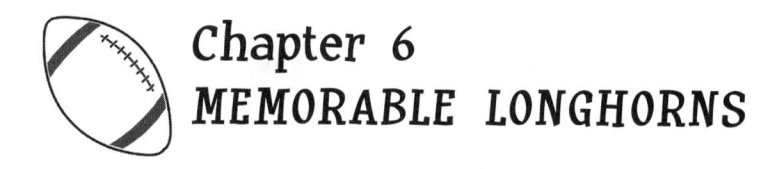

After reading *What it Means to be a Longhorn*, edited by Bill Little and Jenna McEachern, and reading about some other players that weren't mentioned in that book, I thought to myself, How in the heck am I going to choose only a few top players for my top picks? Everyone who played or plays for the Longhorns is absolutely spectacular. I mean everyone!

Even though some of the players have been challenged with negative circumstances during their lives, they are still incredible athletes. My mom has always taught me that nobody's perfect, and that everyone in this world has made a bad decision or two in life. I was also taught by her not to judge others unless I've walked a mile in their shoes, or in this case, cleats. Pass it on!

### Cedric Myron Benson

Cedric Benson attended Robert E. Lee High School in Midland, Texas, and finished his career with 8,423 rushing yards (the most in Texas 5A history and the fourth most in Texas high school football history). Cedric was also a center fielder on the baseball team. As a senior, in District 4-5A games, he hit .361 with 4 home runs and 14 RBIs. Benson was selected by the Los Angeles Dodgers in the 12th round of the 2001 MLB draft.

After a brilliant high school career, Cedric was a four-year starter at the University of Texas at Austin, where he received the Doak Walker Award as the nation's top running back in 2004. He finished his college career with 5,540 rushing yards to rank sixth in NCAA Division I-A history, and second only to Ricky Williams in school history. Benson was a 2004 All-America selection. He has regularly been compared to Ricky Williams due to their similar build, they both played minor league baseball and they both had similar-type dreadlock hairstyles.

After a successful college career, Cedric was selected by the Chicago Bears as the fourth overall selection in the 2005 NFL draft. After a thirty-six-day contract hold out, Cedric came to terms on a five-year, 36-million-dollar contract through 2009. He has suffered several injuries since his signing, but he had a successful year in 2007 playing in 11 games. Cedric carried the ball 196 times for 674 yards on the ground, while adding four touchdowns. He also caught 17 passes for an average of 7.2 yards per reception.

## Derrick "DJ" O'Hara Johnson

Derrick attended Waco High School, where he earned Parade All-American and first team All-Texas Class 5A honors following both his junior and senior seasons. As a senior, Derrick registered 170 tackles (103 solo), 21 stops for a loss, 6.0 sacks, five forced fumbles and two INT's, including one for a touchdown as a senior. Derrick once posted 30 tackles in a single high school football game.

While attending Texas, Derrick registered 458 tackles (281 solo), a school record 65.0 tackles for loss, 10.5 sacks and 10 INT's for 199 yards with a touchdown. This was all in his 40 starts with the Longhorns. He was a very dominant linebacker during his college career which earned him a first-round draft pick (15th overall) with the Kansas City Chiefs of the NFL. He was the Longhorn's linebacker to be chosen in the first round of the NFL draft since 1966.

Although he has only played in the NFL for three seasons, Derrick is developing into one of the most promising young defensive players in the National Football League. Derrick has terrific sideline-to-sideline speed, which allows him to be utilized in a variety of roles. He was the first rookie linebacker to start in all 16 regular-season games with the Chiefs since 1986.

## Earl Christian Campbell

Campbell was born in Tyler, Texas, the sixth of 11 children. In 1973, he led John Tyler High School to the Texas 4A State Championship (4A then was the largest classification in the state).

His nickname is *The Tyler Rose*, a name that refers to his hometown of Tyler, Texas, which is known as the "Rose Capital of America" for its prominent place in the rose-growing industry.

As a collegiate football player at the University of Texas at Austin, he won the Heisman Trophy in 1977 and led the nation in rushing with 1,744 yards. He was selected as the Southwest Conference running back of the year in each of his college seasons and finished with 4,444 career rushing yards.

After an extremely successful college career, Campbell was the first draft pick overall in the 1978 NFL draft by the Houston Oilers, and in that year he was named the Offensive Rookie of the Year by the Associated Press as well as the Most Valuable Player.

Campbell led the NFL in rushing in 1978, 1979 and 1980. He played in five Pro Bowls and finished his career with 9,407 yards and 74 touchdowns rushing along with 806 yards on 121 receptions. In 1980, Campbell's best year in the NFL, he ran for 1,934 yards with four 200-yard rushing games, including a personal best 206 yards against the Chicago Bears. Earl is also a member of the National Football League's Hall of Fame.

## Errick (Ricky) Lynne Williams, Jr.

Williams was born, along with his twin sister Cassandra, in San Diego, California. In San Diego's Patrick Henry High School, Williams primarily played baseball and football, but also ran track and wrestled. On the football field, Williams gained 2,099 yards and scored 25 touchdowns. He was named Offensive Player of the Year by the San Diego Union-Tribune.

Williams was selected out of Patrick Henry High School

in the eighth round of the 1995 baseball amateur draft by the Philadelphia Phillies and played four years at the Class A level with the Batavia Muckdogs of the New York-Penn League and the Piedmont Boll Weevils of the South Atlantic League.

He played college football for the University of Texas at Austin. Williams holds or shares 20 NCAA records and became the NCAA Division I-A career rushing leader in 1998, with 6,279 yards (broken one year later by University of Wisconsin-Madison's Ron Dayne). He also broke the NCAA Division I-A career rushing touchdowns and career scoring records in 1998, with 73 and 452 respectively (topped one year later by Miami University's Travis Prentice), and rushed for 200 or more yards in 12 different games (an NCAA record he shares with Dayne and USC's Marcus Allen). Williams won the 64th Heisman Trophy, becoming the second Texas Longhorn to win this honor, joining Earl Campbell.

He was drafted by the New Orleans Saints fifth overall in the 1999 NFL draft. Head coach Mike Ditka traded all of the Saints' 1999 draft picks to get Williams, as well as a first and third pick the following year. This was the first time one player was the only draft pick of an NFL team. Williams was traded after three seasons to the Miami Dolphins on March 8, 2002 for two first-round picks. In his first season with the Dolphins, he was the NFL's leading rusher and a Pro Bowler with 1,853 yards.

### John David Thomas

Thomas attended Frenship High School in Wolfforth, Texas, and helped Frenship reach the state semifinals in its division in 2000. Thomas excelled at linebacker, running back and tight end for the Tigers, leading some to wonder which position he would play in college. After a heated recruiting battle with Texas Tech University, the University of Texas secured a pledge from Thomas to play tight end for the Longhorns.

At Texas, Thomas broke school records for receptions,

touchdowns and yards by a tight end, as well as for receptions in a single game. Long a favorite (and safety valve) of quarterback Vince Young, Thomas played a prominent role in the Longhorns 41-38 National Championship upset of then #1 USC in the 2006 Rose Bowl, hauling in a game-high 10 receptions for 88 yards.

Thomas was drafted in the third round of the 2006 NFL draft by the New England Patriots. Thomas has been sidelined due to injuries and only appeared in one game during the 2007 season.

## Major Lee Applewhite

A native of Baton Rouge, Louisiana, Applewhite threw for 50 touchdowns and ran for eight more in two years as a starter at Catholic High School.

Applewhite wanted to attend the University of Alabama, as he grew up an Alabama fan and was even named after former Crimson Tide legend Major Ogilvie, but the university's then-head coach Mike Dubose chose to sign two other quarterbacks, neither of whom was particularly successful, over Applewhite. Applewhite was quarterback for the Texas Longhorns from 1998 to 2001. He was the Longhorns' team captain in 2001, and he helped Texas to four straight bowl games — the 1999 and 2000 Cotton Bowls and the 2000 and 2001 Holiday Bowls. He was the Holiday Bowl's offensive MVP in his final college game in 2001, leading the Longhorns to a 47-43 comeback win over Washington.

After a successful college career, Applewhite attended the 2002 training camp of the New England Patriots, but quit prior to the start of the season to pursue a career in coaching.

On January 16, 2008, Applewhite accepted an offer to become running backs coach at the University of Texas. He will also serve as assistant head coach to Mack Brown. Prior to Texas, Applewhite served as offensive coordinator at Rice University under Todd Graham in 2006, and at the University of Alabama under Nick Saban in 2007. He was the youngest offensive coordinator among football bowl championship schools at that time.

## Vincent Paul Young, Jr.

Vince played football at Madison High School in Houston, Texas, where he started at quarterback for three years and compiled 12,987 yards of total offense during his career. He accounted for 3,819 yards and 59 touchdowns as a senior. Senior passing totals included 2,545 yards, 35 touchdowns and four interceptions on 131 of 224 completions.

After his dominant high school career, Young chose to sign with Texas in 2002 for its winning tradition and football prominence there. He was part of a Texas recruiting class which contained future NFL players Rodrique Wright, Justin Blalock, Brian Robinson, Kasey Studdard, Lyle Sendlein, David Thomas, Selvin Young, and Aaron Ross.

As a redshirt sophomore in the 2004 season, Young started every game and led the Longhorns to an 11-1 season record (losing only to rival Oklahoma), a top five final ranking, and the school's first-ever appearance and victory in the Rose Bowl, in which they defeated the University of Michigan. He began to earn his reputation as a dual-threat quarterback by passing for 1,849 and rushing for 1,189 yards.

In his All-American 2005 season, Young led the Longhorns to an 11-0 regular-season record. In the 2005 Rose Bowl, Vince Young put on one of the most dominating individual performances in college football history, accounting for 467 yards of total offense (200 rushing, 267 passing) and three rushing touchdowns (including a nine-yard TD scramble with 19 seconds left) to lead the Longhorns to a thrilling 41-38 victory. This performance led him to winning Rose Bowl MVP honors for the second consecutive season.

Young's career passing completion percentage of 60.8% is the best in UT history. During his career at Texas (2003-05), Young passed for 6,040 yards (No. 5 in UT history) and 44 TDs (No. 4 in UT history), while rushing for 3,127 yards (No. 1 on UT's all-time QB rushing list/No. 7 on UT's all-time list) and 37 TDs (No. 5 on UT's all-time rushing TDs list/Tied for No. 1 among QBs).

Vince was a first-round draft pick (third overall) by the Tennessee Titans of the NFL. In his first season, he earned an 8-5 record as a starter and was named the Associated Press NFL Offensive Rookie of the Year. When Young was added to the AFC Pro Bowl roster in his rookie season, he became the first rookie quarterback since Dan Marino in 1983 to make the team. Vince continues to be a dominant player in the NFL.

# Chapter 7
# THE FOOTBALL LINGO TRIVIA QUIZ

Let's have some fun with this chapter and see what you have learned from my book. If you get the answer wrong or don't know the answer, challenge yourself. Go back to the lingo section and find the answer. Everyone, including you, will be impressed.

1) This refers to when a quarterback, after taking the snap from the center, takes several steps backward into an area called "the pocket" to get ready to pass the football.
   a) Drop back
   b) Encroachment
   c) Place kick
   d) Power sweep

2) A particularly hard block that leaves the blocked player lying flat on the field.
   a) Checkdown
   b) Pancake
   c) Pass defender
   d) Oddsmaker

3) These players are teammates who step up and create opportunities or make big plays when the team needs them the most.
   a) Pylons
   b) Red dogs
   c) Playmakers
   d) Scooby dogs

4) The area of the field that is bordered by the two sidelines, goal line and end line.
   a) The pocket
   b) The sideline
   c) The red zone
   d) The end zone

5) This is what a receiver will run when he leaves the line of scrimmage.
   a) Sack
   b) Inwards
   c) Route
   d) Serpentine

4) This type of foul occurs when a player uses the crown of his helmet to hit another player, resulting in a 15-yard penalty.
   a) Clipping
   b) Tripping
   c) Spearing
   d) Interference

5) This occurs when a defensive player crosses the line of scrimmage and makes contact with a player, or has an unabated path to the quarterback before the snap.
   a) Pooch kick
   b) Encroachment
   c) Fair catch
   d) Holding

6) These players are referred to as second string players who are not in the starting lineup but play an integral role in the football game.
   a) Bench players
   b) Pooch players
   c) Wing formation players
   d) Drop kick players

7) This refers to the name of the facemask worn by football players which has vertical and horizontal bars.
   a) Dog cage
   b) Bird cage
   c) Cat cage
   d) Bunny cage

8) If the quarterback is looking to the right, he will get hit and tackled from the left side and will not see the defender approaching. This term is called...
   a) Gang tackled
   b) Lolly gagged
   c) Bootlegged
   d) Blind sided

9) This pass receiver's route is when a receiver runs straight down the field a certain distance and then stops hard and runs straight back towards the quarterback.
   a) Checkdown
   b) Buttonhook
   c) Coffin Corner
   d) Slew foot

10) This is when as offensive player begins to move laterally along and parallel to the line of scrimmage before the ball is snapped.
    a) Necessary line
    b) Parallel point
    c) Man in motion
    d) On downs

11) A play in which the kicking team tries to recover the kicked ball. The ball must travel at least ten yards before the kicking team can recover it.
    a) On-side kick
    b) Off-side punt

c) Place kick
d) Hang time

12) The loss of the ball by one team to the other team. This is usually the result of a fumble or an interception.
    a) Dime package
    b) Trick play
    c) Turnover
    d) Backfield

13) A play called by the quarterback at the line of scrimmage to make a change from the play that was called in the huddle. The quarterback will shout from side to side to ensure all players hear the change.
    a) Audible
    b) Silent auction
    c) False start
    d) First and ten

14) The only two players in Longhorn's history to win the coveted Heisman Trophy Award.
    a) Vince Young & Roy Williams
    b) Earl Campbell & Jerry Sisemore
    c) Cedric Benson & Eric Metcalf
    d) Ricky Williams & Earl Campbell

15) When did the Texas Longhorn's last win the National Championship?
    a) 1999
    b) 2001
    c) 2006
    d) 2005

16) A long pass play, thrown toward a group of receivers near the end zone in hope of a touchdown. Used by a team as a last resort when time is running out

in either of two halves (usually by a team trailing in the second half).
   a) Yokahama
   b) Gunslinger
   c) Hail Mary
   d) Wheel Route

17) Which Longhorn graduate is the current quarterback for the Tennessee Titans of the NFL?
   a) Ricky Williams
   b) Major Applewhite
   c) James Brown
   d) Vince Young

18) Which formation involves three running backs lined up in the backfield behind the quarterback, in the shape of a Y?
   a) Herringbone
   b) Wishbone
   c) Run and shoot
   d) Power sweep

## ANSWERS

1) A
2) B
3) C
4) D
5) C
6) C
7) B
8) A
9) B
10) D
11) B
12) C
13) A
14) C
15) A
16) D
17) D
18) C
19) D
20) B

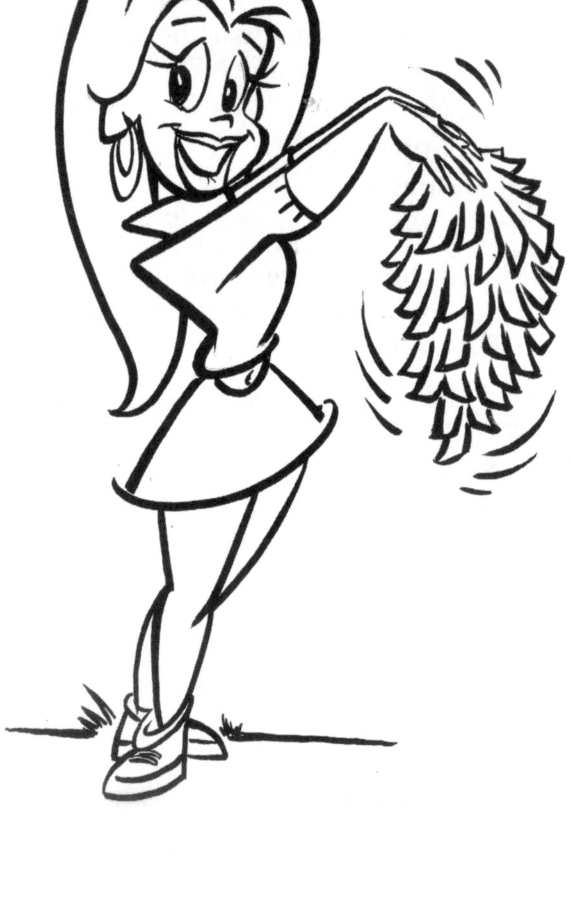

# Chapter 8
# HOUSE & TAILGATE PARTY SUGGESTIONS

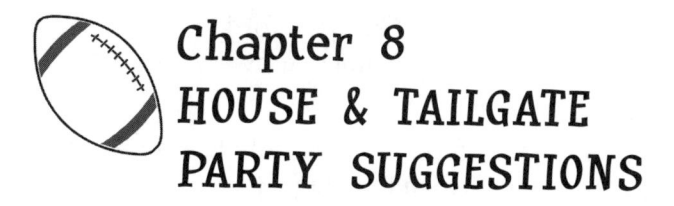

**Ready to have** a kick-off party? Try some of theses MVPS, Most Valuable Party Suggestions.

All teams and players know that in order to have a winning game, you have to be organized and prepared. Here are some "touchdown" ideas that will "assist" you in having a crowd-pleasing party!

> Touch Down Tip – Before organizing your party or any party for that matter, it's always good to get into the habit of asking guests if they have any food allergies.

Before organizing your party, it's always a good habit to ask your guests about any food allergies they may have and then plan accordingly.

## Pre-Game Plan

### Being prepared

Organizing a party is fun and will go smoothly if you are organized and prepared for it. Make a list in advance of the food, snacks and drinks you plan on serving. If you are having children at the party, try and have a designated area in which they can play.

If you have the menu completely under control and don't need your guests to bring any food, have your guests bring any of the following:

Loud noise makers    Foam fingers
Fun hats    Face paint
Tattoos    Funny large glasses

# Longhorn Lingo

Whistles                    Gift bags for kids
Treats for kids             Games/movies/music

## Food time

The goal is to serve food that not only tastes great but won't keep you in the kitchen too long. Here are three great traditions for you to consider.

1) For a fast and easy meal, order:
   - A variety of pizza's and wings
   - A long, pre-cut deli sandwich
   - Fried chicken, a variety of wings and salads
   
   Or buy a vast favorite of sandwich fixings and let your guests put their own creation on sub buns, fresh Kaiser buns or fresh bakery Italian bread.

2) Now here's my favorite! Organize a potluck where your guests bring their favorite dish. It's always nice to have a wide variety of food on the table.

3) BBQ ideas:
   Hamburgers, hot dogs, sausages (simple and takes less time)
   Rotisserie chickens, pork or roast
   Large batch of wings and/or ribs

Regardless what route you take, buffet style is everyone's favorite way to go. They can serve themselves during breaks and halftime.

Make sure you have plenty of chips, pretzels, nuts and dips in front of the TV for the guests to munch on during the game.

## "Warm-up" tips before the game

Most desserts, hot spreads, chili, salads, trays and dips can all be arranged, covered and refrigerated up to two days in advance. Not only does this save you time, but some of the food actually tastes better after the flavors have had time to absorb.

- Keeping the party food warm is easy by placing the hot dishes covered in the oven at 200°F. Reload the buffet table as needed.

- Invest in or borrow hot plates. This is a safe and easy way to keep the food warm.

## Touchdown decorating ideas that will make you the MVP!

- Start the fun by sending out some fun, football-themed invitations to your guests.
- Pick balloons, streamers, paper plates, napkins, cutlery and table clothes to match both teams' colors.
- Cover all or some of your tables with Astroturf, which can be purchased by the yard at any fabric store.
- Have some soft foam bricks and yellow flags on hand so your guest can throw them at the TV when they are annoyed or irritated with the game.
- Pom-poms are a great way to cheer the game along, or you can use them for decoration. If you have children at the party, have them practice cheers in an area far from the crowd and have them put on a show during halftime.
- Try and set up a "socializing only" area for guests that are not interested in the game and would rather sit in a room socializing.
- Rent a mini fridge or two, stock it with cold drinks and place it in the room where the game is playing. If you don't have access to a mini fridge, use a bathtub. If you are serving alcohol, try and have an area for the non-alcohol requests as well.
- Turn over a football helmet and line it first with paper towel and then foil. Place a small bowl of dip, wings, chips or nuts inside. Shape Play-doh on a flat plate to make a base to keep the helmet in place.
- Buy or make your own paper pennants to direct fans to the food. The "Pre-Game" or "First Down" could be the appetizers section, "Halftime" could be the entrees section and "Third Quarter" could

be the desserts section. If you have an area for alcohol and there are kids at your party, make a pennant that reads "Out of Bounds." For the non-alcohol area, you can have a pennant that reads "Inbounds." Make sure you show the kids the "Inbounds" section.
- Use inexpensive plastic whistles with string to wrap around napkins or peanuts that are wrapped in bunches, or use them on the mini party bags.
- On a budget? Be sure to check out the dollar stores for some great inexpensive football party items that were mentioned.

## Dress the party up even more!
- Go an extra yard and write on the invitations that you request your guests to dress as their favorite player or anything that reflects the game. Here are some great suggestions: dress as a cheerleader, a referee, a TV commentator, or a ticket collector. For those who can be party poopers and just don't want to dress up, tell them to dress up as a typical fan that shows up at the games wearing a clown's wig and/or some face paint.

## Clean-up time
Having a party can be a lot of fun and a lot of work. You don't want to be left cleaning up a huge mess. Use sturdy paper plates, plastic cups and cutlery. Have a large garbage bag on hand during the party so your guests can help with their own clean-up. If you have children at the party, cut a hole in the bottom of a garbage bag and also at the sides. Slide the bag over their head. Make sure that the bag is not tight around the neck. Have them put their arms threw the sides. Place a sticker on them that says "Cleaning Crew." If you plan this in advance, have a little gift bag for each child who helps with the clean-up.

# GAMES

It's always fun playing games, whether you're indoors or outdoors. Here are some great indoor and outdoor activities that will give your guests a reason to cheer!

First, have a pile of small gifts for the lucky guests who win. Your guests will not only enjoy participating in all the fun that you organized, but they can also take a small token of the fun they had home with them.

Don't forget to get guests involved even if they are not there for the game but for the wonderful food and company. Chances are they will be the ones screaming the loudest.

## INDOOR GAMES
*Football Pool*

Participants Required: Unlimited

Supplies Required:

– Bristol board or a piece of paper

- There are a few ways you can organize a football pool. Create your own pool by having each of your guests pick; who will be the winning team, along with who will score the most points, who will be MVP or the player with the most points scored, total yards or interceptions etc. Play it how ever you want. Just write the names of the guests that are participating on the Bristol board or piece of paper along with their picks.
- You can have small door prizes for the lucky guests.

*Charades:*

Participants Required: 6+

Supplies Required:

– Pre-made cards or pieces of paper

– A timer

- Prepare your charades words in advance, choosing football-related words such as football, tackle,

halftime, referee, tailgate parties, touchdown, quarterback, defense, beer, chili, spectator, etc. Write each word on a piece of paper.
- Divide your guests into teams and have the teams determine how much time they get to guess the word.
- Flip a coin to determine which team goes first.
- Place the pieces of paper into a helmet, hat of any kind of bag. Just make sure that no one can see inside when they pull one out.
- Ask the first player or team to choose a piece of paper.
- Communicate the number of words and syllables in the word or phrase. Raise your fingers to indicate the number of words. Two fingers equal two words, etc. Raise one finger to indicate first word and then two fingers to indicate that you are working on the second word.
- Start acting. The player must act out or otherwise communicate the meaning of that word to the audience — without speaking or vocalizing to the audience at all. Once you start acting, the audience can start shouting out their guesses.
- Everyone takes turns trying to get their team to guess the football-related word that they're acting out.
- When the correct word or phrase is guessed or the allotted time runs out, the game stops and switches to the next player or team. The team with the most guesses wins!

## *Balloon Poppers*

Participants Required:  Any number
Supplies Required:
– Balloons
– Pieces of paper
- Put a note in each balloon, blow up the balloon and tie it in a knot. Have someone pop one every time a specific event occurs, you decide what. It could be

the person with the most points from the football pool or it could be the first person and/or last person to arrived at the party. Be creative and make sure everyone gets one chance.
- Here are some fun suggestions of what you can put on the notes:
  - The person to the right of you has to get you your next two drinks.
  - You have to stand up and cheer when the other team scores a touchdown.
  - Tell someone on the opposite team his or her team really ROCKS!!
  - You must stay behind and help with clean up.
  - You must have the next party.
  - Wear something from the opponent's team for 30 minutes.

## *Foam Football Toss*

Participants Required: 4+
Supplies Required:
- Foam Football
- Hula hoop or a basket
- Each participant is given four to five chances to toss a football through the hula hoop. The one who can make the target the most times is the winner.

## *Don't Say "Football"*

Participants: Everyone
Supplies Required:
- Labels
- Give each guest a sticker with the word "football" or any word on it and tell everyone that they are not allowed to say that word. If a guest hears someone saying the word, they then take the sticker from the offending party and stick it on themselves. The one with the most stickers on them at the end of the game wins.

## OUTDOOR GAMES

Here are some great ideas for outdoor fun, including tailgate parties!

### Balloon Stampede
Participants required: 2+
Supplies Required:
– Balloons
– String
- Blow up the balloons and then tie each to the participant's ankle using string. At the "Go" signal, all participants are to run around and stomp on and burst each other's balloons. The last participant left with his or her balloon intact is the winner!

### Hula-Hoop Contest
Participants Required: 2+
Supplies Required:
– Hula-hoops
- At the "Go" signal, the participants begin Hula-hooping for as long as they can. Once the participant drops or even touches the hula hoop, they're out. The last participant Hula-hooping wins!

### Football Toss Challenge
Participants Required: 4+
Supplies Required:
– Football
- Have each participant stand at the starting point. The person who tosses the football the farthest is the winner.

### Water Balloon Toss
Participants Required: 4+
Supplies Required:
– Balloons filled with water

- Fill balloons with water and tie them into a knot. Divide the group into teams of two players. Give each team one balloon. Line the teams up an equal distance apart. Players toss the balloons to their partners. Once caught, everyone steps back one step. The last pair with an unbroken water balloon wins.

## *Alka-Seltzer Tag*

Participants Required: 2+
Supplies Required:
– Alka-Seltzers (white is better since color can stain)
– Water guns or cups of water

- Each participant gets an Alka-Seltzer that has been pre-drilled and put onto a string. The participant is to wear it like a necklace. Depending on how you want to play, each participant either gets a plastic cup of water or a water gun filled with water. Larger water guns are best. Be sure to have water on hand so participants can refill when necessary. You can divide the participant into teams or play every man for himself.
- The purpose is to melt the opponent's tablet. The tablet must be in full view at all times and cannot be covered or touched. Once the tablet falls off the string, the participant is out. The last person with his or her Alka-Seltzer still on the string wins!

## *Bigger or Better*

This game is better as a tailgate party game!
Participants Required: 6+
Supplies Required:
– Pennies

- Divide the participants into two teams and give each team a penny. Have the teams, in a one-hour period or whatever time frame agreed upon, go out into the tailgate area and ask for something bigger

or better than the penny. It does not have to be something of great value, just bigger or better!
- After the allotted time is up, both teams are to return to the designated area where they will be judged on which team got the biggest and better item.

*Grape Spitting*
Participants Required: 4+
Supplies Required:
– Grapes (one color only)
- Give each participant a grape. Be sure to give everyone the same type of grape. The green grapes roll differently from the red grapes.
- Have all the participants stand side by side in a straight line. The person who spits his or her grape out to land or roll the farthest wins!

*Limbo*
Participants Required: 4+
Supplies Required:
– A stick or rope
- Have one person hold each end of a stick or a long piece of rope and start by placing it on their shoulders. Each person playing is to try and "limbo" under it. The pole or rope continually drops a notch after every participant has shimmied through. Once a participant falls, they are disqualified. The last person that clears the rope or stick wins!

*Pop Can Roulette*
Participants Required: 2+
Supplies Required:
– Cans of fizzy drinks
- Have about six cans of a fizzy drink set on a table. With no one looking, shake one can so it will explode if opened. A victim chooses a can and may drink it if it does not spray all over him or her.

## Sticky Toss

Participants Required: 4+
Supplies Required:
– One stick

- Gather a group of 4-10 people. Have them choose a partner and stand directly across from each other. Each person takes a turn tossing the stick to his or her partner.

*The Rules:*
1) The size of the stick will determine how the stick must be tossed.
2) Determine which hand will be used first: the left or right hand. Everyone must catch the stick with the selected hand.
3) For the proficient players (optional): Once the stick is caught, the person who tossed it takes one small step back.
   If the person doesn't catch it with the selected hand or if it drops, they may only now catch the stick with one hand. Once someone has lost both hands, the team is OUT! The last couple standing wins!

## Frisbee or Chicken Toss

Participants Required: 8+
Supplies Required:
– One Frisbee or rubber chicken
– Coin for the coin toss

- Divide the participants into two teams. Do a coin toss to determine which team starts with the Frisbee or chicken. The person with the Frisbee or chicken throws it to his teammate. If the teammate catches it, he can take two steps back. He then throws it to someone else on his team. If someone drops it while they are trying to catch it, then the Frisbee or chicken goes to the other team. If it's intercepted, it goes to the other team. The team with the highest score wins!

Longhorn Lingo

*Water Balloon Pass*
  Participants Required: 10+
  Supplies Required:
   – 6 small round balloons filled with water and tied tightly
  • Depending on how many participants you have, divide them into equal teams. Have each team line up one behind the other. The first person in line takes the water balloon and holds it under/between his chin and shoulder. Then the player turns around and faces the person behind him. Without using hands, he passes the water balloon to his teammate. The passing continues down the line until it reaches the last person. If a balloon breaks, the two participants that were trying to pass the balloon when it broke are then eliminated, and another balloon is replaced and given to the participants that were next in line. The game then continues until the last couple is standing.

*Water Balloon Shave*
  Participants Required:   8+
  Supplies Required:
  – Balloons filled with water and tied tightly
  – Shaving cream or canned whip cream
  – Disposable razors
  – Outdoor chairs
  • Select an equal amount of guys to girls. The more you have the better. Have the guys sit in a line in outdoor chair. Cover the majority of the water balloon with shaving cream. Have each guy hold the balloon on top of his head. Give each of the girls a disposable razor and on the "Go" signal, they are to start shaving their balloon.
  • The object of the game is to have the girls shave their balloons clean and without bursting them. Once the balloon bursts, they're out. The first couple to finish without the balloon bursting wins.

If none of the balloons pop, then the cleanest balloon is declared the winner.

## *Hot Ball*

There are no winners or losers in this game. It's just plain fun for everyone!

Participants Required: 6+ (more is better)

Supplies Required:

– 3 – 4 midsized balls

- Have all participants stand in a circle. Have one player take one ball and toss it across the circle to another player. That player then selects a person and tosses the ball to him or her. This is to continue until each person has caught and thrown the ball once. Repeat this several times until each player is comfortable with the pattern of passing and receiving.
- Once all players are comfortable with the pattern, add another ball to the circle following the same pattern.
- Watching four or more balls being tossed like they are hot balls from one person to the next in a constant motion is really cool.

# RECIPES

Everyone enjoys good tasting food. Here are some lip-smackin', finger-lickin' recipes that are sure to make any party a hit!

## Baked Potato Dip

Laura is a wonderful entertainer and always has a ton of great tasting food at any gathering she hosts or attends. We have been over a few times and have enjoyed these recipes she has offered to share with you. This baked potato dip is my husbands favorite and can be used with chips, crackers, veggies…..you name it!!

**Ingredients:**
>16oz sour cream
>1 package of Ranch Dip
>¼ c real bacon bits
>1 c grated cheddar cheese

**Directions:**
>Mix dip with sour cream. Add bacon bits and cheese and stir.
>Serve with crackers or kettle potato chips.
>*Source: Laura Canada*

## Hot Corn Dip

**Ingredients:**
>2 Cans of corn
>¼ Cup grated parmesan cheese
>1 Cup mozzarella cheese
>1 Small can of green chilies
>½ Small can of chopped jalapenos
>1 Cup mayonnaise

**Directions:**
>Mix all above ingredients together in a bowl. Place in Pyrex dish. Bake at 400°F for 45 minutes or until

bubbling throughout and brown on top.

*Note: Add the entire can of chopped jalapenos if you like it HOT.*

Source: Laura Canada

## Jalapeno Poppers

**Ingredients:**
- 6-10 whole jalapenos
- 1 Small tub cream cheese
- 6 Bacon Strips

**Directions:**

Cut jalapenos lengthwise and cut out the centers and seeds. Spoon a small amount of cream cheese into the center of the jalapenos. Wrap with a piece of bacon. Place on grill sheet and grill until soft.

*Note: You can mix bacon bits in the cream cheese instead of wrapping with bacon.*

Source: Laura Canada

## Mark T's Ribs

Mark works with my husband and has a reputation for being the Rib Guy! It looks like a lot of work, but apparently, it's worth every minute!

**Ingredients:**
- 1 Red Onion
- 1 Orange
- 1 Large bag of brown sugar
- 1 Large CHEAP bottle/can of apple juice
- 1 Large CHEAP squeeze bottle of grape jelly
- 1 Pound of hog lard
- 1 Small can of Crisco/equivalent.
- 1 Spice bottle of Paprika
- 1 Bottle of olive oil
- Assorted spices, Tony's Grub Rub, pepper ribs

**Equipment Needed:**

Plenty of pecan wood/hickory briquettes
Tongs
Heat resistant, liquid-resistant gloves
Cookie sheet
Mixing bowl
Aluminum foil

**Directions:**
*Day Before*

Clean everything, including ribs. If possible, pull the lining off the belly side of the ribs. If it's too difficult to do this, make small incisions between each rib.

Begin rubbing down the ribs with the spices and herbs you like. I prefer "reduced salt" spices. Also, I use Grub Rub, which has most of what I like for spices. I also like to take fresh/unprocessed spices and grind them up in my coffee bean grinder. This releases more of the oils, has a fresher taste, and I use less spice this way. *Experiment: Cinnamon or ginger are good spices to use on ribs.* Last, sprinkle with Paprika.

When everything is coated with all the dry rub ingredients, coat the meat with olive oil. This is one of my secrets for any meat, especially steak! Do this to both sides.

Stack the ribs on the cookie sheet and place in the freezer or in the refrigerator if you're going to cook them the next day.

*Day of: Sop & Mop*

Create the "sop," an equal mixture of hog lard (or Crisco) and apple juice. Cut up a whole red onion and the orange.

Add a generous amount of the same spices and herbs that you put on your ribs into this mixture and place it in your smoker or dutch oven if you have one. If not, then place it on the stove and heat the mixture.

Don't let it burn. A slight boil is good for a short period.

Now it's time to Mop: Apply the sop to the ribs. To do this, I use a sop mop. Sop mops are nothing more than a wooden-handled glass-cleaning brush that can be purchased at any grocery store. Use the wooden-handled ones so you don't burn your hand. Put them back in the fridge while you get the fire ready.

### *Prepare the smoker or direct-fire grill*

Fire up the grill (or pit) and create a good bed of coals. Temperature and fire management is crucial while cooking the ribs. If you don't have a thermometer to keep the temperature between 200-250°F., then check the heat by carefully placing your hand about 6" from the coals. If you can't put your hand over it at all, then it's too hot. If you don't feel much heat from it, then it's too cool. I like to use pecan wood or other fruit wood. Hickory briquettes also work well.

### *Cooking*

Pull the ribs out of the fridge. They shouldn't be frozen. Place them on the grill belly side up. Pay attention to the temperature. I like to keep a spray bottle full of water handy in case of flare-ups. This process should take 2-3 hours. Maintain the temperature.

During this process, if you see the ribs drying out, sop them to keep them moist.

After 2-3 hours, it's time to turn the ribs. Before you turn the ribs, make sure they are well sopped.

Cook belly side down for 2-3 hours, maintaining the temperature.

After you've cooked them for a total of 4-6 hours, check to see if the bones are protruding on the end. Bones should look charred, not incinerated. If not, keep on cooking and sopping. If most of the bones are protruding and the meat is starting to brown up, it's time for the "special touch."

Into a mixing bowl, put three handfuls of brown sugar and an equal amount of grape jelly.

Mix together into a paste and slather it on the ribs. Don't forget to coat the sides and ends. Continue cooking with the paste. If the temperature is too cool, the sugar won't caramelize. If it's too hot, then the sugar burns and taints the meat.

This process should take another hour before turning the ribs over and doing the same to the other side for an hour.

*Are the Ribs Done?*

I look for two things when I check to see if it's time to pull the ribs.
1. Are the bones protruding from the sides?
2. Does the meat begin to split when I pick up the ribs from the narrow end?

If these two exist, it's eatin' time. Leave the BBQ sauce alone. You won't need it. You will, however, need lots of paper towel rolls!!

*Note: I recently found heat-resistant, liquid-resistant gloves called "ORCA." They look like an orca whale, have an excellent grip, and when I'm done, I throw them in the dishwasher so they'll be clean for the next time. It usually takes me eight hours and a cooler full of drinks to cook the ribs. This is a lot of work for one rack of ribs, so I usually do multiple racks at a time.*

What I don't eat, I freeze and eat later.

Source: Mark Tolliver


## Canadian Chili Eh!

It wasn't long after we moved here to beautiful Texas that we were invited to our first pot luck football party. I brought some homemade Canadian chili. It was an absolute hit! I hope you also enjoy it!

**Ingredients:**
- 4 Pounds of ground beef
- Olive oil or butter
- 1 (6-ounce) can of tomato paste
- 1 Large can of tomatoes with diced herbs
- 1 Large or regular can or jar of spaghetti sauce
- 1 Large or regular can of kidney beans
- 3 Cups of chopped onions
- 1 Cup of chopped green pepper
- 1 Cup of chopped red pepper
- 1 Cup of chopped celery
- 4-8 Cloves of garlic (to taste), pressed through a garlic presser
- 1 Tablespoon of Worcestershire sauce
- 15 Drops of Louisiana hot sauce
- 2 Tablespoons chili powder, or more depending on how hot you want it
- 1 Tablespoon ground cumin
- 1 Tablespoon dried oregano
- ½ Teaspoon dried sweet basil
- Salt and pepper to taste

**Directions:**

In a large pot, cook ground beef in a little olive oil or butter. I prefer to blend the two. Cook until the beef is no longer pink. Drain excess fat and bring beef back to the pot.

Add remaining ingredients and simmer two to three hours with the lid on. Makes eight to 10 servings. I like to double this recipe and freeze any leftovers.

*Note: I don't like to put too much hot spices in it. It's best to have a bottle of hot sauce on the side so your guests can add their own kick. Also, make this in the crock pot. Be sure to cook ground beef until it is no longer pink and then add it to the crock pot along with the other ingredients.*

Source: Barb Wagner

## Barb's Caesar Salad:

### Dressing Ingredients:
- 4-5 Cloves garlic, depending on the size. Too much garlic with give it too strong of a taste.
- ½ Teaspoon freshly ground black pepper
- 1.5 Ounce parmesan cheese — cubed
- 3 Whole eggs
- ½ Teaspoon mustard
- 1 Tablespoon lime juice
- 2-3 Anchovy fillets (I hate Anchovy's; trust me…you can add them)
- 1 Teaspoon worcestershire sauce
- 1 Cup extra virgin olive oil
- 1 Cup canola oil

### Crouton Ingredients:
- 3 Cups white bread ½" cubes
- 3 Cloves garlic peeled and put through garlic press
- 1 Teaspoon mixed dried herbs (thyme, basil, Italian and oregano)
- ¼ Teaspoon onion powder
- ¼ Cup extra virgin olive oil
- ¼ Cup parmesan cheese – 100% grated

### Salad Ingredients:
- 4-5 Heads romaine lettuce
- ½ Cup parmesan cheese, grated

### Dressing Directions:

Place garlic cloves, pepper, and parmesan cheese in food processor and process one minute.

Add remaining ingredients: eggs, mustard, lime juice, anchovies and Worcestershire sauce and process for about one minute

Continue processing and slowly add oils until mixture becomes thick and creamy. (Use within 48 hours)

*Croutons Directions:*
> Preheat oven to 350°F.
> Mix garlic, onion powder, herbs, grated parmesan and olive oil in a small bowl. Be sure to use the 100% grated cheese. Let sit for 15-30 minutes so flavors can incorporate and absorb.
> Drizzle oil over bread and toss to coat the bread evenly.
> Sprinkle more of the grated parmesan. Place on baking sheet and sprinkle a little more parmesan over the bread. Bake until golden brown, 10-15 minutes.
> Remove from the oven and add more parmesan. Let it cool before adding to the salad.

*Salad Directions:*
> Tear, wash and dry romaine lettuce.
> Place in large bowl, drizzle with dressing and toss to coat lightly. Add croutons, and toss again and serve with fresh parmesan cheese.
> *Source: Barb Wagner*

## Coca-Cola Chicken Wings or Ribs
### Ingredients
| | |
|---|---|
| 1 | Cup Brown sugar, packed |
| 1 | Can Coca-Cola |
| 1 | Large onion, diced |
| 2 | Cloves of garlic, pressed through a garlic presser |
| 1/2 | Tablespoon soy sauce |
| 2 | Tablespoons catsup |
| | Salt and pepper to taste |
| 2-3 | lbs. of chicken wings or ribs |

### Directions:
> In a large casserole or roasting pan, combine all of the ingredients but the chicken. Add salt and pep-

per. Stir until mixed. Place chicken wings or ribs in a large bowl and add sauce mixture. Mix well and place back into the large casserole or roasting pan. Bake at 350°F for 2-3 hours.
*Source: Barb Wagner*

## Apple Crisp

Apple crisp recipes are often handed down from generation to generation. My wonderful mother-in-law, who passed away from breast cancer in March 2000, gave me this no-fault recipe. This is a simple and easy-to-make dessert that adults and kids love.

**Ingredients:**
- 4 Cups sliced, peeled granny smith apples
- 1/3 Cup dark brown sugar, packed
- 1/2 Cup white flour
- 1/2 Cup oats (I use one 1.51 oz. package of uncooked instant apple oatmeal cereal)
- 3/4 Teaspoon cinnamon
- 3/4 Teaspoon nutmeg
- 1/3 Cup softened butter

**Directions:**
Preheat oven to 375°F. Grease an 8x8x2 pan and place granny smith apple slices in the bottom of the pan. Mix the remaining ingredients together and sprinkle evenly over the top of the apples. Bake for 30 minutes.

*Note: You may want to double or even triple the recipe, depending on how many people you plan on serving.*
*Source: Barb Wagner on behalf of Mrs. Julie Wagner*

## Lime Cheesecake

Lise, my sister-in-law, is very picky when it comes to cooking or baking. If she makes it, it's sure to be a hit! Here are a few of her yummy favorite desserts.

**Crust:**
- 1¼ Cups graham cracker crumbs
- 2 Tablespoon sugar
- 1/4 Cup butter (melted)

Mix ingredients together and press into a pie plate. If time is an issue, a pre-made crust is fine.

**Filling:**
- 3 8 oz packages cream cheese
- 3/4 Cup sugar
- 3 Eggs
- 1 Tablespoon grated lime rind
- 1/4 Cup lime juice
- 1 Teaspoon vanilla extract

**Directions:**

Preheat oven to 375°F.

Beat cream cheese until fluffy. Add sugar gradually, beating well. Add eggs one at a time, beating well after each addition. Stir in rind, juice and vanilla. Pour into prepared crust. Bake for approximately 45 minutes or until set in center.

**Topping:**
- 2 Cups sour cream
- 3 Tablespoons sugar
- Lime slices

**Directions:**

Combine sour cream and sugar, mix well and spread evenly over cheese cake. Bake at 500°F for 5 minutes. Cool to room temperature. Chill at least 8 hours. Garnish with limes and serve.

*Source: L. Wagner*

## Banana Cake

### Cake Ingredients:
- ½ Cup softened butter
- 2 Cups flour
- 1 Tablespoon baking soda
- 1 Tablespoon baking powder
- ¾ Teaspoon salt
- 1½ Cups sugar
- 1¼ Cups ripe bananas (4-5 mashed)
- ½ Cup sour milk
- 2 Eggs

### Directions:
Preheat oven to 350°F. Whip butter in large bowl. Sift in dry ingredients. Add milk, bananas, eggs and beat until well blended. Pour into a 10" x 14" cake pan. Bake for 25 – 35 minutes, or until toothpick or knife comes out clean.

*HINT: To make sour milk, put 1 tablespoon of vinegar into a measuring cup, add enough milk to make ½ cup.*

### Icing Ingredients:
- 1 Cup brown sugar
- ½ Cup butter
- 2 Tablespoons cream or milk
- 1½ Cups coconut (flaked)

### Directions:
Place all ingredients into saucepan over medium heat. Stir and cook until melted and well blended. Spread over cool cake while icing is warm (not hot).

*Source: L. Wagner*

# Chapter 9
# JOKES

**Heard any good jokes lately?** I have...

A guy took his girlfriend to her first football game. Afterward he asked her how she liked the game. "I liked it, but I couldn't understand why they were killing each other for 25 cents," she said.

"What do you mean?" he asked.

"Well, everyone kept yelling, 'Get the quarter back!'"

A guy comes home from a football party at a bar one night around 3:00 in the morning. His wife is sleeping, and he is trying to sneak into bed. He's lying in bed for a few minutes and cuts a fart. His wife wakes up and asks, "What in the world was that?"

He replies, "Touchdown, I am winning seven-nothing."

She thinks to herself, "I'm gonna fix him." Then she lets one loose.

He yells at her, "What was that?"

She replies, "Touchdown, tie score."

Now he thinks, "I'm gonna fix her." He's lying there for about 10 minutes trying to work one up. He tries so hard he wets the bed.

## Longhorn Lingo

The wife asks, "Now what in the world was that?"

He replies, "Half time, switch sides."

---

Did you hear about the Aggie terrorist who tried to blow up the Longhorn team bus? He burned his lip on the tailpipe.

---

The huge Aggie freshman decided to try out for the football team. "Can you tackle?" asked the coach. "Watch this," said the freshman, who proceeded to run smack into a telephone pole, shattering it to splinters. "Wow," said the coach. "I'm impressed. Can you run?" "Of course I can run," said the freshman. He was off like a shot, and, in just over nine seconds, he had run a hundred-yard dash. "Great!" enthused the coach. "But can you pass a football?" The freshman hesitated for a few seconds. "Well, sir," he said, "if I can swallow it, I can probably pass it."

---

The Aggies football coach walked into the locker room before a game, looked over to his star player and said, "I'm not supposed to let you play since you failed math, but we need you in there. So, what I have to do is ask you a math question, and if you get it right, you can play."

The player agreed, and the coach looked into his eyes intently and asked, "Okay, now concentrate hard and tell me the answer to this: What is two plus two?"

The player thought for a moment and then answered, "four?"

"Did you say four?" the coach exclaimed, excited that he got it right.

At that, all the other players on the team began screaming, "Come on, coach, give him another chance!"

---

Two guys are talking about their boss's upcoming wedding.

One says, "It's ridiculous, he's rich, but he's 93 years old, and she's just 26! What kind of a wedding is that?"

The other says, "Well, we have a name for it in my family."

"What do you call it?"

"We call it a football wedding."

The first asks, "What's a football wedding?"

The other says, "She's waiting for him to kick off!"

---

At Texas A&M there was a football player who was extremely stupid. He sat beside a boy in class who was really smart, and the teacher knew that he was cheating, but she just couldn't catch him.

One day she was grading a test and she noticed that the smart boy had written, "I don't know the answer" on number 10.

So she looked at the jock's paper and smiled. He had finally given himself away. His answer looked like this:

10.) me neither

## Longhorn Lingo

Two Aggie players were taking an important final exam. If they failed, they would be on academic probation and not allowed to play in the Sugar Bowl the following week. The exam was fill-in-the-blank. The last question read, "Old MacDonald had a _____."

Bubba was stumped. He had no idea of the answer. He knew he needed to get this one right to be sure he passed. Making sure the professor wasn't watching, he tapped Tiny on the shoulder. "Pssst. Tiny. What's the answer to the last question?" Tiny laughed. He looked around to make sure the professor hadn't noticed, then he turned to Bubba. "Bubba, you're so stupid. Everyone knows Old MacDonald had a farm."

"Oh yeah," said Bubba. "I remember now." He picked up his No. 2 pencil and started to write the answer in the blank. He stopped. Reaching to tap Tiny's shoulder again, he whispered, "Tiny, how do you spell 'farm'?"

"You are really dumb, Bubba. That's so easy. Farm is spelled 'E-I-E-I-O.'"

So the reporter asks the Aggie coach, "Is there any truth to the rumor that your new quarterback is dumb?"

The coach replies, "Well, he makes straight A's."

The reporter, suitably impressed, says, "Wonderful!"

"But," says the coach, "his B's are kind of crooked."

"Did your injury happen when you were on the football team?"

"No, sir, it happened when the football team was on me."

---

Morty was in his usual place in the morning, sitting at the table, reading the paper after breakfast. He came across an article about a beautiful actress who was about to marry a football player who was known primarily for his lack of IQ and common knowledge.

He turned to his wife with a look of question on his face. "I'll never understand why the biggest jerks get the most attractive wives."

His wife replied, "Why thank you, dear!"

---

Two boys are playing football in a park in Austin, when one is attacked by a rabid rotweiler. Thinking quickly, the other boy rips off a board from a nearby fence, wedges it down the dog's collar and twists, breaking the dog's neck.

A reporter who was strolling by sees the incident and rushes over to interview the boy.

"Young Longhorns Fan Saves Friend From Vicious Animal," he starts writing in his notebook.

"But I'm not a Longhorns fan," the little hero replied.

"Sorry, since we are in Austin, I just assumed you were," said the reporter and starts again. "Little

Texans Fan Rescues Friend From Horrific Attack" he continued writing in his notebook.

"I'm not a Texans fan either," the boy said.

"I assumed everyone in Austin was either for the Longhorns or Texans. What team do you root for?" the reporter asked.

"I'm a Aggie's fan," the child said.

The reporter starts a new sheet in his notebook and writes, "Little Redneck Maniac Kills Beloved Family Pet."

### College Exam for Aggie Football Players
*\*You must answer three or more questions correctly to qualify.*
Time Limit: One Month

1. What language is spoken in France? _____

2. Give a dissertation on the ancient Babylonian Empire with particular reference to architecture, literature, law and social conditions-OR- give the first name of Pierre Trudeau.
   _____

3. Would you ask William Shakespeare to
   (a) build a bridge          (b) sail the ocean
   (c) lead an army            (d) write a play

4. What religion is the pope? (circle only one)
   (a) Jewish     (b) Catholic     (c) Hindu
   (d) Polish     (e) Agnostic

5. Metric conversion. How many feet is 0.0 meters?
   \_\_\_\_\_

6. What time is it when the big hand is on the 12 and the little hand is on the 5?
   (a) Bed time  (b) 5:00
   (c) am or pm?  (d) Happy hour

7. How many commandments was Moses given (approximately)? _____

8. What are people in America's far north called?
   (a) Westerners  (b) Southerners
   (c) Northerners  (d) foreigners

9. Spell — Bush, Carter and Clinton
   _____
   _____
   _____

10. Six kings of England have been called George, the last one being George the Sixth. Name the previous five.
    _____
    _____
    _____
    _____
    _____

11. Where does rain come from?
    (a) Macy's  (b) a 7-11  (c) Canada
    (d) the sky  (e) Prince

12. Can you explain Einstein's Theory of Relativity?
    (a) yes  (b) no
    (c) He wasn't my relative

13. What are coat hangers used for?
    _____

14. The "Star Spangled Banner" is the national anthem for what country?
    _____

Longhorn Lingo

15. Explain Le Chateliers Principle of Dynamic Equilibrium-OR- just spell your name in BLOCK LETTERS.
   _____

16. Where is the basement in a three story building located?
   _____

17. Which part of America produces the most oranges?
   (a) New York          (b) Florida
   (c) Canada            (d) Europe

18. Advanced math: If you have three apples, how many apples do you have?
   _____

19. What does NBC (National Broadcasting Corporation) stand for?
   _____

20. The Texas A&M tradition for efficiency began when (approximately)?
   (a) B.C.              (b) A.D.
   (c) still waiting

# About the Author

Barb Wagner grew up in Milton, a small town in Southern Ontario. During her childhood, Barb rarely played sports of any kind. About as close as Barb came to a sporting event was when she participated on the middle school cheerleading squad. Later in life, Barb worked primarily in the financial industry in Toronto, Ontario and also founded a motivational company, motivating children competing in the sports field. Barb, also known as "Coach Barb," conducted a successful weekly radio show with Eddie Matthews in Stratford Ontario offering information to parents to help motivate children.

Barb has been married 16 years to a wonderful man who excelled in sports most of his life. Kent Wagner, an ex-pro baseball player in the Montreal Expos organization, a previous Ontario junior hockey player and a scratch golfer, was very well connected and informed with sports his entire life. Barb on the other hand, had very limited knowledge of most sports, unless you call Cheerleading a sport. That was until they decided to have two boys, Dylan and Austin. Barb's philosophy was, "if I can't beat them, I might as well join them."

## Longhorn Lingo

Both of their boys, Dylan and Austin are involved in sports, just like their father. Between baseball, golf and hockey, it wasn't until Dylan's first day on the ice with "Coach Steve" that Barb decided that she'd better learn more about the lingo's associated with the game!

*Cheers to the game!!!*

Cum For Me
An LDP Erotica

Ca$h & Company

**Lock Down Publications**

**Presents**

*Cum For Me*
**An Anthology by Ca$h and Company**

## Cum For Me

Copyright 2014 by Lock Down Publications

All rights reserved. No part of this book may be reproduced in any form or by electronic or mechanical means, including information storage and retrieval systems without permission in writing from the publisher, except by a reviewer who may quote brief passages in review.
First Edition October 2014
Printed in the United States of America

*This is a work of fiction. Names, characters, places, and incidents either are products of the author's imagination or are used fictitiously. Any similarity to actual events or locales or persons, living or dead, is entirely coincidental.*

**Lock Down Publications**

 **Email:** wcp.cash2@gmail.com

**Facebook:** Cash Streetlit Author

**Cover design and layout by**: Dynasty's Cover Me

**Book interior design by**: Shawn Walker

**Contributing Editors**: Shawn Walker, Epic Kreationz, and Sandy Barrett Sims

Ca$h & Company

## Foreword

*This erotic compilation is a first for LDP. Up until now we have only published urban and streetlit novels, but we wanted to give a special seductive treat to our supporters. Now it is time to turn the pages and* **Cum For Me... Ca$h**

Ca$h & Company

Cum For Me

## Obsession
## By
## *Coffee*

*T*here has been a report that millionaire mogul was found dead late Monday morning... More news at twelve.

*A few days earlier...*

"Touch it," Teddy demanded the moment Delilah answered her phone.

"What? You're kidding, right?" She let out a nervous giggle.

"Hmmm," he sexily growled. The sound of his voice was as deep as the ocean and as smooth as velvet. A smile parted his lips. "Do I play?"

Delilah shook her head *no* as if he could see her. She cupped her phone and spoke closely into the receiver. "No, you don't. But I'm at work and there are people around me."

"I'm stroking this hard, black dick and I need you to come sit on it."

*Oh, shit!* Her inner slut echoed. Her pussy began to thump as a sexy image of Teddy using his massive hand to slide up and down the length of his Mandingo thickness appeared.

Delilah looked at her watch. It was 7:15PM. In fifteen more minutes, she could clock out and give him the business privately. "I get off in a few minutes, baby. At least wait until I get in my car," she reasoned.

"You're gonna *get off* now!" He ignored her, breathing heavily into the phone.

She tensely shot up to her feet and looked over her cubicle to see the number of co-workers that remained on her floor.

"Delicious?" He called her by the pet name he'd given her the first moment he tasted her passion fruit.

"Ummm hmmm," she drowned in the silk of his voice as she scanned the office still.

"I don't give a fuck where you are. That's my pussy and I said touch that muthafucka!" he growled. Delilah's heart started racing and small pants escaped her mouth. She sat back down and threw one of her legs over the other in an attempt to slow down the excitement stirring between them for that man. Teddy was the kind of brother who got what he wanted and at that moment he wanted *her*. "Touch it!" He ordered for the final time, startling Delilah from beneath the timid rock she'd attempted to crawl under.

Her chest heaved up and down from nervousness, but his persistence melted her like butter. She had no choice other than to *touch it*.

"Okay, baby," she panted.

She made a fast break to the ladies room on the opposite end of her floor and luckily, every stall was empty. She went into the last one. With her cell phone clutched between her face and shoulder, she came out of her slacks and panties.

Delilah was torn between two emotions, the one that craved the freaky encounter she was about to have and the one that was fearful in the face of being caught because of it.

She stepped back into her heels and propped one foot upon the seat of the toilet. Thoughts of him, of them, had her vaginal faucet running by the time she finally touched her peach.

# Cum For Me

Delilah closed her eyes and snuggled against her phone as if it were him. Her pussy automatically began to pucker when the image of his naked perfection stationed itself in her mind.

"Take a picture of my pussy. Let me know it's real," he demanded.

She could tell from his breathing that he was stroking himself to full excitement. She said nothing as she dropped the phone to do as she was told.

"Sent."

Seconds later, he saw his deliciousness glossed with her nectar. Her chocolate coated lips were the sweetest and juiciest he'd ever tasted. He didn't know his dick could get hard 'til it hurt, but it had.

"Fuck!" His voice echoed off of the walls of his master bedroom suite. "Spit on your fingers. Run them over that clit until it swells up for me." She opened her mouth, but kept her voice subdued. "How that shit feels?" He demanded to know.

"It feels good," she whispered as she felt her pearl tingle under the constant sweep of her fingers.

"I don't believe you. How the fuck does it feel?" He spoke commandingly.

"It feels gooood." She sang in a higher pitch as she quickly rotated her fingers in a circular motion. The hood of her clit grew enormously as the urge to release came upon her.

"Now, slide two of your fingers inside."

"Ummm," she moaned.

"Yeaaa! Get deep in that shit. Grind on them muthafuckas like it's that donkey dick I'm swingin'."

Delilah did just that. She almost lost her balance in the process of executing his sexual instructions, but she regained her footing and began a light bounce to further drive them inward.

Teddy listened to her get lost in the abyss of lust, and like the masochist he was, he blurted his next directive. "Stop!"

"Huh? Baby, I'm on the brink of—"

"And I said *stop*!"

She removed her hand like he'd instructed. "But why, though?" She pouted. Her joy button was tingling, craving to be stroked.

"I don't like how long it took you to obey me. So, I will fly into New Orleans—tomorrow. I'm gonna show you who that shit for. Have my pussy ready when I get there."

Teddy hung up the phone. He didn't need to hear her response because she belonged to him and when he wanted her, he would have her.

*****

The next morning Delilah woke up with childlike excitement. The night before, Teddy had informed her that he would arrive at Louis Armstrong Airport at 5:45PM the next day. She couldn't wait to wrap her arms, her legs, her entire body around her guy.

Her back arched as sexual surges shot through her system. Just thinking about her teddy bear got her aroused. She drifted into a daydream before the chiming of her phone snapped her out of it. Her cell was under the covers somewhere. She scrambled to find it because it could have been Teddy calling and she missed his calls next to never.

Delilah looked at the caller ID and immediate trepidation filled her chest. It was her longtime friend, Suede, calling. Seeing his number reminded her of *their* date that she'd promised him weeks ago for later that evening.

*Shit! How did I forget?* She questioned. "Teddy!" She answered out loud.

She could get so lost inside of that man, she was liable to forget her own name if he didn't call her by it.

She slapped her forehead. *Think. Think. Think,* she chanted.

The ringing silenced. She sighed a breath of relief, but then it started back up. She had to find the most delicate way to back out of her plans with Suede and quickly.

Instantaneously, she felt some type of way because she didn't want to break Suede's heart, but there was no way she would miss her rendezvous with her out of town lover.

Delilah answered the phone in a very drowsy tone, "Hello."

"Good morning. Did I wake you up?" He questioned.

"No, but I don't feel well," she coughed into the receiver.

"What's the matter, La La? Tell me what to do," Suede asked instantly. He was so sincere.

"Nothing I haven't tried already. I'm just going to doctor myself and stay in bed." Delilah was breathing through her mouth to give the stuffy and congested effect.

"La La, the sooner I can get you feeling better is the sooner we can possibly still have our special night tonight. I've put a lot into this."

She could hear his optimism through the phone.

*"Ah—ah a chew,"* she faked. "I'm in no condition to get out of bed. Can't you hear it in my voice?" She sniffled.

That night was Suede's opportunity to show Delilah how much he truly loved her outside of friendship. He'd depleted a good chunk of his savings to buy her a promise ring. A little diamond reminder that his love would be forever.

Things clearly weren't going to work the way he'd meticulously planned them, but he was willing to make adjustments just to make the night happen anyway.

"We don't have to get out. I'll come over to your place. Cook dinner. The whole nine." He offered her his plan B.

*Why are you making this so hard?* She wondered.

"That won't be necessary. I'm contagious and aside from that I just want to sleep in as much peace as I can for as long as I can. You'll do better staying away." She strained the last few words. "We can get together another weekend, okay?"

Suede would have gladly run the risk of getting sick himself if it meant she would feel better, but he reluctantly conceded. "Alright. I love you."

"Always," she responded faintly before disconnecting the call.

Suede hung up the phone, unable to think of anything but his La La. He knew she wanted to be left alone to protect him from her ailment, but he knew what she needed. And that was some TLC—from him.

He stopped at the Walgreens on Morrison Rd. and racked up sixty dollars' worth of various medications that would cure anything from a common headache to the flu. Within the hour, Suede showed up at her house. Although Delilah instructed him not to, she expected him nonetheless. And she was prepared.

## Cum For Me

When she heard the knock on the door, she rolled her eyes and threw her head back. She knew he meant well, but *must he be this insistent?*

Delilah tossed her heating pad in the closet, she sprayed mist on her exposed body with water from her spray bottle and heavily saturated her chest with Vick's Vapor Rub. She looked terrible and smelled sick.

*Great!*

It was a pity, the lengths she'd go through to carry out a lie, but just one night with Teddy was worth it.

She took an abnormal amount of time to open the door and when she did, she leaned against the edge of it for support. "What did I tell you?" She coughed into the fold of her arm.

Suede held the bag at chest level and smiled a gorgeous smile, one that could remove dark clouds from a sky.

He welcomed himself inside through the small space Delilah allotted. She closed the door and fell against it.

*Getting rid of him is going to be exhausting.*

She truly appreciated her friendship of twelve years with Suede, but that was all he was. A friend. But because she knew his feelings ran deeper than the platonic level where her feelings for him remained, it made it difficult to openly tell him about Teddy.

He placed the back of his hand on her forehead. "You're burning up. I should have something in here for that." He rummaged through the medicines.

She sluggishly dragged herself into her room where he followed her.

Hours had passed and Suede was determined not to leave, but he had to. Delilah couldn't have the man who loved *her,* meet the man *she* loved.

Teddy had Delilah wrapped around both his finger and his head. She couldn't resist him for nothing or nobody. Not Tammi, his wife of seven years, TJ, his three year old son, her commitment to Greater Ascension Baptist Church, or Mr. Reliable aka Suede.

Delilah lay in bed staring at the time. Her clock read 3:45PM already. Suede clearly stayed longer than she desired, but she had a mental time frame in which he absolutely had to vacate the premises. She was only a half hour ride away from the airport and Teddy was as punctual as they came. Aside from that, Teddy had a key and she didn't need him bursting through her doors seeing a man there.

"You know I can stay the night," he sweetly offered.

She unintentionally snapped. "But you won't. Listen, I appreciate everything you've done today, I really do, but I'm getting groggier and my attitude is about to jump to a thousand. I just want to be alone." She flipped on her side and nuzzled back under the covers.

*There I finally said it,* she thought.

"That's how it is?" Suede abruptly stood up from the bed. His voice boomed with anger. "I come over to take care of you and this is how you treat me?"

She almost came out of character when he jumped out of the bag on her, but she digressed. "I didn't ask you, remember?"

"You're ungrateful, Delilah, you know that?" He heatedly spat.

## Cum For Me

"No. I'm sick and you should go. I will call you when I feel better." She climbed out of bed and walked into the living room to her front door.

Suede stood in the same position, looking at the bedroom door she walked out of. He was hurt. It just didn't matter how hard he tried, he couldn't get anywhere with her.

"A'ight, then." He yelled out as he stomped his way through her house, stopping mere inches away from her face. "You don't have to call!" He walked out of her door, slamming it behind himself.

She jumped at the piercing sound of the slam and clutched her heart.

Any other time she would have chased him and pacified him because she never wanted to upset him. She couldn't focus on his needs right then and there, though. She would nurse his wounds later, she always could. But now she had to get ready for date night with Teddy.

*****

At 6:30PM, Delilah's doorbell rang and she almost hopped out of her heels. She trotted quickly through her house, pausing briefly at the mirror in the foyer to once over herself for the final time.

Her pussy started pulsating, knowing that only a door separated her from him. *Calm thee hell down*, she giggled as she looked down toward her excitable kitty.

She swung her door open and there he was in his decadent flesh.

Theodore Champion was an undeniable kind of handsome. From head to toe, he stood six feet four and his dark as midnight skin blanketed his muscular frame.

Delilah energetically rushed inside of his opened arms. He leaned down and planted an electrifying kiss on her lips, one that made her knees buckle.

Her sugary kisses made his nine inch python actively snake in his pants.

He backed her inside of the house, bending down to pick up his overnight bag, and crossed the threshold of her door. Dropping his luggage, he pulled her back into his embrace as he kissed her more passionately. He slid his hands over her ample ass to panty check and discovered she had some on.

He kneeled down on one knee and ran his hands over her shapely thighs. She began breathing quickly. "What I tell you about these?" He grabbed her thong on each side and snatched it off of her. Then he tossed it in the middle of the floor.

Now he was face to face with his bush paradise. He placed his nose next to her garden and inhaled the scent of his woman. He kissed her mound and then crooked his head slightly to the side so he could run his tongue over those lickable lips of hers.

"Sssss," she divided her legs and moaned out, gripping his head.

Teddy looked up at her. Her head was thrown back, her eyes were closed and her body anticipated his next move. But he stood to his feet and smooth down her dress.

"Huh? Why you stopped?" She looked confused.

He had to chuckle at her dazed expression. Teddy looked at his watch. "We got time," he teased.

She slapped him against his chest. "Why do you torment me like this?" she pouted.

## Cum For Me

Teddy didn't respond, she already knew the answer. He never did what was expected. It was that edge about him that always kept her burning with desire for him.

He took her by the hand, so he could get a three hundred and sixty degree view of her. He twirled her around slowly and cataloged everything about her exquisiteness.

She wore the Balmain designer dress and Giuseppe heels he surprised her with last week. The note inside read: *You'll know the right time to wear this.*

He loved adorning her with high priced gifts and clothing that accentuated her sex appeal because Delilah was as tempting as her name sounded.

Her baby soft skin was the color of cocoa. Her natural hazel eyes were the symmetry of almonds. Her long shapely legs flowed like a continuous river. Her breasts were like two ripe and juicy melons which drew as much attention as her curvilinear apple bottom. And to top it off, Delilah smelled and tasted like honeysuckle.

"Damn, you're fine."

"And yours," she added. After she looked over her eye candy, she asked, "Baby, why did you ring the doorbell instead of using your key?"

"I must have misplaced them because I couldn't find them before I left. Have no worries, though. They're probably at my office."

"Okay," she gushed as he touched her chin softly.

"One moment." He excused himself, leaving her standing in the foyer of her home. Teddy needed to hide a little surprise that he carried in his overnight bag in her negligee drawer.

As he returned back up front, he slapped and rubbed his hands together. "Are you ready, Delicious?"

Delilah danced in place, gleefully. "What's on the agenda for tonight?" she asked.

"Do I ever disclose that kind of information? Just let your man do what he does," he casanova'd.

"I should have known you'd be tight lipped," she laughed.

She reached for her clutch and punched in the alarm to secure her home before they exited and locked up. Teddy walked ahead of her only to open the passenger door of his custom made 2015 Range Rover.

Ever since he'd met Delilah a year ago, he had reasons to frequently leave The Lone Star State to travel to The Big Easy. To avoid getting a shabby rental, he paid to have one of his vehicles parked at the airport for the occasions he'd be in town.

Delilah learned a long time ago that Teddy did everything big because everything he finessed screamed *boss*. That's specifically why Delilah recalled to the letter the way they first met.

She was set up on a blind date by her best friend, Tempest. She was informed she would meet a gentleman by the name of Michael Leakes for 7PM at Exclusives, one of the most elite and popular restaurants this side of the Gulf.

*Delilah looked at her watch, Michael had already settled on her tongue with bad taste. He was twenty minutes late and no phone call.*

*Despite the embarrassment of a potential duo turning out to be a solo, she decided against calling Suede to be her fill-in date again and stayed for dinner by her lonesome.*

## Cum For Me

*After two glasses of red wine, she toyed with her cream potatoes as she mentally examined her horrible luck in the men's department. For the last few years, she couldn't understand why, she'd become quite familiar with the alone feeling. She'd meet them, and they'd liked her, but no one stayed around beyond the first few dates.*

"Will there be anything else?" The maître d asked, breaking her trance.

"No, just the bill, please," Delilah spoke with mild disdain.

Moments later, he returned. "Ma'am," the waiter addressed Delilah, "your ticket was picked up by that gentleman over there." He pointed across the room to a table of five. He handed her a note then disappeared.

*If I were your man...*

She looked up and saw the most gorgeous smile plastered across the face of the most gorgeous man she'd ever met to date. She hoped that he was the generous guy who paid for her meal and when she saw him casually wave his hand in the air it was confirmed, he was most definitely her pick. Shyly, she waved back.

She sipped on a water and discreetly watched him speak to the men he sat with before he got up from his table and moved toward her. She attempted to rise from her seat like she didn't notice, but he swiftly stood behind her to pull out her chair.

"How are you?" He extended his hand. "My name is Theodore Champion."

She accepted, "My name is Delilah Drieu."

Without taking his eyes off of hers, he kissed her hand. She blushed a little when she gauged the intensity of his stare along with the soft kiss of his full lips pressed against her skin.

"Ummm," she fiddled. "Thank you for dinner."

"A proper thanks is allowing me to sit across from you as we share dinner, desert, or whatever you're craving," he smiled.

She began to smooth over her hair as she sorted through her mind how to respond.

With his eyes still connected to hers, he reached into his wallet and pulled out a business card. "I don't want to pressure you. Take some time to think it over and call me with a yes," he confidently suggested.

And like a cool breeze, he returned to his business meeting. Delilah left knowing that she would call him sooner than later.

 

Teddy glanced over at how tempting Delilah looked with one leg stacked on top of the other, showing just enough of her thickly toned thighs.

As he was riding down I-10, he reached over, pushed her legs apart and eased his strong hand underneath her dress. He began palming her pussy and biting his bottom lip when he felt her instant heat warm his hand.

He allowed his middle finger to glide into her sweetness. She threw her head back against the headrest and grinded on his oversized digit. Teddy glanced between her and the road and became turned on more so than he already was.

Teddy pulled his hand out and smelled her tantalizing scent before sucking the juices from Delilah's delight. So stimulated by the taste of it, he changed their plans slightly.

## Cum For Me

He reached their destination at Club Reign, but he pulled into the back of the parking lot and killed the engine. He said nothing as he opened his door then quickly opened hers. He removed her legs out of the truck and positioned himself in between them.

Delilah said nothing, but then again, what could she say? She knew she was his for the taking.

He hoisted her dress above her ass, slid her closer to him and hungrily began French kissing her pearl. He then speared his long, thick tongue between her pussy lips while rubbing his thumb in a swift side to side motion over her ever swelling clit.

"Oh, shit!" She tried to run, but the console in the truck prevented her from moving further.

He clamped her thighs and pulled her closer to him, locking her this time so she couldn't do anything but take his vicious tongue lashing.

"Ummm," he sounded off as he slurped, smacked, and sampled her nectar.

"Oooh," she moaned, gripping his head. "This is yours—all yours."

He entered her with one, two, now three fingers all the while flickering his whip appeal. The sounds Delilah made turned Teddy on to the max. He was ultra-focused on stamping his name on her kitty by making her cum waterfalls.

"Ohhh, baby! Oh, baby I'm—" Delilah's words trailed off into a soft whimper as she released every drop of her wonder juice into his awaiting mouth.

Teddy lapped every trickle until she was bone dry, inserting a finger inside and pulling out more of her creamy filling to ensure he'd gotten it all.

A few by passers stopped and stared, but Teddy wasn't concerned with anyone except for who was in his mouth. Delilah had drifted too far into an enchanted place to notice anyone as well. Until...

*Whack!*

Tammi hit the back of Teddy's head with her boot. "This isn't the business I thought you were supposed to handle, muthafucka!" She yelled loudly enough for anyone within blocks to hear.

"Ahhh!" Teddy sighed as he grabbed the back of his head. He jumped up from his bent position to face his wife. He leered at her, "Have you lost your goddamn mind?" He asked, standing in front of Delilah, shielding her from the mad woman. "What in the hell are you doing following me?"

"I will ask all the muthafuckin' questions. Not you," she shoved him. "So this is what you do? Eat random bitches' pussies and then come home to kiss me and your child with those same polluted lips? Humph, I knew you were cheating on me. I'm tired of your shit. You so don't deserve me. I hope you die, muthafucka!"

Teddy surveyed his surroundings and in a calm yet stern tone he locked eyes with Tammi. "This theatrical shit you're doing is the exact reason why I'm divorcing your ass! Tammi's mouth flung open and her left eye began nervously twitching. "My suggestion is that you don't make a fool of yourself beyond this point because my decision is the unbendable law."

Almost instantly Tammi balled her fist and swung, but Teddy grabbed that arm and then the other.

"It's done! We're through! " He shook her slightly before releasing her, pushing her backwards with his closing command: "Go home to our son because you have no business here with me."

Tammi was embarrassed and hurt as she watched her husband escort his mistress out of the truck like she wasn't there. Delilah leaned in his embrace ignoring the episode that just happened. Delilah didn't want confrontation with his wife, she knew she had to be hurting. She felt her pain, but she had too much love for her teddy bear and not her, so oh well.

Teddy walked past Tammi as if nothing happened, as if she didn't exist. Her chest heaved up and down as she watched him nonchalantly continue his course with her.

*Her. Him. Them*, she thought. Filled with deadly rage she almost bashed in his truck, but decided she had one better. He'd see. They both would see.

*****

"Are you having a good time?" Teddy asked.

"Of course, with you there isn't a bad one," she refocused her attention back to him.

He placed his hand underneath her chin. "Then why is it that your mind seems to be elsewhere? You're not worried about Tammi, are you?" he questioned.

"Her?" She smacked her teeth. "I'm not sweating her. I thought I saw someone *I* know, but it was just my imagination."

Vado featuring Jeremih's *Bae* came on. Teddy pointed up toward the ceiling. "That's our song. Let's dance."

Delilah stepped down from the counter high stool and followed him onto the floor.

*Swing my way/Let me take you somewhere that I'm heading maybe we can play/Treat you like my hustle you know I be on that all day... You my bae.*

The pelvis bumping from their dancing was intense. The way he placed his hand at the small of her back right above her ass, letting others know silently that he was the man hitting that, made her desire more extreme. She could feel the moisture seep slowly down her inner thigh.

She motioned for him to lower his head. "Baby, I want you," she spoke sexily in his ear."

He looked down at her and smiled a mischievous smile. "I want you too. Let's get out of here."

He opened the passenger door and helped her inside. She assumed they were heading uptown where she stayed, but Teddy proceeded to drive to the Westbank, passing her exit.

"This isn't the way home," she said, pointing at the ramp they were to take.

"We are gonna get there," he smiled.

She exhaled hard, but looked most adorable when she did. He found her appealing when she wanted her way but couldn't have it.

Teddy's theory was simple. Give a little, but hold out a lot. That would break her will to ever pause at his word. They both knew who ran the show, but it was time to etch that shit in her soul.

Ten minutes later, they pulled into the parking lot of Succulence. It was only fitting to dine there since his girl looked succulent.

As soon as she took her seat in the intimate dining room with a beautiful street view of the city, her cell phone vibrated. And again. And again.

## Cum For Me

Suede was calling back to back and he wasn't gonna give up until he reached her. As good of a friend as Suede was, he was oftentimes overbearing. She knew his intentions were good, although she wished he gave her breaths to breathe, especially tonight.

"I have to go to the ladies' room." She excused herself, pecking him on his lips.

Delilah saw a glass on a table and brought it with her into the restroom. She hated lying to him yet again, but she knew she had to save face.

*Good grief,* she mouthed before dialing him back.

"I saw you called."

"Yeah, I did. I'm still pissed from earlier, but I couldn't help but wonder if you were alright?" Agitation was in his voice.

"It's still the same—" she paused for a second to exaggerate her performance, "—from earlier."

"What's that echo I hear?" Suede questioned.

Delilah emerged a finger down her throat, tipped the water from the glass into the toilet and started making regurgitating noises. "I'm in the bathroom," she gagged.

"Delilah, I'm coming over to take care of you!" Suede reprimanded.

"No!" Delilah raised her voice an octave. "I am sick and I'm cranky. I am about to get some sleep, so I am cutting off my phone. I'll talk to you later."

Delilah grabbed her chest as she felt her heartbeat accelerate. If she wasn't clear about her relationship with Suede, she would have sworn somewhere along the line they were dating.

*When Teddy leaves, I'll give him extra time*, she thought.

"I thought I was gonna have to come in there and get you," Teddy joked when she returned to their table.

"Why you say that?" She uneasily chuckled.

"You were in there long enough. You have a boyfriend you have to report too?"

Delilah stiffened her face slightly, but relaxed once she heard him laugh soon after. "There's no one for me but you," she reminded. Which was the truth, Teddy was her everything and more.

Teddy stood from his seat and bent down to kiss Delilah. Her neck rolled back right after her eyes did. His tongue danced sensually with hers, creating so much friction and chaos in his pants he couldn't torture himself by making her wait any longer.

The waitress approached their table. She cleared her throat to get their attention. "Can I start you two off with our house wine? It's—"

Teddy lifted a finger to quiet her and reached into his wallet. He pulled out two twenties, dropped them on the table and grabbed Delilah's hand. She left the restaurant knowing this time they were indeed going home.

*****

The moment he stepped out of his vehicle, he met Delilah on the passenger side and threw her against the side of her house and ravished her in kisses. Grabbing at her breast as she reached for her house keys to continue their twenty-four play, Teddy decided it was time to take the show indoors.

She pushed the door open, but was startled when she didn't hear the beeping sound of her home alarm.

## Cum For Me

"I could have sworn I set the alarm?" Delilah looked back at Teddy who immediately took off searching each room of the house as she waited by the door.

After ten minutes of searching her entire twenty-five hundred square feet home, he walked up on her. "Nothing looks out of place and everything checked out. Maybe you forgot to press the enter button being in a rush," he reasoned.

"I'm certain I set it, baby." Delilah was confused because she never left without it being on.

"You're safe with me," he assured.

Those four words were intoxicating. Nothing was sexier than a man who could make a girl feel safe, so she was back focused on the L that was about to go down.

He began tugging at his tie, loosening it up before he pulled it over his head. He took off his blazer, then unbuttoned his shirt and tossed that too. Delilah watched him unwrap himself out of the rest of his clothing and without thought she came out of her dress as well.

She was about to step out of her heels, but he waved his finger side to side silently telling her to leave them on.

He stood before her looking like an ebony god. Body so well sculpted one would have thought he was pieced together with the finest selection of men from around the world.

Teddy extended his hand and she placed hers in his. No words were needed. His eyes, his words, his body movements, and good gawd his sledge hammer communicated what she was to do, and she always listened.

Delilah stepped out of her dress and followed his lead into her bedroom. He ushered her into the room first. "Stand over there and face the mirror." He turned on the light and pointed to the dresser. "Now close your eyes."

They clamped shut the moment he said it. A smile stretched across her lips as she stood in anticipation of what was to come. Teddy walked up behind her, pressing his slightly crooked dick against the small of her back. Delilah tilted her head slightly behind her and closed her eyes tighter.

He leaned down to kiss her collarbone. "Who do you belong to?"

"You." She rolled the answer off of her tongue very seductively.

Teddy admired her cocoa brown skin in the reflection in the mirror. He ran his hand across her breast and down her stomach, resting his hand over her pussy mound. He took pride in her submission to him.

Teddy reached into the top drawer and pulled out both boxes. Her eyes were still closed and she dared not open her mouth to say a word although she wanted to ask him what was taking so long.

He unbuttoned the rectangular box and removed the very exquisite diamond piece and placed it around her neck. The weight of the seventy carat necklace hung perfectly between her breasts. Drop pearl shaped diamonds cascaded down toward her breastplate like a waterfall of diamonds.

She began to bounce from anxiety. It was hard to keep her composure when she knew he'd just surprised her with a girl's best friend.

"Open your eyes."

Her eyes opened brightly and she gasped, touching her jewels delicately. She never saw anything as tasteful and expensive as the piece that sparkled like a million stars. Delilah turned to face Teddy and thank him, but gasped at the sight before her.

## Cum For Me

Teddy was on one knee with an open box exposing a stunning ten carat antique platinum solitaire. "I meant what I told Tammi. I'm divorcing her because I want to marry *you*. So will you? Will you marry me?"

Tears streamed down her face and dripped onto her breast. She couldn't do anything but shake her head *yes*. Teddy placed the diamond on her finger, kissing her hand.

"You're mine," he boasted.

Still in the kneeling position, he turned Delilah around and parted her legs in the shape of a V. He separated her ass cheeks and ran his tongue from the tip of her pussy to the point of her ass. She grabbed at her hardened nipples as tiny orgasmic spurts shot throughout her body.

"Oooo," she howled as she rubbed on her clit.

After he dined between her thighs for a few minutes, he stood to his feet. "Grab your ankles, baby."

Delilah leaned forward and held on tightly. Teddy grabbed his dick and ran it along the course of her sopping wetness before he plunged himself inside of the softest place on earth. She yelped in excitement.

He secured her by the waist and began grinding against her grinds. Delilah's sex from behind was likened to watching a stripper pop her ass at just the right speeds and at the right times.

"Who dis pussy for?" He slapped her bubble booty.

"Aaaahh. Aaahhh. Ummm." Delilah was in her own head, unable to hear the call of her man.

He smacked her ass cheek so hard this time the stinging traveled up her back. He pulled the length of his inflexible muscle out and teased her entrance, then he rushed it back inside.

"Who. Dis. Pussy. For?" He growled, thrusting inside with every word to make sure she heard and felt him.

"It's your pussy," she cried.

"Say it again." He needed to hear it. It turned him on to know that he controlled her.

"It's yours!" she shouted.

He grinned as he hunched over to massage her breast and he continued to bump and grind his python in then out, in and then out.

When Teddy pulled his dick out, she stood up to face him with her hand buried between her legs, playing with her pearl.

He stroked his black, glistening, hard as steel dick. "Who dat ass belong to?" he smirked.

Delilah's mouth dropped open and she began panting short breaths. She motioned for her bed, placing a pillow underneath her stomach. With her ass tooted in the air, she spread her cheeks, "Come see."

Teddy walked over to the bed and climbed in. He looked at her chocolate mounds and caressed them slowly before he allowed his spit to hit the bull's-eye. He toyed with her clit from underneath and her back dipped into a deeper curve as a pleasure reflex.

"Ohhhh," she moaned.

He pushed his thumb at the entrance of her ass as he continued rubbing the juices around her engorged clitoris with the other.

"Tell me to fuck you," he said in a sexy baritone voice.

"Fuck me. Fuck my ass now!"

"Awww, shit!" He reached for his throbbing dick and perched it at the opening, then he began easing it inside of her tight hole.

## Cum For Me

"Owwww! Owww! Oooh!" she bit into the second pillow.

"Take this dick, baby." He massaged half of the dick already inside of her back and forth to loosen her up for the rest. "You're Daddy's good girl?" He slow stroked, pushing a little more in each time.

"Uhn. Uhn." She shook her head side to side. "I'm his nasty bitch. Now fuck me!"

"Hell, yea!" With no further hesitation he pushed the rest of himself inside of her awaiting asshole.

"Aaaahhhhhh," she wailed at the acceptance of his full girth. "Fuck it like it's your pussy, baby."

He instinctively grabbed a handful of her beautiful curly hair, pulled her head backwards and began fucking her as she'd instructed. She rotated her fingers over and inside of her pussy as he punished her from behind.

"I want you to cum in my ass, baby. I want you to cum in my assssss," she repeated over and over as she summoned her own orgasm.

Teddy enjoyed dominating her. It was the greatest pleasure to know that he not only owned her heart, but her body as well.

"You want me to bust off in that ass?" His breathing became labored and his pumps grew quicker.

"Yasss! Yassssss!" she bellowed. *"Cum For Me."*

"I'm about to cum, baby. I'm gonna shoot this nut deep inside of you."

"Oh, shit! Do that shit!" Her pearl was on the verge of exploding, it had grown so large. "I'm 'bout to cum. I'm 'bout to cummmm. I'm cumming," she sang in a high pitch.

"Grrrrr," Teddy roared as his machine gun let off round after round, blasting off inside of her. "Ahhhh, shit! Fuck!"

As their releases came to an end, neither could breathe. He collapsed on top of her and kissed the nape of her neck.

"Oh, I love you, Teddy."

"I love you too, Delicious."

After their breathing regulated, Delilah went into her adjacent bathroom. She got a soapy towel to wash both her and him off with.

"Do you have it in you for another round?" she asked erotically.

Teddy looked at his soldier saluting in response to her question. He grinned at it and then looked up at her. "What you think?"

She giggled, jumped out of the bed to turn off the light and climbed on top of her stallion.

If it hadn't been for all the commotion Teddy and Delilah made, they would have heard the faint and uncontrollable noises of a man's whimper a few feet away. Suede watched Teddy pour himself into Delilah as he died on the inside.

He knew something was eerie the way Delilah had acted earlier. And when he stalked around her house long enough after she had put him out, he was able to see that eerie was named Teddy or *Ohhh, I love you, Teddy,* to be exact.

He knew when he saw him partake of her goodness in the parking lot he should have confronted her fraudulence then. Instead, he tortured himself by following them inside of the club and then onto the restaurant.

## Cum For Me

    Suede was compelled to see what Teddy did differently than him which gave Teddy a chance at her love and him nothing but a big, dramatic show of lies.
    Suede was furious, enraged, and heart broken. Everything he had ever done had been for her and to see her genuine love for Teddy ripped at his soul.
    He'd blankly stared into the restaurant where he saw Delilah's arms drop to her side like she was helpless under the spell of his kiss and that sent him overboard.
    Teddy just crossed lines that were off limits.
    Suede had hustled to his car and slammed the door once he'd gotten inside and pounded his hands against the steering wheel. He began crying because the thoughts that swirled in his head weren't good. He sat there emotionally torn between two decisions.
    He wiped his eyes to clear his vision because he knew his answer. He was heading to Delilah's place. He wasn't sure what he would do once he got there, but he headed her way.
    Once inside, he disarmed the security system. Delilah was unaware he knew her code, she was unaware of a lot concerning Suede.
    He noticed her panties were lying in the middle of the floor and he shook his head in disgust as he picked them up and examined them through the strain of the seeping moonlight.
    Suede walked into her bedroom, switched on the light, and stared at her bed. He wondered if they were intimate, so he smelled her pillow. There was no scent of the man she was with on them, but that did little to comfort him because it was very clear Teddy had his sexual way with her before and he will again.

He walked over to Teddy's bag and was about to rummage through it before he heard them stepping inside. Quickly, he turned off the light and ran into her clustered walk in closet where he hid and heard more than he ever wanted to know.

It was four a.m. when Teddy and Delilah were finally knocked out and he was freed from his six by six prison. He walked over to where she lay happily in his arms, staring angrily down upon them. He wanted to ask her so desperately why she couldn't love him the way he loved her, the way she'd just loved Teddy? Instead, he turned around and left the room undetected.

Quietly, he placed a hand on the front door lock to disengage it, but it was unlocked already. He thought nothing of it as he exited the house, his mind swirled with other contemplations.

Suede jogged the two blocks to where his car was parked and peeled off into the dark of morning. Then five miles into his ride home he slammed on his brakes and shouted to the roof of his vehicle.

"Fuccckkk!"

He began burning with jealous fury. Flashes of their love making plagued his mind and he went ballistic.

*How the hell could his proposal be better than having a life with me? I was the one who loved her for better or worse, not him!*

"Him!" Suede growled.

There was no way Suede was going to idly standby and watch his world dissolve. In his mind, she really loved him, and Suede was going to give her the uncrowded time to see it.

After he cried hard, then laughed maniacally, he sped off with an agenda.

### *A few days later…*

There has been a report that millionaire mogul, Theodore Champion, was found dead late Monday morning. More news at twelve.

Delilah heard Lynn Carmichael, the reporter of Channel 13 News, tell the world that her fiancé was murdered. In a state of shock and disbelief, her glass slipped out of her hand, shattering upon impact against the wooden floor.

"Noooooo!" She screamed hysterically.

### *The end?*

## Island Lust
## By
## *Linnea*

Neveah, Kaylanie, Caileigh, and Brooklyn hopped out of the cab in front of the The Courtleigh Suites in New Kingston, Jamaica. The first cousins had been planning the vacation for about a year and it was finally time to have some fun in the sun.

Kaylanie slid her sunglasses up her nose as she emerged from the vehicle with a look of disdain on her face. This wasn't her type of hype at all. As they passed through several areas of smaller, row houses and roads that gave them an idea, she was convinced this part of the island was not for visitors. She knew trusting her sister, Caileigh, to make arrangements without verifying them thoroughly was a mistake, but she had already spoken her piece on the way so she wasn't even about to go there all over again.

*Leave it to her adventurous ass,* Kaylanie huffed to herself.

Wait a minute," Caileigh stretched her arm in front of the others girls' chests to stop them in their tracks. "Before we leave this airport something needs to be said. What goes on in Jamaica..." Caleigh waited for a response.

"Stays in Jamaica," the other girls excitedly chimed in unison.

"Good because what I am about to do Tyrus *cannot* find out about," Caileigh emphasized the seriousness of her baby daddy discovering her plotted indiscretions.

She loved him, but their sex life since the baby had become so routine. She needed spontaneity and adventure, both of which had disappeared over the last few months.

# Cum For Me

Caileigh opened her purse to reveal the numerous condoms she was carrying. Neveah and Brooklyn teasingly shielded their eyes as if the sunlight and gold foil gave off a blinding glare.

"That's a damn shame," Kaylanie turned up her nose.

"Whatever, with your siddity ass. Let's not forget that you got your modeling career off the ground by doing favors on the couch," Caileigh reminded her.

"Y'all don't start that mess, please. We are here to have a good time," Brooklyn, the baby of the group refereed the fight between the two sisters. At twenty-one, she had barely made the cut for the trip. The other cousins were banging on the door of the thirties club and extremely skeptical about bringing her. After some begging and pleading, they agreed that she carried herself in a mature enough manner to tag along.

After entering into the pact, Caileigh almost knocked them down, eagerly trying to get into the hotel and check in. Careless, she paid no mind to the fact she left her bags for the others.

"I swear this girl gets on my nerves at times." Kaylanie shook her head. "Those bags will sit right there if she waiting on me to bring them in. I'm not a damn bellhop."

"You know this is all she has been talking about for weeks," Brooklyn laughed.

"Whooptie do." Kaylanie's size two frame had enough struggles with her own bags to be concerned with carrying her sister's.

She packed just like the fashion model she was, always ready for a runway moment. She was five feet, seven inches normally, but most of the time she wore heels that made her at least six feet. She had a mocha chocolate skin tone and a shoulder length bob with a Chinese bang that hung low, accentuating her alluring almond shaped eyes. She wore corn chip shorts with a wife beater that was tied in the back and coach tennis shoes.

Neveah paid the driver and then picked up her and Caleigh's bag, walking into the hotel behind the other girls.

Caileigh had already found her prey at the front desk. "So what part of the island are you from?" She leaned onto her elbow, sliding the keys from desk attendant's fingers.

"Rema," he responded in his thick island voice. He was medium height, bulkily built, cappuccino colored man with curly hair and a perfectly aligned set of molars.

"Umm hmm. And how far is that from here?"

"'Bout fifteen minutes."

"Maybe you can show me the city when you get off, Duran," she read his name off of his gold lapel. "You have my room number." She winked at him.

"Definitely, Fluffy." He licked his lips, imagining what Caileigh's treat might taste like.

"Fluffy?" She creased her brows at the nickname, wondering if he was insulting her because she was thickly shaped woman. She was five feet, two inches with big breasts, thick thighs, and a small pouch that remained after the delivery of her six-month old. She had short hair which she wore spiked, and doughy brown eyes.

She hoped he wasn't trying to take a jab at her because she was confident in her shape. Her beauty came from within and not from what people judged by the naked eye.

## Cum For Me

"Babes, a jus caah u body fluffy. U shape well good," he explained why he had called her the name.

"Uh huh." She joined the other girls at the elevator.

The two bedroom penthouse suites sat a few feet from the elevator. Sitting the bags on the floor, Neveah walked across the living room to the balcony, breathing in the dry summer air. She took in a deep breath, inhaling the fresh island air as the palm trees stirred lightly, attempting to give off some cool air.

This trip was so needed to get her away from her life. Working a full time job and managing her master's degree schedule was far more difficult than Neveah anticipated. She tried to keep her mind focused on the payoff her hard work would yield, but at that moment all she wanted was some peaceful time alone on the island to relax.

Brooklyn toured the inside of the suite. "This is amazing," she gasped, going back and forth between the bedrooms.

Each bedroom was furnished with a king sized bed, thirty-two inch wall mounted TV's, an ottoman, and a breakfast set that sat in front of a massive wall length window. A breathtaking view of the city sat below, surrounded by the clear blue water and green hill sides that could be seen with the curtains drawn. The bathrooms had glistening brown granite marble counter tops and high glass showers.

Brooklyn stopped admiring the attractive views once she heard a knock at the door.

"Y'all ready?" Caileigh asked. Neveah came off of the balcony, closing the sliding door behind her.

"For what?" Brooklyn questioned.

"To go out. We didn't come all the way here to be locked up in no damn room. I need to see what this place is about, so come on," Caileigh demanded.

"I need a few to get ready," Brooklyn said.

"I want to lie down. So y'all go ahead without me. I'll do whatever is planned for later," Neveah replied lethargically.

"Girl, bye with that bull. You're not tired. You're stressing over lover boy." She corrected Neveah's lie. "You do as you please, but you better stop worrying about that nigga because believe he ain't thinking about you." Caileigh served Neveah with the harsh truth. "I'll be downstairs in the lobby waiting for you. Hurry up," she huffed at Brooklyn, allowing the door to shut.

She was right. Once Caileigh stepped out of the room, Neveah lay across the bed, checking her phone for his messages. She had texted him when she got in, but he'd had yet to respond.

"Ughh!" She threw the pillow across the bed in frustration.

Neveah knew she needed to end the relationship with her grad school department chair holder, William, but she couldn't. He had specifically told her he wasn't looking for anything serious, but she'd caught feelings for him anyway. Now it was a complicated mess.

Neveah knew she was far too beautiful to be wasting her time with his old, shriveled up ass anyway. Her peanut butter complexion and bedroom eyes were eye grabbing. Her full juicy lips and natural, golden colored-locks hung to her mid-back. She could catch a man quickly without trying. She just had to make it up in her mind to leave William alone.

## Cum For Me

Caileigh exited the elevator, peering in the direction of the desk. She planned to occupy her time flirting some more with her first island treat, but Duran was nowhere in sight. She headed across the lobby toward the shelves that displayed the brochures of different attractions the city offered. From what she had seen online, New Kingston was similar to the French Quarters in New Orleans.

Walking further into the lobby and past the office, she heard Duran on the phone having a heated conversation with someone. She nosily snuck around the desk and put her ear to the door to listen in. His back was to the door as he looked out of the open blinds onto the street.

"Yuh bettah av mi money wen mi reech." He threatened the person on the other end of the line with the consequences if they didn't.

A devious idea crept into Caileigh's mind. *You only live once.* She shrugged her shoulders at that thought and tip toed into the office, peeling off each of her clothes until none remained.

Duran hung up the phone and turned around to an ass naked Caileigh, standing in the middle of the floor. He licked his lips, approving of the woman before him.

"I thought why wait 'til later for what we can do now." She slowly walked over to him, allowing him to take in her nakedness a little more.

"Damn, Fluffy," he nodded his head as she walked across the floor. He wanted her badly. When she reached him, he gripped all her of ass, pulling her into him and passionately kissing her. Their tongues intertwined in a tango as the room disappeared.

Caileigh's hands left his back in search of the reason she came. Unfastening his pants, she stuck her hand into his boxers, pleased with what she found. *Jackpot,* she thought at the feel of the nine inch hook she discovered. Moans expelled from Duran's mouth as she gently tugged up and down his full length until he stood at full attention.

Duran picked her up, placing her onto the office desk, ready to fulfill his earlier desire. Bending over, he flicked his tongue over her clit gently, savoring her honey. The more he quickened his pace, increased impulses of satisfaction coursed through Caileigh's veins. He slurped on her juices, enthralled by her pleasure.

"Oh, shit!" She seized the back of his head tightly, summoning him to continue. He began sucking on her womanhood, trying to extract all her nectar.

"Fuck!" She cried out, lifting her body off of the desk. He cupped her ass checks to hold her in position, then inserted three of his fingers into her pothole as he continued. Caileigh laid back, clenching the edge of the desk for dear life. Duran gulped on the saccharine that poured out of her beehive. Caileigh's body quivered as she panted heavily, trying to catch her breath. It felt as if all of the oxygen in the room had been depleted.

"Duran, please." She squirmed from the bliss he was giving her, but the stronghold he had on her wouldn't allow movement. Unable to hold the ecstasies that streamed through her, she released sighs of delight onto his tongue.

"Umm," Duran hummed as he licked her clean.

Rising from the floor, he pulled her by the legs and across the desk to him. Her mind briefly wandered to the thought of the condoms she had left upstairs. *Shit on it at this point,* she thought. Massaging his Mandingo against her pearl tongue, he joshed her sopping wet passageway with only the head. Her warmness felt better than he could have ever dreamed.

## Cum For Me

He eased further into her with each motion, coating his shaft with her wet offering. He moved his lower extremities in a tidal wave motion, giving her surges of delight. He wanted to savor every dripping, wet stroke that Caileigh's pussy allowed.

"Give me all of you," she called for more of him to enter her.

"Shhh, Fluffy. 'Nuh worry uself." He prolonged honoring her request.

Her funnel swallowed every bit he gave. His head fell back as he quickened his pace slightly, her muscles contracting to control his entrance and exit. Their bodies shivered from the pleasure being exchanged. He leaned over her body, planting sensual kisses down her neck and body. Caileigh reciprocated, placing pecks onto his shoulder blades. She dug her nails into his back, scratching his skin.

"Take this like it's yours." Caleigh pushed back onto him to ensure he knocked down her walls. The curve of his dick tickled at her G-spot.

She placed her legs around his neck, forcing herself onto him which drove him into a frenzy. Duran grasped her wrist, elevating her off the desk. Caileigh resembled a pendulum dangling back and forth over the floor as Duran thrust violently into her. Their bodies slapped together brashly, giving round of applauses in appreciation of the work they were handing out.

Perspiration trickled from Duran's forehead onto Caileigh from the intense heat their bodies expelled. The sweat mixed with the warmth drove Caileigh into an insane trance. She screamed as the second rapture of bliss emanated from her gut. Duran prodded her burrow until he could no longer hold back. He placed her in the computer chair, ejaculating his seeds all over her stomach.

Caileigh remained positioned in the chair for a minute to get her mind right. A few minutes later, Duran extended his hands, showing her to the bathroom where she could wash herself up. She quickly put on her clothes, knowing that by now the girls would be in the lobby waiting.

"Thanks for an awesome time." She kissed his cheek.

Kaylanie and Brooklyn sat in the lobby, impatiently waiting on Caileigh. She made such a big ordeal for them to but ready, but disappeared.

Moments later they spotted her, "Where the fuck you been?" Brooklyn interrogated.

"Minding my damn business. Let's go." She walked off without another word.

The two ladies shook their heads at each other then followed their bossy cousin. Sometime later, they headed to the Bob Marley Museum for a tour.

Caileigh was still lurking to fulfill her hoeish mission, so she collected at least two other numbers from two fine ass natives.

"They don't make them like this at home," Caileigh laughed as Kaylanie and Brooklyn refused to entertain her charades. "Anyway, ole' boy said we need to check out a club called Quad and some ole' mansion called the Devon House.

After the museum, they had dinner at Scotchies Jerk Center and from there they took a quick nap before they got dressed for the club. By their outfits, it could easily be seen what each woman was searching for.

## Cum For Me

Caileigh wore a white peplum top with matching tights that had lace from the waistline to her ankle. Her ensemble was accompanied by red, wedge heels. A blind man could see she wore no drawers and her breasts were damn near to her chin courtesy of push-up bra. She left no doubt that she was ready for some fucking while the others could care less about the island men. They just wanted to have a good time and chill.

Kaylanie sported a knee length, blue and grey bandage dress with sling back grey heels. Neveah had on a bright green floor length skirt with a matching top that fell directly above her navel and gold ankle cuff sandals. Brooklyn had on a pair of dark denim capris with a black halter top that matched the red and black Jordan's on her feet.

"Just in case I need these." Caileigh patted the small clutch she'd tucked two condoms in.

The girls shook their heads at her thirsty comments.

Neveah checked her phone for the millionth time, but she had no response from William. She huffed in aggravation and placed it on the desk.

*He just don't damn care,* Neveah told herself.

Catching a cab, they stood in front of a three story, grey stucco building with a neon blue sign that read: Quad. After a fifteen minute wait, they made their way to the more exclusive top floor of the club, or so the bouncer had said. The club was live.

"Hey, Champion. Wah yah get?" The bartender flirted with Caileigh. He would definitely show her a good time on the island if allowed. Thicker women were highly attractive and desired among the men.

"I would like a shot of Hennessey and my girls would like..." she paused, turning to them for their orders.

"Peach Ciroc," Neveah responded.
"Guiness Stout," Brooklyn said.
"Water," Kaylanie replied.

Caileigh rolled her eyes. "How much?" She went into her bag for the money after the bartender handed them their drinks.

"It's on me. Nice up yuhself." He bid them to enjoy themselves. They raised their cups in a toast to him and began sipping.

They caught a table on the side of the dance floor and took a seat. The reggae music blared through the speakers and the deejay hyped the crowd up on the mic. Girls popped their ass and pivoted their hips to the island's most popular songs.

Sipping wasn't getting Neveah the effect she was looking for, so she took the Ciroc straight to the head, quickly returning to the bar for a second round.

"You better slow down," Brooklyn warned her.

"I'll be fine," she brushed her off. She moved a couple of feet away from the table to spare herself any possible lecture. She returned to the bar once more before losing all count of her alcohol consumption.

The Ciroc began to take her to a happier place, erasing her thoughts about what William was doing. She rocked her hips to the beat of the music.

"Yow browning, yuh look good enuh." A young boy spoke into Neveah's ear. He was a tall, lengthy, dark, milk chocolate specimen with short dreads. He wore a multicolor, patterned, button down, collar shirt with a pair of skinny jeans and black tennis. He had a neatly lined fade and beard that framed his face.

Judging that he was no more than twenty-two, she redirected her attention back to the floor, hoping he would move along because she definitely wasn't interested. He held his hands up in surrender as he backed up some. Neveah closed her eyes, refocusing on her drink and the ambiance of the space, bobbing her head from left to right as she felt the liquor take control.

The darkness did something that heightened the effects of the alcohol. The club had a totally different vibe about it. She felt incredible as she soared in the clouds. She increased the swivel of her hips as the music infiltrated her soul. The young man took advantage of the opportunity he saw unfolding. He grabbed her sides, pulling her backwards onto him. She rotated her hips like a hula hoop against his pants. He piloted the sway of their bodies until they became in perfect sync.

Neveah gave him a tantalizing exhibition that caused his manhood to thicken within seconds. Feeling his bulge, she immediately desired compensation from her work. She faced him, maneuvering his hand to tame the throb coming from between her legs. He palmed her pussy, ready to tear her insides wide open. Taking her by the hand, he escorted her outside of the club into the alley on the side. Her mind said what she was doing was irrational, but the pulsation in her core sought relief.

About fifty feet into the alley, he pinned her to the building, savagely kissing on her body. He snatched her shirt up, freeing her breasts from the bra that imprisoned them. He completely demolished them with the heat of his mouth, indulging on her nipples.

"Mmm," Neveah whimpered at the gratification of him reaching her hot spot. Her sprinklers activated, causing a dampening in her pit.

He ferociously tore her thong from under her skirt, discarding it like garbage. Her skin singed in bliss at his animalistic behavior. She wrapped one leg around his waist, leaving the other to anchor her to the ground. The sound of his pants unzipping made her crave his dick. Spitting on it for extra moisture, he rubbed it onto his pole before he forcefully shoved it inside of her wet vessel.

"Mi browning, u dis mi." He was about to punish her ass for even considering that she could dismiss him. Her bare back scraped against the stucco building as he hammered her canal. She wrapped her arms around him as her knees threatened to give out.

Sensing he wasn't going as deep as possible, he instructed her to face the wall and assume the position, spreading her legs extra wide with his foot. The liquid from her lair flowed liberally. She braced her palms on the wall, preparing for impact. He wrapped her dreads in his fist, snatching her head back as he pummeled her pussy unmercifully.

"Hit this shit," she shouted.

He bit into her back, accelerating the propulsion of his pole. She closed her eyes, shaking her head defiantly at the fact that anything could be that good. The pain mixed with pleasure was cosmic. She wanted to scream his name from the top of the highest mountain. The friction from the stabs of his spear caused her skin to tingle and shudder.

Neveah opened her eyes to a crowd of onlookers at the end of the alley, they had stopped to admire the scene. The temperature of her heat box rose to supernova, enough to eradicate mankind from the earth. The strength of his jabs were filled with the lust from when he first noticed her on the dance floor. Unable to contain it, she released her first sign of pleasure onto his pipe. He licked his lips in satisfaction, but he was far from finished.

"Ey gyal, ole u ankle dem." He commanded her to hold onto her ankles. He eased his rod in and out, pulling her into him once he had fully entered. He wriggled his hips to ensure she took in every piece of his shaft. Taking one of her hands off of her ankles, she applied pressure on her stomach.

"Nuh, my girl," he pushed her hand away.

She obeyed his summons as he applied enough force to almost crush her bones as he unceasingly explored her tunnel. The sky opened and the universe cried the tears that would not fall from her own eyes in her moment of ecstasy. The warm rain slid down her back into the crack of her ass while he continued his lunges into her deep center. His youthful stamina showed no ending in sight to the lashing he was unleashing into Neveah's cave. She was in paradise.

*Whap!*

The sound of his hand smacking her ass roared like thunder. Her ass cheeks jiggled like Jell-O on impact. The sting from the force of his hand mixed with the downpour of rain intensified the mood. He seized her dangling breasts, pinching her nipples between his fingers. Her eyes appeared colorless as her pupils retracted back under their hoods.

He continuously plowed in her at a rapid pace. Her legs shook violently and her pussy ached in the most divine manner. Voices in her head sang the praises of the stranger. He grunted, taking custody of her love handles to steady her balance, almost ready to spit his seeds. Pulverizing her with all his force, she held onto the wall to shield her head from banging into it. She was ready to hose down his rod for the second time.

"Ahhh," she screamed, irrigating her valley.

She came so hard the second time that he could no longer hold his own nut. With a few prods, he pulled out, jacking his nut onto the pavement.

"Mmm," he grunted.

Neveah caught her breath before fixing her outfit to head back inside. As she proceeded down the alley, he called out to her.

"U nuh waah mi name?"

"Nah. You've served your purpose." She continued walking without looking back.

*Damn, when the island boys can put it down, you already knooww...* she sang, smiling to herself.

Making her way back to the floor, Kaylanie and Brooklyn were standing on the sidelines. Brooklyn was conversing with an island guy while Kaylanie ignored his friend who was trying hard to make conversation. Neveah stood within eye sight of the table so they could see she was back.

"Where have you been? We started to put out an APB on you," Brooklyn spoke in a reprimanding way to Neveah.

"Ma'am, last time I checked, I was grown." Neveah waved her concerns off. "You're the damn child here."

"Uh huh." Brooklyn made her way back to the guy waiting for her at the table.

Neveah looked around for Caileigh, but there was no sign of her. "Where is Caileigh?" she asked Kaylanie.

"Girl, I be fuck if I know. Most likely in the bathroom letting one of these island men fuck her more stupid that she already is. I know I'm ready to go, though," Kaylanie spat.

## Cum For Me

"Well, we can't leave without her, so we better start looking. Let me get Brooklyn," Neveah huffed before heading over to retrieve her people.

Searching the club, they saw no sign of Caileigh anywhere. Brooklyn tried hitting her phone, but it went straight to voicemail. She hit her a few more times receiving the same result. On the verge of exasperation, she had the deejay do a call out like Caileigh was a lost child in a department store. Twenty minutes later, Caileigh was still M.I.A.

"Ohhh! I swear that girl gets on my last damn good nerve," Kaylanie complained. "She clearly isn't here and I don't have time for this shit with her. Let's get the fuck out of here." They walked out of the club toward the hotel.

The girls nervously retired to their rooms. Neveah called the police on their way to the hotel but there was nothing they could do just yet.

Kaylanie tried to watch TV to calm her nerves, but her ears kept playing tricks on her. She jumped up each time she thought she heard the door handle, ready to lay into Caileigh's ass. She had done some reckless shit before but this made no sense. Eventually, she paced the floor worried about her sister's whereabouts. *Why would she leave the damn club without saying something to someone and then not answer her phone?*

Kaylanie's head began to pound from the agitation of Caileigh disappearance. She needed a drink, something she haven't done since their dad had been killed by a drunk driver. She grabbed her wedges she had placed next to the sofa and headed downstairs. She couldn't wait for Caileigh to walk through that door. The tongue lashing she had for her would probably end in a fist fight. Her hands flailed as she played the scene out in her mind, walking through the hotel lobby. Caught up in her own head, she paid no attention to where she was going. She fell down the two steps that led to the hotel's bar. Her foot bent in the opposite direction, twisting her ankle.

"Shit!" She winced, gripping her ankle to stop the thudding pain.

"Yuh arite?" The bartender came from behind the bar to check on her. He offered his hands to aid her, seeing the grimace on her face. She accepted his hand and he pulled her up, being careful to lift her slowly. They stood face to face, staring into each other's eyes.

"I will be fine. Thank You," Kaylanie sprang backwards a little.

"Come siddung," he put her arm around his neck as she hopped on her right leg. He retreated behind the counter and filled a clean towel with some ice.

"Mmm hmm," he mumbled, placing it onto her injury.

The swelling made her release a slightly painful moan. She requested something strong to distract the pain, so the bartender made her a Jamaican Rum Punch. To amplify the effect he added an additional shots of Jamaican White Rum straight from the distillery.

The first sip of the drink burned but the rest went down smoothly. While she nurtured her ankle, she asked a few questions about the area. Hopefully he could ease some of her concerns about Caileigh's safety. He didn't give the best report but not the worst either. He was curious as to why she would ask, but figured she didn't want to talk about if she hadn't said.

Kaylanie had another drink and decided it was time to go back to the room. Her ankle felt numb from the ice and relaxed for the most part, but she wanted to soak it to hopefully help with the swelling.

The bartender came around the bar top to help her when he saw her attempt to get up off of the barstool.

"I can manage," she held onto the chair, fixing her shirt that had lifted up slightly, showing the bumble bee yellow thong she wore.

"Yuh wah mi wahk wid u gi yuh room?"

"No. I have it," she began bouncing out of the bar. She held her arms out to keep herself steady, but still wobbled.

"Nuh worry, yuh criss," he assured her that she was good. "Mi soon fawud," he let the other bartender know he would be back. He got in front of her, bringing her hands down and leading the way. His touch was so soft and tender. Kaylanie wanted to object, but he shook his head and put a finger on her lips before she could utter a word. He brushed his finger across them delicately.

"Shhh," he directed her and walked backwards to maintain eye contact with her. His stare mesmerized her and she followed his lead without another objection. He escorted her through the lobby and to her room.

"Weh di key?" he asked.

"Right here," she took her hands from him and patted over her left breast. She braced herself with the wall and dug in, but couldn't find they key. "Damn it," she fumed at herself. She remembered that after she had returned from the club she'd tossed it on the end table next to the sofa. That's where it still was.

"Mi ago get annada wan." He went toward the elevators to retrieve another key from the front desk.

Kaylanie leaned against the wall and watched him walk away. But sexual urges started to arise within her.

Maybe it was the alcohol that lowered her inhibitions or her need to be distracted from the issue with both her sister and her ankle, but she was steaming with desire.

    It had been a hot minute since her last man. Her control issues caused her previous relationship to end. She demanded to know where he was, who he was with, wanted to pick out his clothes and was close to coaching their sex. No longer able to handle it, she came home to find a note from him and all of his things gone. While she was happily single and in control of her life, she could use some sexual release. Her essence began to seep at the thought of fucking the bartender.

    He returned about five minutes later with her key in hand. Kaylanie licked her lips as he came toward her. *Yep,* she answered the question in her head. The locked clicked and he helped her inside.

    "Thank you. Uhhh," she looked for a name tag. "I'm sorry. What's your name?" She wrapped her arm around his neck, hopping on one foot into the room. He helped her onto the sofa.

    "Eason," he replied.

    'Thank you, Eason. Let me give you something for your trouble. Have a seat," she invited, patting a spot for him.

    "Nuh. Mi affi guh elp lack di bar." Eason knew the other bartender would be looking for him to close up.

    "Don't be in such a hurry, I have something nice for you." She got up off of the sofa and boldly straddled his lap. Peering at him with sultry eyes. She began unbuttoning his shirt, running her hands down his perfectly carved torso. Her eyes glowed at beholding his eight pack. She gazed into his eyes and with no spoken words he gave her permission to proceed. He leaned up as she pushed his clothing over his shoulders, revealing the tattoos that ran up and down his well-built arms.

He lifted her off of his lap, effortlessly carrying her into the bedroom. He started to place her on the bed, but had a more creative idea. He sat her down on the bed as he dragged the ottoman out onto the balcony. Able to place a small amount of weight onto her ankle, she limped behind him, meeting him. She pushed him back, requesting he have a seat in the chair. Eason submitted to her request and slid back.

She slowly crawled up the ottoman like an animal preparing for an attack. She brushed her body against his before gingerly placing both feet on the floor and standing up over him. Eason reached up, pulling down her cotton shorts as she removed her shirt. She unfastened her bra, tossing it to the side of the chair, allowing her breasts to be emancipated. She grabbed the band of her thong to remove it, but Eason shook his head in rejection.

"Lef it ahn," he charged.

She pushed them to the side willing to grant one of his requests. Ignoring the pain in her ankle, she eased down in the squatting position, hovering above him for a minute. He reached up to pull her down by the waist, but she knocked his hands away. She would be in control of how it went down.

Kaylanie removed his pants, slinging them across the room as her eyes feasted on his hardening member. A couple of strokes from her delicate hands had him standing tall. She slithered her body down onto him gradually until she devoured his entire shank. The unloosening of her tight, underground chamber sent waves of stinging indulgence throughout her frame. Fully breached by his length, she sprang up and down on him like a pogo stick. She maneuvered herself in a different direction each time she came down onto him. Kaylanie's body twitched in exultation, allowing him to leave no area un-stroked. Her storm surge barrier vaguely ruptured, discharging a stream of her fluid.

"Mmm. Mi uh na." Eason moaned, grumbling inaudible speech.

She about faced, riding him doggy style. His thick, long mass filled her space entirely. Eason reached around, whisking his finger over her clit, heightening the intensity. "Fuck, Eason!" She shouted so loud she knew somebody heard his name. She imagined people coming out at any moment to catch a glimpse of the scene.

He yanked her off his stake, not ready to spit his contents into her. Placing her on the edge of the balcony, Kaylanie leaned back, gripping onto the wooden rails. Her body hung like a chandelier, viewing the island in awe from her upside down position. She could see the glowing water shooting high in the air from the lit fountain that sat in the middle Emancipation Park.

The danger of her slipping invigorated her, causing slight spasms of jubilation. Eason's mouth hung up as he barreled into her vault with all of his power, trying to destroy the latch of her lockbox. Her body rebounded back into him with each slam dunk of his pole into her basket.

Eason pulled her up, lying her body face down under his on the ottoman. His upper body strength was off the chain as he rapidly performed pushups in her cave. He was relentless as he pumped in and out. He swept her ears with his tongue when his body came down on top of hers. He was conquering uncharted territory with his advances. He increased his thrusts to almost the speed of light. A sense of galactic awareness penetrated her soul.

"Grrr," he growled, releasing himself into her hollow. He kept going, realizing she had not reached her climax. Kaylanie was only a minute behind.

"What the fuck?" Her body appeared to go into an epileptic fit, submerging his staff with her precipitation.

They lay under the illumination of the full moon and stars until Kaylanie dozed off. Eason had forgotten all about closing up the bar. He secured her in his arms and carried her to the bed. She stirred, having a nightmare about Caileigh's whereabouts.

Checking her phone, she saw that Caileigh had finally texted her back. She'd had the islander from the front desk scoop her up for another session of his good wood. She would be back in the morning and they would head to a few more spots in the area.

One down, seven more to go, Kaylanie told herself as she turned over, cuddling in Eason's arms.

*The End*

## Seductress
### By
### *Tonya Holley*
### *(MsWriterForLife)*

## Chapter 1

Delshawna Brown had an unusually high sex drive. Actually, she was a nymphomaniac with a sexual need that exceeded what was normal for nymphos. And when you threw in the fact that she was try-sexual—meaning she would try *anything* sexual—you were dealing with one depraved broad.

At that moment Delshawna was very horny, which was saying a lot, and blaming her body's extreme need on the lack of fulfillment from the man she'd made the huge mistake of spending the night with. *I need some bangin' dick and a cup of coffee after the night I had with that weak fuck, Darrel,* Delshawna, known as Sasha, thought as she walked into an unusually empty Starbucks.

Her nerves were bad and her body was in a carnally deprived frenzy as she reflected on how long it had been since she'd had a bang that actually satisfied her.

"What can I get you?" The female server asked as she stepped into Sasha's line of vision, flooding her view with nothing but sex appeal. And almost as if in protest, her pussy thumped, reminding her that it was in desperate need of pleasure.

"I'll have a triple, chocolate chip mocha," Sasha said as her eyes involuntarily drank in the sexy woman before her. Just looking at her had Sasha so aroused that her nipples ached and became erect. In fact, her entire body suddenly joined her pussy in a protest that was going on hot and heavy. "And my name is Sasha," she flirted a little.

*Since I couldn't get good lovin' from Darrel, maybe I can get it from this beauty*, Sasha thought as she added a smile to that flirt.

"Hot or cold?" The woman responded with a welcoming smile of her own and Sasha's libido jumped for joy. *If I made an advance, would she be receptive?* Sasha wondered. She was finding it hard to concentrate on anything that didn't lead to her having sex.

"Hot, please." *Maybe I can convince her to let me turn her out,* she thought as she checked out and checked the woman out at the same time.

As the line server went in the back and prepared her order, Sasha allowed her vision to absorb the woman's slim waist, nice, round booty that was hugged by her black Capri pants, and C cup breasts that were revealed through her snug uniform shirt.

Sasha groaned in pleasure as she felt her core become wet and her nipples grow so firm they ached at the mere touch from her bra. Her skin was ablaze and her tongue involuntarily licked her lips as it ached to sample something just as wet as she was.

"Hot, triple, chocolate chip mocha," the sexy body was accompanied by a sexy voice and an equally sexy look as she made eye contact with Sasha.

There was something in that look and Sasha wanted whatever it was that the look held.

"Thanks," she said as, yet again, she licked her lips in a seductive way. Then she waited to see if the woman would give her the okay to press forward with a possible sexperience. When she didn't, Sasha simply smiled. *I'll be back*, she told herself before grabbing her drink and going out of the door.

With extreme disappointment flooding her at the missed sexcapade, and her mind trying to figure out a way to get at the line server, Sasha was shocked when she heard a male voice say, "Oh!" just as her drink suddenly splattered her shirt and drenched her aching breasts beneath.

*Oh, no this motherfucker didn't spill my drink on me!* Sasha looked at her stained, white halter top and black, Baby Phat, jeans.

"My bad, ma. I didn't see you there."

*How the hell could you not see a whole human being right in front of you?* She wondered. Then she looked up at him, ready to cuss him out. But after getting a good visual of the handsome stranger before her, illicit thoughts ran through her head and intense sexual tension ran through her body. She couldn't help but to let the man slide as she immediately prayed that he would slide into her.

"It's okay, I'll be fine," she said, her body reacting violently to his sexiness.

"Nah, let me buy you another drink," he insisted.

*Please! Baby, you can do a lot more than that for me,* she thought as a desire to fuck him hit her so strongly and so powerfully, her pussy clenched brutally.

"No, I'm not trippin' off of that," she spoke in her most seductive voice. "But maybe you can help clean me off," she spoke boldly as she dipped her finger in the whipped cream that sat on her chest.

She hoped he would take the bait she was throwing out when she seductively licked the cream off of her finger. Then she looked at him wantonly and dipped that same finger into the cream again. After getting a load of first the line server and then him, her body was on the verge of a sexual collapse. And if she didn't get some soon, Sasha knew she would lose it and jump on anything for fulfilment.

When his eyes revealed that he would indeed take the bait, Sasha stepped back through the doors from which she had just exited. Then she snatched him into the coffee shop and licked the cream off of her finger with her tongue right before taking her shirt off. The nympho in her was ready.

She didn't care that they were in a public place, or that they could be seen by anyone who decided to suddenly walk through the doors. The exhibitionist in her lived for moments when she could display herself at her most salacious point. So the more public the place, the harder she would get off.

"Oh, really?" He asked in surprise of her bold actions as he first looked around to see if anyone was there. When he saw that it was just them and the woman behind the counter, who looked every bit as interested in Sasha as he was, he turned back to her and observed each inch of the upper body she'd wasted no time in exposing.

"Yeah, you made the mess, so get to cleaning," she told him as he stared longingly at the bare breasts she was fondling.

"You ain't said nothing but a word, baby," strange guy said as he wasted no time stepping to Sasha and licking the cream off of her twin delights.

Sasha moaned as his tongue came in contact with sore nipples. "I hope you know what you're doing," she said as he licked her breasts until they throbbed in pleasure-filled pain and her core leaked until her panties were drenched. Then he made a trail of kisses down to her jeans.

Pulling them off of her, he lowered his lips to her lower lips and began attacking her juicy pussy.

It took only a few seconds and a few naughty licks for Sasha to know that dude knew what he was doing. *Oh my God! His tongue game is thebomb.com.* "Ahh, oh! Shit! Damn! Keep licking right there!" She screamed out in the pleasure she had been so desperate to receive.

The man's tongue had taken her to the end zone so quickly that she was on the verge of her first orgasm when he suddenly stopped and rose from the floor. That drove Sasha mad. But before she could go off on him, without warning, he picked her up and placed her on the counter near the cash register.

"Are you ready for this, ma?" He asked her as he noticed the cashier at the entrance of the shop, locking the door. The aroused expression on her face told him that a threesome was in the making.

"Stop talking shit and give me that *dick*," Sasha said as sexual frustration had her yanking him towards her when her pussy kicked into overdrive. Her intense need for the dirty deed was making her crazy as he moved ever so slowly while unbuckling his pants.

"You want this?" He smirked at the desperate look on her face.

"Duh!" She practically shouted as the nympho in her went berserk.

Without further delay, dude whose name she didn't care to know roughly slammed his nine inch dick in her.

"Ooohhhh!" She screamed out as she bust at penetration, her body going into epileptic spasms.

"What's wrong?" He taunted her as her juices coated his thick, marble-like shaft. "I thought you wanted this dick," he teased as he kept her cumming by hitting all of her hot spots.

Sasha wailed like a dying animal as she tried to get her bearings, tried to handle the fact that old boy she didn't know was giving her the fulfillment she'd been craving for a long time. But he never gave her the chance to handle anything. Instead, he quickly held her arms over her head with one hand and placed one of her legs on his shoulder. Then he drove his dick into her abyss and delved like he was deep sea diving for lost treasure.

*Damn, he's putting it on me*, she thought as her ongoing orgasm intensified.

Then, "Do you mind if I cut in?" The female line server asked as she stood naked beside them. "Go ahead," he told her as he slowly pulled out. "I got her all juiced up for you."

The line server moved over to the counter and stood in front of Sasha, bent her body until her face was between Sasha's legs, and wasted no time tasting what she'd craved the moment Sasha had walked into her place of employment.

All Sasha could do was scream as the debauchery she loved continued.

"So good," server lady said as she slurped the juices that were pouring from Sasha's sanctum. "Mmm, I could eat you all day, every day," the woman whispered as she suddenly felt nameless cat use the dick he'd pleased Sasha with to pleasure her.

And the moment he rammed his shank into her, she came just as quickly and as hard as Sasha did. Dude knew what the hell he was doing.

"Aaaahhhhh," coffee maker chick moaned on Sasha's clit as someone knocked on the door of the shop.

Sasha turned her head and focused her barely open eyes on the door and the crowd that had suddenly gathered and was watching the show. Some of the people were looking at them in shock while others looked on in disgust and kept it moving. Sasha didn't give a fuck about their opinion of her, all she cared about was the tongue slurping her slit and the sight of mystery man giving java mama the dick.

Then, as she became even more turned on by watching the crowd watching her, she came. Hard and loud. "Oooooooooo, shiiiittttttt!" She screamed as neither she, nor he ceased from their pleasure. Once her body stopped shaking and her mind returned to normal, she spoke. "Come here," Sasha told him as she ignored the crowd. "And give me that whipped cream," she moaned as she prepared to give the onlookers a show. "You," she said to mocha maker, "on the counter, on top of me, facing me."

When man she'd never met before pulled out of espresso empress, he neared her and handed her the cream. At the same time Sasha gripped his dick, bathed it in cream, and placed it in her mouth, lady licker moved as instructed.

"Fuck!" Horny dude moaned as exquisiteness inhaled his dick.

"Yessssss," cappuccino countess cried out as Sasha placed her own fingers on her body where a man's dick would be and finger fucked the sexy vixen. Sasha demonstrated such expertise with her hand that caffeine queen immediately began bouncing up and down on her digits. "Oh my God, yesss, right there!" She screamed out in pleasure, on the verge of cummin'.

"...cummin'..." was all strange dick could say.

## Cum For Me

"That's right, cum on my fingers, give me those juices," Sasha said to them both as she continued mouth fucking him and finger fucking her.

"Shiiit, I'm cummin!" He moaned as simultaneously they both bust. He unloaded his healthy babies into her mouth just as coffee creamer leaked her sweetness on Sasha's fingers.

Together, both of her prey collapsed as if exhausted, breathing heavily while Sasha got dressed. "We should do this again sometime," she licked line server's cum off of her fingers before grabbing another drink and exiting the coffee shop.

*Now that's how you start a day off, with an insane orgasm appetizer, an exhibition entrée, and something sweet to drink for dessert,* Sasha thought as she was walking through a nearby park, texting her boyfriend Deshun. There were a few females that she'd seen earlier, shaking their heads at her, but Sasha didn't let the hating get to her because the exhibitionist in her loved being the center of attention, even if the attention was negative

"Hey, baby. Welcome home," Deshun greeted Sasha as she walked into their bedroom.

"Hey, I told you I'd be home soon."

"Yes, you did." He sighed. "I missed you," he said before trapping her into a kiss. *I really am not in the mood for his boring dick game,* she thought. He backed her up towards the couch, started ripping her clothes off and fell back.

"You been waiting for me, huh?" She asked and giggled as he attacked her neck, putting hickies everywhere.

"Turn over," he demanded. She did as he asked, getting on all fours. Without foreplay or anything, he plunged into her so hard that she screamed out in pleasure and pain.

"Ahhh, shit," she moaned and threw that ass back as he fucked her faster and harder. *What the hell has gotten into him?* Sasha silently questioned herself as Deshun fucked her like he was a sexpert.

"You like that? You like that don't you?"

"Deshun, oh, Deshun. Yes, don't stop. Ahhh!"

"I'm never going stop," he groaned as he pushed harder into her.

Deshun was so turned on that he quickly and roughly flipped her over. Then he placed her legs up in the air and her head upside down, pounding her hard and fast. He moved Sasha's hair to the side and bit her neck, keeping her hands pinned down. *Oh, my God! It seems like he's getting a lot bigger. I'm going be in so much pain later,* she thought as, for the first time since they'd been dating, he satisfied her just the way she liked it.

## Chapter 2

A phone call from her boy toy Rex is what had Sasha looking extra tasty in her revealing, white, mini-dress as she walked out of her house to her red Suzuki sports bike, heading straight toward Benning Road in DC.

It had been her full intention to stay home and chill by herself for once, but Rex's temper tantrum at being told no, and his persistence at getting the pussy turned her on so much that she gave in and told him she'd be there shortly. Well, that and the fact that his dick game was without question the best.

"Damn, ma." Rex said when she pulled into the parking lot of his place. He licked his lips and undressed her with his eyes as she got off of the bike. "Yo, y'all, I'm out," he said to his boys that were standing on the corner of the complex in which he lived.

Three minutes later Rex was moaning like crazy. Ohh, shit! Damn, Sasha," he moaned as she sucked and licked his dick.

"Be quiet or I stop," she warned him.

Rex tried with everything in him to keep silent, but when Sasha opened up her throat and swallowed the head of his dick, he couldn't help the moan that flew violently from his mouth.

That's when she stopped.

"Come on, baby. *Please*," Rex begged her.

"No," she looked at him seductively as his dick throbbed painfully.

He was becoming distraught as she kneeled over him, looking at him with those come fuck me eyes. Her mouth was less than an inch from his throbbing mushroom head.

"Please," he pleaded.

"No," she reiterated. "I told you to be quiet. You should have listened."

"I'm sorry. I'm sorry," he pressed "I'll do anything."

"Anything?" she questioned with a smirk.

"Anything," the word rushed from his mouth before he had time to think about them. And knowing Sasha the way he did, Rex knew that he might have made a big mistake agreeing to that anything.

"Okay," she finally gave in. "But if you move or say one word, I'm going to stop."

He shook his head in agreement, refusing to say a single word.

Before he could comprehend what was happening Sasha had her mouth back on his hard, marble pole. And the head of that pole deep down her throat. As she massaged his dick with her throat muscles, she moved her head faster and harder, faster and harder until he thought he would explode.

His orgasm was right there, on the edge, pulling at him. But Sasha was doing something with her mouth that wouldn't give it to him. He wanted to scream like a bitch, but he knew that if he did she would stop and leave him with blue balls for days. So he bore the tortuous pleasure in silence.

Then he felt it. The ass fingering he hadn't been expecting. To his surprise, he liked it and that pissed him off. The moan that wanted to bust through his teeth, Rex kept at bay. No way way did he want to allow the woman to bitch him out like that, but the combination of her throat assaulting his dick and her fingers tantalizing his ass was enough to keep him silent as he enjoyed Sasha's freaky pleasures.

"She can't do you like this, can she?" Sasha whispered before torturing him some more. Rex was one of those guys that had a little freak in him and Sasha loved that about him. That was why she didn't understand how he ended up in a relationship with Ms. Goody Two Shoes.

"Noooo, ohh shit! She can't," he moaned when her throat massaged his shaft and she fingered him harder. His body jerked in ecstasy as his eyes practically rolled into the back of his head. "I can't take it anymore!" He tried to make her stop before he came too fast, but she slapped his ass hard.

"Stay in position and take it, bitch!" Sasha showed him no mercy.

"You're the fucking best," he said as she raised and lowered her head harder and harder, allowing him to fuck her face. Fuuuccck!" He grunted loudly as an orgasm tore through him, causing him to grip her head tightly as he came hard in her mouth.

Almost as if angry that she'd bitched him out, he jumped up, grabbed her and walked towards the bed. Then he proceeded to take some of his manhood back from her by slamming angrily into her and putting it down on her.

"Ooh, ahh! Yeah, right there!" Sasha screamed out in pleasure as Rex was punishing her, teasing her by filling her to the brim and hitting all of her spots.

"Right here, huh? You like that shot?" he demanded.

"Yesssssss," her moan satisfied him immensely.

"Beg me for this dick," he demanded.

"Pleeeaassseee!" she begged when he deep stroked her so good she thought she would go insane..

He love hearing her beg every time they fucked, and this time was no different.

So he plowed her like the open field she was, fucking her like hers would be the last pussy he ever got.

## Chapter 3

"Hey, girl, what's up?" Symphonique asked Sasha as they sat at the bar waiting for their drinks. Symphonique was rocking a pink see through dress with pink pumps to match, but Sasha was wearing cut out Baby Phat jeans and a lace top that revealed her cleavage.

"Nothing much, I'm just doing me," Sasha said. *And when you're not around, your man does me too,* she thought as a wicked grin appeared on her face. "What about you?"

"Girl," Symphonique immediately began telling Sasha all of her business, "lately Rex has been sexing me a lot differently. I mean, *girlll,* it's mind blowing. He's been doing all kinds of freaky tricks and to tell you the truth, I kind of like it. It's almost to the point where I can't get enough of him!" Sasha remained silent and drank her Sex on the Beach while searching the waterfront club for some new dick. Symphonique continued to talk, but her words were no longer heard until, "...started fingering my ass!"

That brought Sasha's attention back to her friend. But before she had the chance to respond in anyway, a deep, masculine voice whispered in her ear and said, "How you doing?"

Immediately, as her body went into nymph mode at the seductive sound, she turned her head to the left and saw a sexy ass man that bore a striking resemblance to that ghost character off of the TV show, Power."

"I'm doing fine." *And I'll doing be even better if I get to play with you.* "How about yourself?" She asked.

"Good, now that I'm talking to you," he said.

She laughed. "That is the corniest line I've ever heard."

"Yeah, it was kinda corny, but I'm not a corny man when I go after what I want," he said as he got in her personal space.

"Oh really? Well, I hope you're not a corny dancer," she said and sashayed out to the dance floor where Chris Brown's, *No Bullshit* played.

Alone, in the middle of the dance floor, Sasha danced seductively as she the handsome stranger moved toward her.

"It's not that much fun when you're dancing alone," he said as he wrapped his arms around her waist.

"That's why I asked you to join me," she said, and then started to grind on him just enough to turn him on and keep him that way.

Hours later, after they had rubbed and rolled one another to intense arousal, Sasha wanted to get to know him better. "I would like to get to know you a little bit more," he said.

"I was just thinking the same thing. So how about we start with our names?"

"Mine is Mizzo," he told her.

"I'm Sasha. And I want to fuck you." She spoke her mind without regret. He was taken aback by her forwardness. "Unless you have a problem with that."

"No, I'm all for it," he said as she turned and walked out of the club and he followed suit.

Arriving at Mizzo's condo, Sasha had not a care in the world. The only thought in her pretty little head was dick and how much of it she was going to get. Once inside of his place, although she was impressed with how he was living, that wasn't why she was there. So she got straight to the point.

"I hope you're not afraid of what I'm planning on doing to you," she said as she dropped to the floor, on her knees, and began taking his member out of his pants.

"I think I can manage."

"If you say so," she smiled wickedly before placing him in her mouth.

"Oh shit," he moaned as her dick sucking expertise became quickly apparent when she swallowed him whole and her lips and his balls became one. "Shit," he said as he gripped her head and began to thrust into her mouth. "Yeah, suck this dick baby!" He wasn't expecting the heaven she was taking him to and as a result he pushed his dick further in her mouth.

Mizzo'd had his dick sucked plenty of times, but Sasha was like a damn Hoover and he knew that if she stayed on her knees long enough she would suck him dry, to the point of dehydration.

"Damn, baby," he said as he grabbed her head when she pressed those suckable lips round the head of his dick and sucked like a baby sucks a bottle. He could feel his soldiers marching toward her tongue and Mizzo began a hard thrust in her rmouth, forcing his dick back in her throat. Most women would have withdrawn at that, but not Sasha. She closed her throat around his shaft and allowed him to plow as if she was trying to get him to plant his seed there.

Suddenly, every muscle in his body began to tense, he could feel his head pounding into her trachea. And then she began to hum and the vibrations almost made him blast.

"If you don't stop I'm gonna cum," he warned.

That's the only thing that made her stop.

"Lay down for me," she whispered and he quickly followed her direction. "I wanna feel what that tongue can do."

Sasha wasted no time sitting on his face, facing his hard as steel manhood. Then she lowered her body and put her mouth back to work. But she wasn't expecting his mouth game to be almost as good as hers. And when his tongue twerked on her clit, her body began to shake.

"Shiiiitttt!" Her vocal chords played a climactic tune on his dick.

That's' when Mizzo gripped her ass cheeks and pressed her face hard onto his orgasmic orifice. "Ride my face," he told her as he slurped her flowing juices. Sasha almost died.

His licks were fast and furious. The French kiss he gave her lips down under was enough to make her bust in his mouth. And the way he nursed on her clit made Sasha think her essence was his fountain of youth.

"Aaahhhh," Sasha moaned as they continued to serve each other.

Then Mizzo grabbed her waist and without warning. "If your mouth feels like that, I gotta feel that pussy."

In no time at all, he flipped Sasha over. She looked at him in shock, primal lust crawling all over her as he climbed on top of her.

"Give me that hot beef injection," she taunted him as he slid himself inside her wet wet. "Ahhhh!" She arched her back and screamed as her walls gripped his dick.

"Fuck!" Mizzo hissed as he thrust forward while pushing one of her legs toward her chest with one hand and placing the other hand on her quickly swelling clit.

"Ahh! Oh! Shit!" Sasha moaned and wiggled under him as he fucked her without mercy like a jackhammer.

# Cum For Me

"Whose pussy is this?" He asked as he used his sex tool like a battering ram.

"Oohhh god!" That was all she could say.

He smacked her ass as he delved her depths. "Answer my question. Whose pussy is this?"

"Ohhh, shit! It's yours, Mizzo. It's yours, it's yours!" She screamed as she felt her orgasm rampaging through her core, trying to make its volcanic debut. "Oh, my god! Don't stop. Right there. That's my spot. Shit, you're going make me cuuuuuum!"

And like Sasha pleaded, Mizzo didn't stop until they both became satiated citizens of paradise.

## Chapter 4

"What's up, bitch?" Sasha greeted Symphonique as she walked towards their table. She was mad at Sasha for ditching her at The Waterfront Club, but Sasha had ways of making her get over that.

"You're in a good mood. I guess that means you got some good dick, huh?" Symphonique said as she rolled her eyes in her friend's direction.

"Girl," Sasha began proudly, "I think I'm in love with this new dick that I served all night." Sasha couldn't get what Mizzo had done to her out of her mind. "And I know that you've never heard me say those words before, but the way he handled me was... Ohh... Hmm... I can't even put it in words!" Sasha said.

"It's good that he put it on you like that. Maybe now you will leave my man alone!" Symphonique snapped, making everyone in Cosci look in their direction.

Sasha was completely unfazed by Symphonique's revelation, She had no idea that Symphonique knew, or even how she knew, but Sasha was sure Ms. Perfect's feelings were hurt. However, she wasn't about to sit back and let Symphonique go ham on her, hurt feelings or not.

"You better calm your ass dawn," Sasha warned.

Symphonique ignored Sasha. "Why you been sleeping with my man?"

"You haven't been satisfying him, so I did. No big deal."

"No big deal? You're my friend. He's my man. What the fuck is wrong with you Delshawna?" Symphonique belted, using her government name.

"Nothing is wrong with me, I was just giving you a push," Sasha calmly replied as she searched the place for some dick. Mizzo might have been good, damn good, but the nympho in her still needed more.

"You were giving me a what? *A push?*" Symphonique was infuriated. "I don't need your slutty ass trying to give me tips on how to keep a man happy. I know how to keep a family together. Not like you who's out there trying to break up relationships or make a name for your trifling self out in the streets!" Symphonique yelled.

"Girl, you are taking this way too seriously, He's just some dick to me. Nothing more."

"And that's the fucking problem. You don't care about anyone but yourself. People are right about you. You're a selfish ho!"

Sasha chuckled. "Please! Do you really think that I care about what people call me? I don't care about those haters. I'm a *don't give a fuck* type of bitch."

"Apparently that includes not giving a fuck about your best friend."

"Look, get out of your feelings, okay. It happened and I can't take it back. Besides, he didn't have any regrets so why should I?"

"Because I'm your friend!" Symphonique looked at her girl in disbelief. She wanted to strangle Sasha, but Sasha shook her head as if she didn't care, because truthfully she didn't. She knew that Symphonique would definitely get over it, she never stayed mad at people. Especially people she was cool with. Knowing that, Sasha didn't even bother with a reply, She simply stood, and walked out, going to find someone else fuck.

"You're going to regret this!" Symphonique yelled after her.

"Okaaayyy," Sasha sang out as if she had not a care in the world.

## Chapter 5

When Sasha finally made it home that evening, all she wanted to do was take a bath. "It's been an interesting day," she said to herself as she got to her apartment door and grabbed the small stack of envelopes from her mailbox before heading in.

"Ooh, shit! Girl, fuck this dick!" Deshun groaned from the bedroom as Silk's Freak Me Baby played repeatedly in the background.

Sasha looked in the direction of where she heard her boyfriend's voice and the music. Then she chuckled, *I can't believe he in here fucking another bitch.* But instead of being angry, curiosity took hold of her and she eased her way silently down the hall, determined to get a good look at the source of the sounds that were turning her on.

"This is so wrong, but you feel so damn good," she heard a woman say. Sasha slowly opened the door and it was then that she saw Symphonique riding the hell out of her boyfriend in reverse cowgirl position.

The sound of the door opening made Symphonique slowly open her eyes. She stared at Sasha, hoping to see pain and hurt on her face. But all she saw was lust as she continued to fuck her man.

"Fuck, Symphonique, you got that good pussy!" Deshun moaned as if in ecstasy.

Hearing her man moans fill up the room turned Sasha on like crazy.

"You enjoying yourself, baby?" Sasha asked Deshun, who had yet to notice she was there.

"Oh, shit!" He moaned as he continued stroking in and out of Symphonique. He wasn't in shock to see his girl standing there. He and Sasha added other people to their bed all of the time, that was part of what had kept them together for so long.

The fact that it was his girl's friend was kind of a surprise, but hell, pussy was pussy and at that moment Deshun was getting some of that good-good. "This shit dope, baby."

Without wasting another second, Sasha started taking her clothes off. Then she stood in the door for a few minutes, fingering herself as she watched Symphonique to see what she was working with, as she watched her man to see if he was being satisfied. When she realized he wasn't, Sasha seductively sashayed towards the bed. It was time to show Symphonique why Rex was addicted to fucking her.

Before Symphonique had the chance to move or protest, Sasha was in her face, then latched onto her breasts like a puppy Pitt Bull on its mother.

Symphonique tried with everything in her to move the woman away, but the sensual assault Sasha was performing on her beasts had her resolve slowy dissolving. "Mmmm," she moaned lightly as Deshun slow stroked her pussy. "Aaahhh," she moaned again.

When her friend's body was no longer stiff and rigid with protest, Sasha eased in for a sensual kiss. And it didn't surprise Sasha at all when she felt Symphinoque's tongue enter her mouth. She had always known that one day she would turn that broad out.

Slowly, methodically, as Symphonique slowly rode her man's dick, Sasha eased the woman's body back until Symphonique was lying with her back flat on Deshun's chest, her legs wide open and bent at the knees, feet flat on the mattress.

## Cum For Me

"Fuck him," she told Symphonique as she watched her friend raise and lower her hips, easing his dick sensually in and out of her.

As if her mouth was a heat seeking missle, Sasha lowered her face to Symphoniques private place and as her man fucked her, Sasha ate her.

"Ooohhhhh, shiitttt! Goddamn!" Symphonique wailed.

"You like that?" Sasha asked.

Symphonique replied with only a scream as the intensity of a dick and a mouth at the same time became too much for her. She bucked her hips in wild abandon as Deshun continued his tortuous slow strokes and Sasha continued sucking her slit with vigor.

"Ohhhhh," Symphonique moaned yet again, on the verge of insanity.

Sasha chuckled as she continued. Licking, Sucking. Nibbling on her swollen lips. She extended her tongue, made contact with Symphonique's clit and flicked it up and down so fast it practically vibrated.

"Shiiiittttttttttt!" Symphonique moaned, practically groaned as an epic orgasm forced its way toward her center.

Symphonique bucked wildly. Deshun reached his arms down and gripped her hips to hold her still. Sasha gripped her thighs and pinned her down as well. Deshun thrust, Sasha sucked. Deshun thrust, Sasha sucked.

"I... I.. can't. I can't..." Symphonique tried to speak, but the pleasure was too much.

In Deshun's dick went.

Up Symphonique's slit Sasha's tongue went.

Out Deshun went.

Down Sasha's tongue went.

"Aaahhhhh!" Symphonique screamed as her orgasm was fast approaching.

That's when Sasha's lips latched on to her friend's engorged clit.

Symphonique's body bucked with all of its might.

In Deshun's dick went harder.

Sasha sucked the clit harder.

"I'm cummin, baby," Deshun moaned as his soldiers shot out of his extremely hard cannon and knocked down Symphonique's walls as they flowed through and out of her core.

"Ohhhhhhhhhhhh!" was all Symphonique could do as her body seized, jerked, bucked and exploded. "Ooohhhhhhhhhhhh!" Her eyes rolled into the back of her head and her toes curled painfully, as her juices fled her body and flowed straight into Sasha's waiting mouth.

*Now this bitch knows that I'm the baddest bitch in bed,* Sasha thought *as she prepared for round two.*

**The End**

## Never Enough
### By
## *Lady Stiletto*

### Chapter One
Reminiscing

Starr sat on the edge of her bed watching the newest XXX rated movie, *Cum For Me* by Ca$h and Company while smoking on a wine tipped cigar.

Watching the raunchy film reminded her of the encounter she had with Devin the night before. She loved how he had fucked her six ways from Sunday. And then a sinister grin came across her thick, pouty lips as she thought about her other sexcapade. A quickie she had with Semaj prior to her meeting with Devin. That was on her lunch break by the storage containers of an abandoned parking lot.

Starr had a high sex drive and nothing was ever enough to please her sexually. She sat back on the bed and started to reminisce about what lead up to her steamy sexcapades with Semaj and Devin all the while opening her legs and inserting Big Black Jack back inside her creamy center.

*Starr was at work, sitting at her desk, dispatching calls when her phone began to buzz. She looked down at her phone and saw Devin's name flash across her screen. A smirk came across her face, but she sent the call to her voice mail. At the moment, she had other calls coming in. As soon as the call volume slowed down, Starr asked one of her co-workers to take her calls while she went to the ladies room. She retrieved her cell phone and went down the hall to the restroom. Closing the door behind her, she quickly drew the pattern to unlock her screen, then dialed Devin's number.*

*He picked up on the first ring.* "At work, huh"?

"*Of course. That's why I hit the end button, silly,*" *she responded.*

*You got that pussy marinating for Daddy tonight or what?" Devin asked in a seductive tone. She put her head down and formed a slight smirk, then stuck her tongue out between her perfectly glossed lips and spoke.*

"*You so nasty, boy. But you know I can't wait to feel that tongue in this wet box, Daddy,*" *she said.*

"*I like when you talk that shit, baby,*" *Devin retorted.*

*Reaching down to her tight fitting shirt that read Verizon, Starr began to massage her breasts listening to the sound of Devin's voice. She was thinking that maybe she could bust one quick nut before she was missed.*

"*You know I'm going have this kit kat nice and juicy for you, baby. Tell me how you can't wait to suck the honey out of these sugar walls,*" *she said.*

*Continuing to imagine his full lips over her breasts, she sat down on the couch in the employees' restroom and unfastened her pants.*

*She could now see the rings in her pierced nipples through her shirt.*

*Devin whispered in her ear,* "*You know I'm going to slither this tongue all up and through that hot pussy of yours, shawty.*"

"*So, your place or mine?*" *Starr asked in a low whisper while pulling down her pants. Then she let her fingers wander down to her now swollen clit.*

## Cum For Me

*Devin had one of those deep, sexy voices that when you heard it, it instantly made you wonder what sex would be like with his fine ass.* "Yours," *he said.*

*My wife will be home, baby girl. You know that. Starr's face instantly frowned as she thought about how butt ugly his wife was. That was the reason he'd been filling her up every chance he got.*

*The mood to masturbate was now on pause as she stopped caressing her clit and threw a little bit of shade his way.*

*"Humph, then why you keep wanting to dick me down when you got her dumb ass?" She spat.*

*Devin started laughing in her ear. He knew every time he brought up his wife, she became jealous. He responded, "Because you a fucking freak, shawdy and you love sex just as much as I do. Plus, I can have my way with you."*

*She hated having to put her hot box on the waiting list when it came to him, but she loved the way his tongue game made her have multiple, uncontrollable orgasms.*

*"Well, okay, baby. I was just saying. I'll leave the door open for you. See you later tonight when you're done playing the loving husband." She smiled. "Then we can play naughty sex games."*

*He smiled harder than the Kool-aid man. He knew she had a strong appetite for sex and he couldn't wait to push his dick up inside her hot furnace and coat her sugar walls. Even though Devin wasn't the only dick that ran through Starr, he knew he was the only one she let sex her without a condom.*

*They had been friends since junior high school and even then he was smashing her ass at school and getting head in the boys' locker room. That's why she was salty* about him marrying that cross eyed bitch, Melody, instead of her.

"A'ite, baby. See you then."

Before Devin could finish, she hung up. "This nigga must not know I got game and good pussy," she mumbled.

Scrolling through her phone, Starr went to Semaj's number. Now, she had only known him for a couple months, but she fucked him the first day they met and had been meeting up with him on occasion for some hot, erotic sex. When she got that itch, she had to feed her sexual appetite, and she had a list of dudes that could satisfy her in different ways. She typed a quick text message to Semaj and hit send.

Starr then pulled up her pants and adjusted her clothes, looking at herself in the mirror to do a once over. She unlocked the door to the bathroom and walked back to her desk.

As soon as she was about to sit down, her phone began to buzz. Before looking down, she thanked Mia, her co-worker, for looking out for her. She placed her headset back on and sat down. Unlocking her phone, she had a reply message. Opening it up, Starr couldn't help but blush as she read his text.

Semaj: Hey sex pot. You know I got you baby girl. Take them panties off and get it nice and creamy for big daddy so I can beat that pussy up like I hate you!

Starr knew from that text she would be riding his Mandingo for lunch. She smiled in anticipation.

She'd met Semaj at a traffic light a while back, they both were playing catch up with their cars. Semaj had a

## Cum For Me

royal blue Z-350 with nice rims and Starr noticed him trying to get her attention as they sat at one of those lights. But every time they tried to catch each other's eye, the light would change. Finally, Semaj got the words out for her to pull into McDonalds' parking lot.

She pulled into the parking lot in her burgundy Infinite Q45. They both got out and admired each other. Now, Semaj knew off the top he wanted to fuck the girl just based on her appearance. Starr was five feet five inches, light skin and had a slim but thick build. She had thighs, hips, a nice plump ass and a flat wash board stomach.

He made sure to let that be known through the advances of their conversation. Plus, the little pink shorts she had on hardly left any room for the imagination which made his manhood wake up and pay attention. A nice redbone he planned to have bent over some furniture soon while he went surfing around in them guts and had her screaming his name. He just didn't know how soon he would execute his plan.

But Starr was not like some females, you didn't have to run game on her to get in those panties. She was a sex addict and when she got that twitch between her legs it was uncontrollable. Whoever she could get to feed her insides was a target.

Starr didn't waste time asking the handsome stranger what he was doing later.

He responded bluntly, "You, cutie, if you're game." He licked his sexy, full lips.

"Oh, I am definitely game, handsome. I see something I like," Starr responded.

As Semaj moved closer to her, he started feeling on her.

"Damn! I can't wait to have you cumming all over my dick. I am going to split you in half," Semaj promised. Starr began to giggle, moving in closer to him. Semaj grabbed her by the waist and reached straight for her plump little ass. "Nice," he stated.

She reached up on her tip toes and wrapped her arms around his neck. "Mmm, you smelling and looking all good. I'm Starr, by the way," she whispered.

"Semaj," he responded. "Look, Ma, you got my man all excited and shit," he told her while looking down at his dick print. "So won't you meet me back at my apartment in like an hour," Semaj said.

"Let me see what you working with, Daddy. I want to know if it's worth my time," Starr responded.

Semaj grabbed her tiny hand and placed it on the print of his basketball shorts. Then he let Starr's hand explore. Her mouth fell open as she felt the length and thickness of what he was working with.

Semaj grinned at her reaction and spoke, "That's a full, grown man hanging down there, baby. You sure you want to go there with me? 'Cause I'ma bust that ass wide open. Literally," he stated.

With a chuckle, Starr began to feel her temperature rise and started to crave the Mandingo the stranger had between his legs. She fidgeted, trying to stop herself from jumping on his anaconda right there in the parking lot. Once that itch came, she couldn't control herself.

"I better go," she exclaimed.

They quickly exchanged info and Starr jumped into her car and pulled off. Moments later, reaching her parking lot, she started to hyperventilate. It had been too long for her to have not had some guy's shaft or tongue inside of her hot box. She sat in her car, trying to fight that demon called lust. The demon was often so strong that she could have been ganged banged moments before and it would not have been enough.

Putting the car in park and turning off the engine, she began to feel on her thighs and breasts. She liked the way her hands felt as she bit down on her top lip. Leaning her head back on the headrest, she began rubbing on the crotch of her shorts. Entering into her own world, rubbing her clit in a hard circular motion, Starr never saw Semaj pull up behind her.

She could feel the heat and moisture she'd created. Opening her legs as wide as she could, she placed one of them up on the gear shift between the seats and stuck two fingers inside of her wetness. Then she began to finger fuck herself.

Semaj walked up on her only to catch the show. He was instantly happy that she'd left her purse on the back of the car when she pulled off. Fully interested, he watched as long as he could before his hard, erect shaft wanted to join the party. Tapping on her window, Semaj noticed that the sound didn't even frighten her when she looked up and saw the stranger who she was getting ready to masturbate while looking down at her.

She used her free hand to wind down the window. "May I help you?" She asked in a discombobulated state, not even bothering to stop what she was doing.

I have your purse, little mama. I had to chase you down so that you could have it back. Glad I did, "he responded. "Can I be of some assistance to you, Ma"?

Starr looked up at the handsome man with lust in her eyes, and spoke, "Thanks for bringing my purse. What else you got for me?"

Shawty, making this too easy, he thought.

"Let's take this show up to your apartment," Semaj spoke.

Within minutes Starr had Semaj in her house and they were ripping each other out of their clothes. Semaj still couldn't believe how much of a freak she really was and Starr couldn't wait to feel him inside of her inferno. Retrieving his wallet, he took out a magnum XL condom and placed it on his thick, mushroom head, then rolled it down his rigid shaft. Starr eagerly anticipated what was to come, so she fell back on the couch and started to rub on her clit as she watched him put on his love glove.

"I want you to fuck me so hard, baby," she whispered.

As she continued to pleasure herself, Semaj walked over to her and grabbed her off the chair. He sat down and pulled her on top of him.

"You gonna ride this big dick," he said.

Starr took a deep breath as she got in the straddle position. Slowly, she lowered herself down on his huge monsta and cried out in a pleasurable pain, taking him inch by inch. Semaj grew tired of the slow, drawn out process and wanted to show her no mercy. He was eager to see just how big of a freak she really was. So he pulled her down until she hollered out in pain.

She felt her pussy stretching to accommodate the size of his member as it made its way into her stomach. The pain was unbearable, but Starr had to feed her craving. The wetness and tightness of her honey pot sent Semaj into overdrive. He began to bounce her up and down as he pushed up inside of her with a raging speed. Even though it was a little uncomfortable at first, she had to admit, Semaj felt good as he brought out her sex demons. Then she began matching his strokes.

# Cum For Me

*"Oh, my Gooooddd! You feel so fucking good, baby. Beat this pussy, Daddy" she exclaimed. "Yes, Semaj, yea. Yea, just like that, baby, Oh shiiiit"! You going to make me cum all over this big dick, baby" she cried.*

*He sexed Starr all over her apartment, making her have multiple orgasms all over his dick that night. And since that moment, they'd been nonstop. Whenever she needed her fix, Semaj was there to oblige.*

*Snapping out of her trance, Starr looked up at the clock. She was ready to go on break so she could meet up with Semaj at the old U-Haul lot so they could get a quickie in. The time was passing and Starr could feel her temperature rise as she fidgeted around at her desk. She couldn't wait for the clock to hit 12:30PM. As soon as it did, Starr removed her head set and sent the calls to the main call center. Grabbing her purse and getting ready to exit, she was stopped by Mia.*

"Hey, boo, we are about to go to Nando's for lunch. You want to come?"

*I'm about to cum repeatedly on Semaj's dick and this heffa is blocking me, Starr thought.* "Nah, Ma, I'm good. Meeting up with a friend, so y'all go 'head," *she said with a smile, brushing pass Mia heading toward the exit.*

*As Starr jumped in her car and pulled off, Marry the Pussy by R Kelly bumped through her speakers as she headed to meet up with her sex buddy. She retrieved her phone and dialed Semaj's number, after a couple rings, he picked up.*

"Yea," *he answered.*

"Are you on your way?"

"I will be there, shawty," *he told her, then he hung up.*

Starr pulled into the abandoned parking lot that was just a few blocks from her job. Pulling around to the back of the building, placing her car in park, she wasted no time taking off her sneakers and sliding off her work pants, tossing them on the back seat.

She had on some black boy shorts and a shirt which she took off. She was wearing a wife beater underneath and you could see her perky, pierced nipples through it. Letting down the visor to look in the mirror, she made sure everything was in place. She applied lip gloss and sprayed her favorite perfume.

Starr slid her seat back and thought about meeting up with Devin later. Devin had been smashing her off for a while and he was the only dude that she had some type of feelings for. Starr loved Devin's head game, his snake-like tongue sent her into convulsions. Just thinking about him made her start to touch on herself as she wished Semaj would hurry up.

Minutes passed and she had gotten herself nice and hot. Hearing the bass blasting, she knew Semaj was there. She looked up and saw him turning the corner, pulling into a parking space in front of her. Her vagina muscles instantly started to do Kegels as she waited on him to get out. When Starr saw that both doors of his ride swung open, she stopped what she was doing and sat up in her seat.

Semaj exited the driver side looking yummy as hell, but no one got out of the passenger side.

As he walked over to her car, Starr opened her door. "You brought someone with you, Semaj?"

He began to smile, "Yes. And you looking real sexy there, Dirty Red," he said, trying to skip the subject. "We going in the storage space, right? Well, get your sexy ass

## Cum For Me

out, then." As he reached for her hand, Starr realized she was pressed for time, she only had an hour for break. Slipping her tennis shoes back on, she took Semaj's hand and stepped out. "Dayum that thang phat, Ma. I am going to punish that ass," he said as he walked her in the direction of the old storage room they occasionally visit to get a quick nut.

"Who is in your car?" she asked.

"Just one of my homies. I'm going to drop him off after I fuck the shit out of your freak ass," he replied.

As he felt on her ass, they reached the storage space and walked in. Semaj wasted no time groping her and slipping his tongue into her mouth. As he pushed her up against the container wall, raising her arms above her head, he took off her wife beater exposing her breasts. Instantly, he grabbed on her nipple rings and started playing with them as he pushed his tongue further down her throat.

She could feel her body heating up with every touch. Semaj's hands and his tongue were like the tentacles of an octopus, leaving nothing unattended. Sliding her boy shorts to the side and raising one of her legs up, he slipped his index finger inside of her honey pot. Their tongues continued to do a forceful slow dance as Starr began to roll her hips on his finger.

"Fuck me, Semaj," she whispered.

He moved his head and started sucking on her pierced nipples. The sensation of him licking and sucking set her furnace on fire. Starr was now ready to feed into her lustful desires as Semaj hoisted her into the air and slid his dick inside of her creamy center.

She moaned out as she took him inch by inch."Oooo, fuck!" She exclaimed. Semaj pounded in that *juicy pussy of hers. He had her ass pinned up against the wall. As he touched them guts, Starr cried out, "Oooo, shit, baby. Fuck this pussy, Daddy. Just like that."*

*Starr was in her zone as Semaj pumped that big monsta inside of her. "You going to cum on this dick for Daddy, Red?"*

*The two were so into each other, neither one of them heard nor saw Wood standing there, catching an eye full. He couldn't believe his man was wilding by fucking that girl almost out in the open like that. But his shock didn't stop him from watching and pulling out his phone to record the show.*

*Wood was a straight up pervert to say the least. Wood could start to feel his own manhood grow from watching them get it on.*

*Semaj had his back turned, fucking her up against the container wall. Starr, for a moment, opened her eyes and saw the stranger watching.*

*Wood and Starr locked eyes and she gave him a smirk that indicated she knew he wanted to be next. As she bit down on her lip and continued to beg Semaj to fuck her harder, she never once alarmed him that whoever he had with him was standing there stroking his dick, watching her perform for him.*

*Wood licked his lips and kept his gaze on Starr with his fully erect penis in his hand.*

*Starr moaned the words, "I want you to come for me, Daddy." Steadily looking into Wood's eyes, then suddenly that demon of fire was burning for him.*

*Because Semaj never noticed his man standing there, he kept his stroke game going while Starr cried out, "Cum in this hot pussy, Daddy!"*

## Cum For Me

*Within minutes, Semaj yelled out, "Here I cum, baby!"*

"Me too, Daddy! I—I—I'm cumming!" *Starr cried.*

*Semaj brought himself and Starr to an uncontrollable climax as she brought Wood to his. Looking over Semaj's shoulder at the stranger, she saw that Wood had nutted all over his hands and jeans. She smiled at him, and after winking his eye at her, he disappeared before Semaj could release her from against the wall.*

*"Damn, girl! You going kill a nigga with that voodoo pussy," Semaj said, trying to catch his breath while pulling off the condom.*

*Starr laughed, fixing her clothes. "What time is it?"*

*Semaj looked at his watch and responded, "You still have twenty minutes to freshen that thing back up." He began to laugh and she joined him in that laughter.*

*Then she pushed him on the shoulder playfully. "Shut up, boyyy. Let's go," she said.*

*Walking back toward his car, they both noticed that the passenger door was now closed. Neither one saw the passenger, "Man, where the fuck this nigga go?" Semaj said aloud.*

*"Well, I have to go, baby. But I will hit you when that itch for some more Mandingo comes back, "Starr said.*

*Pulling her close, Semaj stuck his tongue in her mouth and again let his hands wonder over her ass.*

*Pushing him back, "Stop it, Semaj. You know I can't get hot when I have to go back to work. We going be fucking again, right here on the hood of your car," she replied.*

*Semaj shook his head and was about to speak when he saw Wood coming out of the bush's. "Nigga, what the fuck you doing coming out of there?" Semaj asked.*

"Shit, I had to go piss, you took so long back there," Wood said.

"Oh, shit, my bad," Semaj replied.

"I'm going to go, talk to you later," Starr said.

As she turned and walked back to her car, she made sure to give both of the guys a show by adding a little more twitch in her hips. She jumped back into her vehicle and decided to head to her home girl, Monica's, house to freshen up.

She pulled in her friend's driveway and saw her car parked. "Good, her ass is home," she said. Grabbing her pants out of the back seat, Starr slid them back on before getting out of the car and grabbing her overnight bag, which had quickly become her after sex bag.

Walking up and ringing the door bell, Starr felt like she'd been doing a thousand crunches. Semaj's dick would literally be in her stomach and afterwards, her shit would be tight like she had eight pack abs. She was feeling a little sore also, but planned to go home and soak in some bubbles to take care of that. Before Devin got there later that evening to break her off, she wanted to set the mood.

Monica finally came to the door and like her usual self, she had something slick to say. "Girl, you been out here a good minute and you still got them pants on. I thought if I took too long you would be out here trying to hump my Cherubs."

"Move, bitch," she said as Monica began to laugh. "I need to change."

Starr pushed her way into the house and Monica teasingly questioned her. "Who dick you had that fish tank on now, hooker?"

Starr kept ignoring her friend's sly remarks as she walked to the bathroom. "Fuck you, bitch," Starr snapped.

*"If I had a dick, you probably would,"* Monica snapped back.

*Starr went into the bathroom, undressed, and took a quick bird bath. As she reached for her pants, she saw a piece of paper fall out. She bent down and picked it up, unfolded it and read it.*

*Hey, Lil' Mama,*
*Thanks for the nut. Me and you would make a helluva team if we came together. So if you can't get me out your mind, like I can't stop thinking about you, hit me up.*
*Wood.*

*Starr had totally forgotten about the strange man that she'd made cum just by giving him a show as he'd watched her fuck Semaj. Thinking back, she looked up into the mirror and saw an image of her letting Wood fuck her. "Damn, not again," she said. Starr could feel her temperature began to rise and that tingling feeling she got was emerging.*

*Knowing she had to go back to work, she couldn't risk calling someone else. She looked around to see what she could use to quench her lust. Seeing nothing but a toilet brush, Starr grabbed it, sat down on the toilet seat, and inserted the handle into her vagina. Pushing it in and out, Starr felt an adrenaline rush and after a few more strokes, she started to hit her sexual peek. She inserted it a few more times until the urge for Wood had passed.*

*Quickly, she pulled on her clothes and rushed out of the house. Back at work, Starr couldn't wait for the day to be over so she could go home and relax.*

*Hours later, the day was finally over and she rushed home. She could now relax. Stripping down, she ran a tub* of hot water and filled it with her favorite Japanese Cherry Blossom bubble bath. The hot water felt good and helped with the soreness she was feeling. All she could do was think about Devin and couldn't wait for him to eat her out.

Starr had to admit she had some hidden feelings for Devin, but sex was her addiction, not feelings. She began to drift off to sleep when she was awakened by the ringing of her phone. Jumping out of the tub, Starr realized that an hour had passed. Checking her phone, she saw that she had missed a call from Devin and proceeded to call him back.

He picked up on the second ring, "I been calling you. What's up?" he asked.

"I was in the tub and fell asleep. Are you still coming?"

"Yea, I will be there in a little bit. Get that shit nice and hot for me, baby, so I can dive in head first."

Starr let out a giggle. "You know it, Daddy. I'll leave the door open for you and the only thing I will be wearing is my natural juices."

"Mmm, that's what the fuck I am talking about with your freaky ass. How bad you want me?" Devin wanted to know.

"Come find out," she told him as she clicked off the line.

Starr wanted to set the mood a little bit, so she pulled out some scented Strawberry candles, popped a bottle of Pink Moscato in the freezer, and groomed herself. Since Devin liked her naked, Starr sprayed on her favorite perfume, Guilty by Gucci, and lotioned down. Then she fluffed her hair and applied lip gloss.

Looking at herself in the mirror, Starr admired her body and struggled to wrap her head around the fact that she was a Nymphomaniac. She knew she wasn't capable of

## Cum For Me

loving anyone because she used sex as a means of numbing things in her life. She broke her train of thought when she saw the paper that Wood had given her folded neatly on her dresser. Grabbing the note, she looked at the number and felt the urge to call.

After deciding to call, the phone only rang twice before a man answered. "Hello," the voice on the other end spoke. Starr didn't know whether to hang up or speak, but before she could react, Wood spoke. "Is this my naughty girl from earlier?" he asked.

"Hey. Yeah, I'm Starr," she responded.

"I know, I heard an ear full about you, little mama."

"Is that right"? she asked. At first she was in her feelings about Semaj telling his friends about their sex life, but then quickly realized that she really didn't care. After all, he wasn't her man. "So why you give me your number if you know me and your boy smashing on a regular? She was curious.

Wood began to laugh, "Look, shawty, I ain't going to beat around this bush with you. I came there to see firsthand. Semaj been told me about you the first day y'all fucked, he said you was a stone cold freak.

Starr became angry and responded, "Apparently you are too. Who watches their friend have sex and masturbates to it?"

"I wasn't watching him. I was watching you and you gave me a show I want to see up close and personal, baby," Wood stated.

Starr began to smirk before she spoke, "You think you can handle me?"

Wood looked around his room to the chair where he had a girl tied up and gagged. He was into the bondage and submission life style and Starr had no idea that she might have met her match.

"Baby, I don't think you ready for a nigga like me. I'll have your body responding to me and doing things you never done before," Wood replied.

Starr could feel that monkey on her back rising and thanked goodness that Devin was on his way. The more Wood talked the hornier she became. She wanted to see for herself what his dick would feel like inside of her pussy next.

"Well, I have to go. But maybe we could talk again sometime," she said.

"Before you go, come to this party tomorrow night at Club Wett." Wood gave her the address. She wrote it on the same paper he wrote his number on and then they both clicked off the line.

She walked toward the kitchen and took the bottle of Moscato out, deciding to start without Devin. Sitting on the couch, the lights from the candles and the buzz from the wine had her feeling hot. That itch came as she started to caress her bare nipples and pull on her rings, giving her the ultimate sensation.

Taking another sip of her wine, Starr heard the elevator open and knew it was Devin. She placed one leg over the arm rest so her glistening peach would be the first thing he saw. Then she began to rub on her clit as the door to her apartment came open. There stood her baby, looking good in basketball shorts, a wife beater, and Timbs.

"I see you have desert already waiting for me," he said, closing the door behind him. Devin rubbed his hands together and walked over to where she was seated on the couch. As he kneeled down in front of her, Starr reached *out for him and wrapped her arms around his neck. Pulling him closer to her, she stuck her tongue in his mouth.*

*They began to kiss as Devin removed her hands, replaced them with his own, and started feeling on her breasts. Taking his tongue over each nipple and sucking on them sent Starr into her zone. He worked his way down to her stomach and went past her love hole. He kissed and sucked on her inner thighs which drove her crazy.*

*"Taste this pussy, Daddy," spilled from her lips as she grabbed his head and guided it to her vagina opening.*

*Instantly, Starr could feel his long snake-like tongue circling her swollen clit. She licked her lips and moaned out in pleasure. He began to slowly tongue kiss her fat pussy lips, then he sucked on her clit until he felt she couldn't take any more.*

*Starr pumped her love box on his tongue, faster, urging her climax to erupt. Devin flicked his tongue up and down causing her secretions to make a splashing sound. She could feel her climax nearing and began digging her nails into his wavy hair as her eyes rolled back in her head.*

*"Ooooo! Right there, don't stop! Eat this pussy, baby! You feel so fucking good, Papa," she gasped.*

*Devin's head was between her legs like he was enjoying his last supper on a platter and she was his main course. Devin devoured her juicy core like it was a ripe Georgia peach gently nibbling on her seed. He could feel her legs shaking as she grinded harder on his wet tongue.*

*Star shook uncontrollably as the heat from Devin's breath and the motion of his high speed tongue created the ultimate pleasure. As he brought a shaking Starr to ecstasy, she grabbed his head, holding him in place while she released her sweet juices in his mouth. He didn't miss a drop as he licked the platter clean.*

Scooping her up off of the couch, Devin flipped Starr onto her stomach. He wasted no time stripping out of his shorts and placing his wife beater behind his neck. She knew what was to come so she reached back and began to rub her clit. Ready for insertion, he kneeled down and spit in her love box. Then he placed the head of his penis right at the mouth. When he rammed his rod inside of her, her sexual appetite went up by a hundred degrees.

As Devin pounded his way in and out of her warm, sticky center, she yelled, "Fuck me, Devin! Just like that!"

Lifting her up off the edge of the couch, he placed her round ass in the palm of his hands and pumped in and out of her like a raging race horse. Her pussy was so wet and hot like a furnace it sent him over the edge. "Whose pussy is this?" he asked.

"It's yours, Big Daddy!" She yelled.

Starr could feel her legs start to shake as they were placed over her head for what seemed to be hours. Whenever she decided to give Devin some, she was prepared to go two hours strong because it took him forever to bust his first nut. And she craved the way he put it down too. He was the only nigga who made her squirt multiple times and she loved every moment of it.

Starr had plenty of lovers, each fulfilling her sexual appetite.

Devin kept pounding away inside of Starr's wet box as he was close to releasing. Starr yelled for him to fuck her harder, and so he did, filling her up with his hot semen. And when she felt him release, Starr squirted all over his dick.

And that's how her sexcapades went with Semaj and Devin.

## Chapter Two
### Club Wett

The next day Starr thought about the invite Wood issued her to come out to the club. She wasn't the club type, but she had all types of things running through her head. The most serious thing being Semaj and the fact that he might have set her up. *Did he bring Wood with him to watch her during their sex session?*

She needed answers.

Starr found the paper with Wood's number on it and dialed him up, but he didn't pick up. Instead, it rang and then went straight to voice mail. She thought about it and hesitated, finally deciding that she was just going to stay in a have a date with Big Black Jack. As soon as her mind was made up, her phone buzzed on the night stand. She picked it up and saw that it was Wood.

"Hey there, beautiful," he said.

"Hey," she responded.

"So what's up? You coming or what?" Wood asked her straight out.

"Is Semaj going to be there? Are you two setting me up?"

"Hold up, little mama, slow down," Wood said. Nah, Ma. He don't get down like me. He just fuck freaks, but I create them.

"Oh, yeah?" she asked. Well you can't create me then," she began to laugh.

Wood smirked on the other end. "You right, but I am going to make your body respond to my demands and take your high sexual appetite" to an all new high," he stated. "You have the address, just come through and let your mind explore. It's up to you, no pressure. Oh, there's one rule for females to get in, though."

"What's that?" she asked.

"No panties. If you decide to come, whatever you wear, no panties allowed," Wood spoke.

That instantly made Starr curious as she got that tingle she always needed to feed.

"Okay, see you soon," she replied and clicked off.

Deciding to go, Starr got dressed and an hour later headed out the door. Arriving at the location, she realized that it didn't look like a club, it just looked like a regular building. She excited the car and walked up to the abandoned building, looking down at the paper to see if she was at the right place.

Once inside, she saw a set of stairs and walked down them until she came upon a corridor. She continued walking until she saw a huge man standing at another door where she could hear music and people moaning and screaming in ecstasy. Approaching the man, Starr cleared her throat and asked if she was in Club Wett.

The giant man looked down at her and smiled. "Why, yes, pretty lady, it is."

Relief ran through her as she tried to go pass the man, but he blocked her way.

"I thought you said this was it? Why can't I go in?"

The man looked down at her again and asked, "Who invited you, beautiful? And did they tell you the rule to get in?"

Starr remembered what Wood said. "Oh, yeah. I was invited by Wood and he said no panties for females."

"So, let me see the goods, baby," the man responded.

## Cum For Me

Without hesitation Starr lifted the tight fitted, red, leather dress she wore and showed she could follow directions. The man opened the door for her and once inside, she could not believe her eyes.

The club was dimmed with red lights and she saw girls in cages. Some had leashes around their necks with men walking them like animals. For the first time in her life, Starr thought that something was beyond her level of freakiness.

As she kept walking, she could see people standing around watching pornos and having sex and she had to admit that she was suddenly turned on. Men were lined up in the hall, groping her as she walked past them. She was wondering where Wood was until she came face to face with him. For the second time their eyes locked and this time she was fixated on what *he* was doing.

The man that had once masturbated as he watched her had a girl's hands tied behind her back. That same girl was strapped to a chair and blindfolded while she gave him head. He smiled at and winked at Starr just as he'd done when he watched her with his friend. Now it was Starr turn to watch him.

The vision of the girl slobbing on his dick and Wood holding her head in place while pumping his dick in her mouth, watching her gag on it, had Starr feeling that lust demon coming up out of her. She couldn't shake the urge.

Wood, seeing the lust in her eyes, left the girl tied up and walked over to Starr. Backing her up against the wall, he forcefully separated her legs with his foot. Taking his hand and moving it up under her dress, he roughly stuck two fingers in her pussy and began fingering her. Starr felt that twitch between her legs as her vagina began to pulsate.

Feeling her body react just as he wanted it too, Wood placed his hand around her neck. Starr got a little frightened with him doing that, but Wood told her to relax and just let her body respond.

Removing his member with the other hand, Wood positioned the head of his penis to her second set of juicy lips. Starr was in a whole other zone of lust and didn't realize he didn't put on a condom. Removing his fingers, he slid his uncovered dick right up inside her sugary walls.

Starr was so hot and wet that he couldn't help but slow stroke the pussy. She let out a moan and whispered, "Damn, this dick feels so good. Wood, don't stop, baby."

Wood tightened his grip around Starr's neck and began to lightly squeeze as he went in and out of her. Starr couldn't believe how he was making love to her and she began to squirt all over his shaft. As she wrapped her legs around his waist, he gave her a slow but hard screw up against the wall. Between the pressures he applied around her neck and his slow but hard strokes, both of them skyrocketed into an explosive climax together.

### *The End!*

## Can Redd Ride?
### By
# *Forever Redd*

### *Legend*

She was masturbating. I could tell, by the breaths she was taking her voice had become low and oh, so sexy.

"Redd, you touching yaself, baby?"

"Yes," she whispered.

"Can I help you? Can I take you there?"

"Yes."

"Put ya thumb on ya clit and rub it real slow. Think about my tongue licking it up and down. You like that? Is that pussy sweet? Taste it, Redd. Put ya thumb in ya mouth, pretend it's my dick and suck ya essence off."

"Mmm, I taste so good. Can you taste me?"

Of course I couldn't taste her, in the physical, but her scent was on my clothes and it was strong. It was so strong that I could practically taste the hibiscus in her herbal essence shampoo. I savored the warm saliva that had composed in my mouth and swallowed hard. Damn right, I tasted her.

"Yea, I taste ya, Ma. That pussy real, real juicy. Put two fingers in that thang and slide 'em in and out. Think of all this dick creepin' through ya insides."

"Yeeessss," she whispered.

"Push 'em real deep and spread 'em apart. Feel that pussy openin' up, Redd? Use ya other hand and slide two more fingers in there. Feel that?"

"Fuuuuuuck," she screamed.

"Oh, don't worry, I plan on doing just that."

Redd was finally able to calm her breathing and locate her voice. "Damn, you make me sick." She fussed, after getting her shit off.

"Sick? Why? Because I make that pussy hot like fever, or because I make it drip like a runny nose"

"Okay, so you got me. I knew I wanted you from the moment I laid eyes on you. Do I want the dick? Yes I do, but let's cut the bullshit. The same way I want you, you want me too, so don't fight it. Come get this pussy, your pussy. I won't hurt you, unless you want me to. I won't bite, unless that's what you like. Now me, I like all that shit. So tell me, Can Redd ride it?"

"Leave ya panties on the floor, unlock the door and I will be there in fifteen minutes."

*****

I made my way to the unlocked door and stepped inside. I followed the flickering candlelight to Redd's bedroom. She was ass naked, sprawled out on top of some red satin sheets. She had one leg cocked to the side with a bend in her knee and the other was straight out. The soft white light that was cast by the flames allowed me just enough visual to see the sticky trail that made rest between her lower lips. Her curly mane was wild and spread all over the pillow, giving her a predator appearance, but the pouty mouth and baby face told a different story.

A small hand drifted from the mattress and took up residence between her legs. Every so often, a small *ssss* would escape her parted lips.

I stood in the doorway and watched the epitome of sexiness buried deep within the throws of self-pleasure. She was beautiful, imperfectly perfect.

"Lemme cum on your dick." I heard her say.

## Cum For Me

"I didn't think you knew I was here," I replied, walking over to the bed. I lifted Redd's hand from her tender pussy and sucked her juices right off, then licked her palm for good measure.

"Oh, I knew you were here. I smelled that Issey Miyake the minute you reached the kitchen."

"Funny, I thought the same thing about you," I said as I inhaled the fragrance that was left on her fingers.

"How long you gone make me wait?" Redd asked.

"Until it's time. Let me touch you, feel your mind. Let me taste you while I feed from your thoughts. Let me hear you, learn the rhythm of your heartbeat."

"No, no, no. We didn't come in this with feelings. This was supposed to be about fucking. Me pleasing you, you pleasing me. Plain and simple. Remember the discussion?"

"Of course I remember the discussion. But I don't wanna just make love to the pussy, those nice slow strokes, the ones the ladies like. I wanna fuck ya mind. ."

"Okay and what's that gone do?" she asked curiously.

"Dismantle the head and the body will crumble. I will do shit to ya body that will leave you paralyzed, but I can leave your head with images that will make you cum on command. Don't play with me, Redd. You not ready. "

"Whatever you say. Uuummm, who you supposed to be again?" She joked.

. "Shiiit, allow me to reintroduce myself. My name is Legend."

### *Redd*

I would never forget the day I met the infamous *Legend*. It was Memorial Day weekend and Black Bike

Week was jumping. He was standing amongst the River Cape Assassins, a bike club out of South Carolina. I noticed him as soon as I stepped out of my hotel room and I could tell he noticed me too. His half shut eyes remained on me the entire time I walked across the parking lot. It was as though he lured me in with the sleepy browns. He had a deep dimple that rested in his left cheek and as soon as I saw it, I wanted to stick my tongue in it. He greeted me when I was close enough to reach out and touch him and that was just what I planned on doing.

"What it is, sexy?" he asked as he licked his lips nice and slow.

"You got it." I replied.

"Naw, baby, I ain't got it—at least not yet," Legend replied.

He was talking my talk and my pussy was definitely listening. I could feel the contraction every time he licked his lips. "So, tell me, what is it you haven't gotten yet?"

"Whatever you tryna give me, shawty. I don't just up and take shit."

"I know that's right. I'm no thief, but I know a few things I wouldn't mind taking."

"Is that so? Run that math and I'ma call you after our last ride. I'ma put a lil' something in ya ear."

"Well, how ''bout this, I'm in room two four nine maybe you could drop by and put a lil' something in my panties." I flirted.

"Damn, shawty, yo lil' ass is crucial. What you getting into tonight?"

"Me? Nothing. Would *you* like to discuss what could be getting into *me*?"

Legend shook his head and smiled. "I take it nobody ever told yo ass not to play wit a grown man

Consider this a lesson and a warning. You ain't ready," he replied confidently.

"You right, I'm not ready," I headed across the parking lot where my girls were standing making nice with a few of the bike club members. I knew he was watching me walk away, everybody else did when I walked by. There was something about my twenty-eight inch waist and forty seven inch hips that kept heads turning. Surely, Legend would be no different.

"Aye, yo! Aye!"

I heard him, but I wasn't going to turn around. I wanted the dick and he was playing.

"Aye, yo, Redd. You wanna ride?"

I stopped my stride and turned in his direction. "I thought you'd never ask." I let my girls know I was out and walked back over to Legend.

I stepped on the back peg and extended my leg to straddle the Kawasaki Ninja ZX 10R. Once I was on, Legend pulled out of the hotel's parking lot, joined the rest of his team and cruised the strip of Myrtle Beach. I didn't know if it was the cool breeze coming off the ocean, the wind in my hair, or the manly scent that drifted from his body but whatever it was, I was dripping wet. The vibration from the tail pipes did nothing but intensify my desire to be fucked.

We rode through the city, stopping here and there to pose for pictures and show off the bikes. Each time we stopped, Legend's attention was focused on me and I enjoyed every minute of it. He was definitely getting the pussy. The afternoon was coming to a close and the sun had begun to set. Everyone went their separate ways in order to prepare for the night time turn up.

We arrived back at my hotel and Legend parked. He turned around and straddled his bike backwards. We were face to face and practically body to body. He drew my lips into his mouth and the heat from his mouth seemed to set my soul on fire. He was a bottom lip sucker and very talented too. His kiss was sweet and he handled my oral cavity with precision. We tongue wrestled a bit before his lips ended up nestled between mine. Legend brought his hands to my head and began to massage my scalp. It felt so good, my pussy tingled.

He removed his lips from mine and placed a kiss on my cheeks, forehead and neck. As he helped me off of the bike, the look in his eyes said more than thanks for a lovely evening, so I grabbed his hand and ushered him to my hotel room.

Once inside, I turned to face him, and was quickly greeted by a tongue in my mouth and those magical hands. back in cranial roots. A firm shove of his body to mine forced my back against the door and a hard dick to my midsection. I wanted Legend in the worse way, right then, right there, right on top of the hotel carpet.

Legend allowed his hands to drift from my scalp to my shoulders and then to the small of my back. He ran his hands up the back of my shirt and unclasped my bra, then brought his hands around to knead my full breasts. He rolled my nipples between his index finger and thumb and just as my body began to shake Legend lowered his hands to the button that held my shorts together and opened that too. The anticipation was killing me and I felt like I was one step closer to the dick. The only thing standing in the way of me and that pleasure piece was his zipper. Legend slid a hand inside the waist of my shorts and around the top of my panties. When he reached the back, two fingers fluttered across my ass crack and I almost fainted. He ran his fingers down, then up the partition of my ass cheeks, removed his tongue from my mouth and placed his lips to my ear.

"I bet that pussy wet?" Legend whispered.

With my eyes still shut and my bottom lip sucked in, I nodded my head *yes*.

"I figured it was," he said as he kissed my cheek and prepared to exit.

"Wait, you gone just leave? You did all that and you gone just leave? Who does that?" I questioned.

"Me. I told you "bout that mouth. Now be ready 'bout nine, I'ma come scoop ya." Legend turned the doorknob and walked out the same way he walked in, leaving me the same way I arrived, pussy soaked.

*****

Legend and I went to a bar for drinks, then a club and finally a walk on the beach. The night was perfect I felt the effects of the alcohol and I was ready. We found a small corner of the beach with little to no traffic passing through and we took a seat.

"How long you here for?" I asked.

"'Til Tuesday. You?"

"Monday." I replied.

"Sooo, I guess that means we gotta make the most of our time here, huh?"

"I guess so." Our lips met. I barely slid my warm tongue against his lips just enough to slightly open them. I could taste the fading traces of Bud Light being replaced by peppermint and I guided my hand to his dick.I gave the bulge a quick squeeze and my eyes widened in shock, he was so thick. "Can I kiss it?"

"Easy, Tiger. How you gone just bring me out here like I'm some piece of meat?" Legend feigned shock. "Now, enter at your own risk, this is all about pleasure."

"Understood," I replied as I lowered his zipper.

"No strings, no extras," he reclined back.

"None," I licked my lips. "Just let me taste it," I whispered.

"Taste it, Redd."

I opened his jeans and nestled my nose to the slit in his boxers and inhaled. I loved the scent of a freshly showered man. Not the scent of his cologne, but the scent of his manhood, one that could not be masked by fragrances. I could feel the brown Cyclops awaken and rise to the occasion as I licked dead center of the eye. One long, slow, wet lick. Then I wrapped my lips around the head and sucked him out of his boxers. As I slid my head back, I admired his spit covered shaft, inch by inch. It was beautiful. His skin was as soft as satin, as smooth as marble and he tasted like the finest of chocolate.

I tickled his head with the tip of my tongue, sucked in my jaws and forced his dick down my throat. Any loose skin would involuntarily tighten as I increased the suction on his dick. The tighter the skin, the harder the dick. I loosened my oral grip when my chin reached his balls, then licked the main vein from bottom to top. When I reached the head once again, I took note of the Cyclops crying. A single tear had escaped that one eye, so I dried it—with my tongue.

"Two minutes. Hold on. Two minutes," Legend stated while out of breath. It ain't 'bout to go down like that, Redd."

"What you mean?" I asked, with a devilish grin.

## Cum For Me

Legend flipped me over and ripped off the lacy thong that was once under my skirt. I didn't even get a chance to protest before he was face first in my pussy. My cat was open and staring directly in his face. There wasn't a single hair in sight, no traces of a razor, she was nice and bald which would make it easier on the pallet. He lowered his face to my garden to taste my fruit. He kissed the small mound before him and allowed his tongue to explore her split. He was careful not to part my awaiting petals, as he first savored the nectar that had begun to collect at my opening.

"Mmmm," he moaned. "Just as sweet as I knew you would be. Ripe, wet and juicy. Kinda like a peach."

Legend parted my lips with the tip of his tongue and pecked at my clit. Back and forth, he slid his tongue from his lips to mine and I was already trying to back away. He put my thighs in a choke hold and planted my ass firmly into the sand.

"Legend,pl..pl..please, lemme just…"

"Ssshhh," he hissed, never taking his lips my box. The warm breath that exited his mouth soothed the naughty kitten before him. "I know you want some dick, but right now," he licked my pussy once more, "you…*lick*… not…*lick*… ready." He continued on his course, navigating me to the promise land.

"Fuck me, Legend! Oh, my God. Wait. No. Please don't stop." Legend was putting in work and I was clueless as to what I wanted him to do next.

My thighs shook and they snapped shut on his head. I was surrendering to the tongue and feeding him the cat. My body tensed and I screamed. "Leeeeegend."

All my gooey goodness leaked out of my body and into his mouth. He used the tip of his tongue to slightly penetrate me and my river flowed freely, straight down his throat.

"Please, don't move. Stay right there. Do not move, please, please," I breathlessly whispered.

Legend didn't flinch. He didn't tear at my thighs to try and pull them apart either. He was mellow and every so often I could feel a tiny breath bleed from his lips. Slowly my legs drifted apart and Legend was free to move. He plopped down on the sand beside me to calm his breathing.

"You still want this grown man dick?" Legend asked, never even opening his eyes.

"That depends, can you handle this big girl pussy?"

"Redd, talk that shit to somebody that ain't just had you runnin' and shit, beggin' and carryin' on. Now, if you really want me to, I'll bend that ass over rat now."

"No, I really don't want you to bend me over, Legend. Sorry, if that's what you thought."

"Aaaww shit, here comes the feelings. Let me guess, you have never done this before and you can't believe I brought you out here just tryna fuck?"

I listened to Legend go on his rant for a full three minutes about how all girls are the same and some other bullshit about feelings that I stopped listening to.

"Are you done talking? Because I'm done listening."

"Are you ready? Because I am."

"Yes, Legend, I'm ready. I been ready. Can I ride it?" I asked, unbuttoning my top.

"Button that shit back up, girl. Come on let's go!"

Legend grabbed my hand and pulled me from my seated position. We hurried up the beach and back to the

## Cum For Me

parking lot where we hopped on his bike and zipped up Ocean Blvd.

By the time we got to the door, my bra was opened, my shoes were off and I was fumbling to get the key out of my clutch. Legend was behind me with his dick pressed in my back causing me to have even more difficulty getting the door unlocked.

"Legend, stop it. I got the key right here, just let me—"

"Let you what?" he asked, sliding a hand up my skirt.

Just as his middle finger slid inside of my moisture, I got the door open. Legend pushed me in the room and slammed the door shut. One solid swipe of his arm and all my bath time essentials were thrown to the floor. Legend grabbed my arm and turned me around and pushed my head down to the dresser.

"Legend, you gone fuck this pussy Baby? You wanna make me cum? Tell me you like that, all this ass in ya face, touch it."

"Oh, don't worry, I'ma do more than touch it. I'm 'bout to beat the brakes off that thang."

"Mmm, is that right, Daddy?" I moaned.

I heard the small packaging tear open and I prepared myself for Legend to tear into me. He placed his hand in the small of my back to add more depth to my natural curve to ass ratio, then aimed his meat directly into my center.

The moment of penetration was perfect. I felt my pussy expand to accommodate his girth and I felt him travel places that had yet to be explored by someone else. The moment he slid between my thighs the barely audible breaths started. He inhaled one breath and slowly exhaled as he settled inside my middle. Slow was the down stroke and rigid was the up. As his pace increased, Legend grabbed a fist full of my hair and pulled my head up. My back was pressed to his chest and my ass to his stomach.

"Look in the mirror, Redd. I wanna watch you take this dick. "Open ya eyes, shawty." I wanna watch you, watch me, watch you handle this meat. I wanna see you when you when you cum, you gone cum for me Redd? Uh huh, eyes open. Now watch."

Legend was so deep in my pussy, I was standing on my tip toes. He reached around with his free hand and wrapped it around my throat.

*Oh…my…God.* I thought, as I was being lifted in the air by merely my hair and my neck.

"Open ya eyes, Redd. You know if I move one time." Legend eased back off the gushiness of my G spot, then tapped it once again. I was paralyzed, I couldn't move. He pulled back once more, then back it and found his resting place.

"Open ya eyes and let's watch me make that thang drip."

He watched and I came.

*****

Legend carried me over to the bed and laid me down. "You good?" he asked before rubbing the length of his nine inches.

"What you mean am I good? Is it supposed to stop there? Like are you finished? Because where I'm from pussies don't just purr, they leak. You asking me if I am done? As in finished? Baby, I'm fuckin' 'til my pussy get dry."

## Cum For Me

"Really now?" Legend said as he slid his body between my legs. "And when you think that's gone happen?" He kissed my lips.

"I don't know, it never has before."

Legend made a grand entrance into the pussy yet once again. The lamb skin that shielded us from raw flesh on flesh was so thin, I could feel every vein that pulsated beneath his surface. His thickness was enough to stretch my walls and he had more than enough length to deliver the *act right*. Legend hoisted my legs onto his shoulders and in one stroke the head of his dick gained control of my body. He knew what he was doing, the pleasurable pain was etched in my face. My eyebrows furrowed, my forehead wrinkled and my eyes squeezed tightly. I held my breath as I anticipated his next move.

"Relax, Ma, I ain't gone fuck wit it, but I want you to know, I ain't gon forget where your spot it's at."

I exhaled as Legend pulled back and began the slow stroke. The further back he pulled the more I raised my hips, I didn't want his meat anywhere, but in my womanhood.

"Legend," I moaned.

"Sshh, Redd. Don't talk."

"Legend, turn over. I wanna ride it. Please."

Legend stopped his stroke and sighed. "Damn, Redd, really? You gotta do this right now? I don't wanna change positions. Unless I can get that back shot?"

"Only if you laying on yo back. Switch."

As soon as we attempted to switch positions, Legend grabbed me around my waist and pinned me to the bed. He laid on top of my back with his meat threatening to enter me at any second.

"No Legend, we not goin' there. Let me do my thang, let me ride it."

Legend laid flat on his back and I wrapped a thick thigh around his waist. I pulled my legs closer to him and welcomed him into my secret space. Up and down round and round was the motion of my hips, slow and precise. I placed my hands on his chest and pinched his nipples, I could feel the pressure build up as Legend gripped my back. I slid up his shaft leaving nothing more than his head between my lips to give him a small kiss, from me to him. As soon as I heard him exhale as though he was relieved I didn't keep going, I slid back down on his dick, hard and rough. My ass cheeks jiggled at the contact made between his balls and my soft exterior.

"Mmm," Legend moaned, as soon as I hit bottom.

"You like that?" I whispered in his ear.

"Mmm, yes! You feel so good. Ride it Redd. Ride that dick, Ma," he said as he tightened his grip on my ass.

I placed my mouth to his and silenced his pleas, then popped a very juicy coochie all over his dick. His strong hands grabbed my backside so tight, I could feel my flesh swell between each one of fingers. When the kiss was broken, I squatted over his pelvis and bounced my ass up and down on his meat.

"Redd, I'm 'bout to cum."

"Not yet."

I turned my ass to Legend's face and locked my legs around his neck. He had nowhere to go, but face first into my snatch and for me, him down my throat. My tongue teased the eye of the Cyclops and my hand gripped his balls. He placed his hands in my tresses, pressed me down on his manhood and I swallowed his dick. I wanted him to feel the clench and release of my tonsils as he dropped all

## Cum For Me

of that meat in my throat. My gag reflex was nonexistent and I could feel him as he slid down the slippery slope of my esophagus. His entire shaft had totally disappeared as I rendered subtle licks to his balls. When I brought my extremely wet mouth up his shaft, my jaws were clenched so tight, I damn near sucked a baby out his nut sack.

Satisfied with the oral pleasure, I took the position reverse cowgirl style and ran my hands down the length of Legend's legs. He had a bird's eye view of how it really goes down in the south.. I clapped my ass cheeks together, then one at a time. I came up fast, then went down slow all the while massaging his feet. I glanced back at Legend and I watched him watch me take all his dick.

"You still wanna see me cum?"

"Yes," he whispered, palming my ass.

"Cum for me." I demanded.

The twitch I felt deep in my core let me know Legend was on the brink of cuming and I was prepared to do the same. The buildup was so intense, I stretched my body all the way out and added the extra curve in my back. The pressure applied to my clit and Legend lost inside of my body, sent showers of my love potion spraying all the way up to his neck. Legend dug his fingernails in my rear and his body went limp.

"Damn, damn," was all he managed to say as he attempted to catch his breath.

Legend laid in silence before peeking over at me. Ya know Redd that shit felt good as Hell. Damn Ma, my dick still twitchin' and shit.

"Sooo, can I ride it?"

"Anytime you want, Redd."

\*\*\*\*\*

## *Legend*

I couldn't believe me and Redd been going two years strong. Today is our anniversary and I am gon' surprise her by reenacting that time so long ago. I was gon' gas up the truck, load up the trailer and ride her down to the beach. I was gon' take her to the same spot where we got it popping the first time and fuck her brains out. I wanted to give her a heads up that I would be there shortly to pack for the trip.

"Hello," she answered.

"What you doin'?"

"Nuttin, Why? You missing me?"

"I always do when we are apart."

"Mmm, is that right?" She questioned. "You know that's right. What, you thought? I stayed wit you cause you nice?" I joked.

"Ha ha. You stayed because you love this pussy."

"I do. I'll be there in five minutes, where ya panties at?"

"Just where you like 'em, Daddy. They still in the drawer."

"Leave the door unlocked," I said to Redd and released the call.

When I entered Redd's apartment, she was playing with her kitten while R. Kelly played in the background. I walked over to the bed and removed her hand. I placed her sticky fingers onto the growing beast in my basketball shorts.

"Lemme do that. You gon' toot that thang up for Daddy?"

## Cum For Me

"Don't ruin the moment, Daddy. Can I ride it?"

I inserted two fingers inside Redd's love nest and instantly I felt the drip from my dick. She was hot and sloppy, just how I liked it. From her pink insides that glistened underneath the glow of the fluids that dripped from her core and saturated her epidermis to the smack of the sodden flesh, the lapping of her juices, and the ever present moans that escaped her lips. Oh, yea, Redd could most definitely ride it

I grabbed her by her waist and flipped her over, there were no holds barred on this one. I pressed her face into the pillows and lifted her stomach from the mattress. Propped up on her knees and looking back at it, Redd gave me a mischievous grin. With no latex, no barriers, I slid into her life and rearranged all her business.

That one spot, that she kept locked away, the one place she never allowed a man to go, I violated it with vengeance. I knocked at that door to no avail, she squirmed and twitched, but she wouldn't succumb to the visit from my dick.

Redd was on one and I was enjoying the rejection from this fighting cat. Since she wanted to fight it, I decided to take it. I placed one hand in the small of her back and two fingers in her mouth. I delivered rapid shots to the back of her domain. I slowed the pace, then gave her the death stroke, all the way out and straight back in. The stroke was long and measured. Redd was shaking so much, her ass cheeks jiggled against my thighs.

"Cum for me, Redd."

Her legs locked and the most pleasurable scream escaped her lips as the spasms of satisfaction plagued her body. Sweat cascaded down her forehead and all across her back as she put her ass in the air to accept all of me. And she did just that. She took in all my length, my girth and all my kids. Redd's body jerked ferociously as she came all over my dick. Once she lowered her breathless body to the mattress and snuggled into the pillows and I slapped her on her juicy booty.

"Whaaaaat?" She screamed.

I laid down beside Redd with my dick looking like a lil old lady creeping out of church, pointing to the Heavens. I looked at it, then looked at her.

"Did you like that? Did Daddy fill that pussy up?"

"Yes Baby, yes," Redd replied, snuggling into the pillows.

"Nah, Redd, we fuckin' 'til yo pussy get dry. Remember you said that?"

"Yes, Daddy, I remember," she replied.

"Good, now ride it!"

***The End***

## Wet Memories
### By
# *Royal Nicole*

### Nicole

I studied his face intensely, taking in every single feature from his darkened caramel skin tone to the tip of his pointed nose right down to his full lips. What I wouldn't give to feel his lips kiss my pussy just one more time.

My hand traveled over my 38 DDD breasts pausing to tweak the nipples before continuing its journey to its destination, a little town best known as *ecstasy*.

My soft fingers glided over my button as it went a little further into my dripping wet honey spot. I eased my index and middle fingers inside of my saturated pussy, imagining it was his dick sliding deeply inside of my tight walls.

As the minutes ticked on, it was no longer my fingers I felt fucking me. It was now his dick sliding in and out of me. I could feel his breath on my neck as the tip of his tongue swirled around in small circles on my hot spot. I moaned louder as I felt his steel push deeper inside of my slippery walls. The back of my head pressed further into my pillow as my back arched off of the bed in sheer ecstasy. Miss Kitty was almost at her breaking point as water drooled out of her mouth. Before settling down and relaxing, my body jerked as if someone was playing tug of war with my limbs

The last thing on my mind before sleep had finally taken over was the thought of knowing I'd finally gotten to see the face I had just visualized in my head. I just hoped I would be brave enough to act on my feelings, or better yet I hoped my feelings would be reciprocated.

*\*\*\**

*Buzzzzzzz*

I heard my alarm going off in my ear.

*Damn, 9 a.m. came fast as fuck,* I thought.

My brain started circulating and my mood spiked to a hundred. Today was the day I would see him.

For a moment, my mind took a trip down memory lane. I could remember him always asking for my number every time he'd see me walking through the neighborhood. Each and every time, I would smile politely, say no, and keep on moving. At the time, I was dating this cat named LJ, and there was no way I was going to cheat on him.

After almost four years of him asking me for my number, one day, I finally stopped long enough to give him some convo. We politicked for a few and agreed to meet up later on that night. My best friend, Sade, had come up to visit me from Durham, NC, so we decided to do a double date type thing.

Later that evening, when the sun had given the moon its time to shine, we stepped out ready for whatever.

Ole boy stayed with his baby's mom and at the time he'd said they weren't together.

My home girl and I were both nervous about going to knock on his door, so we sent one of the lil' bad ass chaps who hung outside his door 24/7.

Next thing I knew, Mr. Man was coming down the stairs smashing the game wearing a crisp black Tee, a gold chain that hung loosely around his neck, some black jeans that hung a little baggy, a black fitted and some J's on his feet. He wore a gun holster on his waist with his Glock tucked safely inside.

*This nigga is the fuckin' truth,* I thought to myself.

I watched as he approached the car and then hopped in the back seat beside me. Sade had her boo, Will, in the front seat so we were set.

Music cranked to the max, we pulled out and headed to a little spot called The Lake. It was in the University area of Charlotte, NC. The shit was fuckin' gorgeous at night. There were bars and restaurants surrounding the boardwalk. Lights were lit to illuminate the pitch black darkness of night.

We got out of the car laughing and joking about something Sade had said.

Once on the boardwalk, we parted ways. I was with my potential new boo and she was with her dude. As we walked and talked side by side, Mr. Man and I walked slowly around the lake, under the wooded trees, passing other couples who were also strolling.

*"What happened with you and ole boy? I mean, I've been tryna get at you for a long time and you never had much holla for me until now. So, I assume you and him had a fall out. Am I right?"* he asked as we sat down on a bench and looked out at the lake.

*"Me and LJ aren't together anymore. He's about to move away to be closer to his family and I don't do that long distance shit, so I had to let that go. Plus, I felt we both needed to explore other relationships first before we decide whether or not we really wanted to be with each other for the rest of our lives. We been together about as long as we been in high school, plus some. I didn't wanna wake up one day married to a man who would blame me*

for making him settle down early, and then use that as an excuse to start cheating. It is what it is," I said.

"That's what's up, Ma." He put his arm around me and pulled me closer. It was already warm outside, but when he pulled me closer to his body I swear the temperature went from hot to scorching. "You know a nigga tryna wife you up right?"

"So you say," I replied with laughter.

"So I know," he emphasized with sincerity, pausing, he looked around his surroundings before finishing up his thought, "this shit is beautiful, Ma. I ain't never been to nothin' like this. Thank you."

"You're welcome. You've never been out here before? Everybody comes out here."

"Not everybody," he said as he peered down at me. "Come 'ere, Ma."

I scooted as closely to him as our bodies would allow.

"Let me taste them lips," he stated almost a whisper as he leaned down closer to my lips.

For a slight second he paused before taking my lips and devouring them like a man who had been starved. His hand glided down to my plump ass.

Before I knew it, I was straddling his lap out in public, and at the moment, I really didn't give a damn. At the time, the hunger of my kitty was driving me insane and she was determined to be fed. I wound my hips against his groin. I could feel his grown man come to attention and salute the very essence of my womanhood. His hand made a path to the center of my parted thighs. He firmly rubbed my va-jay-jay through my jeans, not too hard not too soft. He rubbed it just the right way.

# Cum For Me

He pulled away from my lips, put his mouth next to my ear and whispered, "You like that shit, Ma?"

A moan from my plush lips was my only reply. I was jolted out of my moment of ecstasy when I heard voices getting closer. I moved to jump off of his lap so fast you would've thought I had gotten caught red handed doing something I had no business doing. Before I could hop all the way off, he grabbed me around the waist with a strong arm and held me in place.

"Where you going woman?"

"People are coming."

"So what! They be fuckin' too."

I burst out laughing and playfully smacked his shoulder. "You know what? I can't take you serious right now. You play too much." I giggled.

"You know it's the truth. Come on, Ma, let's go find ya girl." We laughed and joked some more as we made our way to find Sade and Will so we could leave.

A short while later we all got in the car and headed home.

## Shareef

I watched Ma as she got out of the car. Damn, her ass was phat. I was determined to bust her pussy wide open before I went in the house tonight.

I had chased shorty literally for damn near four years and to finally have her within my grasp, I'd be damn if I didn't grab her and hold on to her tight. I'd be a fool to let her go. I looked her body up and down, eyes stopping at her ass. The way her hips were swaying in them jeans had my member rocked up. I was ready to put in overtime now. Fuck waiting.

I caught up with her, grabbed her hand and pulled her along with me practically, dragging her. I needed her body now.

"Shareef, what's wrong? Why are you walking so fast?" she questioned but I gave no response. I just kept walking.

As soon as we turned the corner behind my apartment building, where it was pitch black, I stopped and pulled her into my arms. The wooded area concealed our bodies as I picked her up, pinned her up against the wall and went in for the kill. I attacked her lips with the hunger of a lion. I lifted her up and she wrapped her legs around my waist tightly. With a hunch in my back, I grinded my hardening manhood against her valley.

Damn, I need to feel her insides. This dry humping shit ain't what's up.

I placed her feet on the ground, unbuttoned her jeans and pulled her pants and panties down in unison. She seemed to have caught on to what was about to go down and began to unbuckle my belt. She unzipped my pants before undoing the button then pushed them down with her petite hands.

I picked her back up and placed her back against the wall. Her legs wrapped around my waist. I ceased all movement to look her in her eyes to make sure there was no hesitation while giving her a chance to back out.

"Once this happens, ain't no going back, understood?"

"Overstood."

I looked her deeply in her eyes once more then slid inside of her tight, wet pussy. The way my breath caught in my throat, I swear it felt like my soul was being snatched out of my body. Never had I ever felt something that felt so good. Hell yea, her ass was mine.

"This my pussy from now on, you hear me?"

"Yaass," she hissed out between moans.

Her head titled back in ecstasy as I continued to pound her insides like a boxer pounded his opponent's face. I slowed down a tad bit so I could enjoy the feeling of her walls wrapped around my stick. I was 'bout to give her a lesson in what her body could do. I used my tool as a GPS to find her G spot. It took no time for me to find it. I was like Master Splinter when it came to the pussy. I knew how to train that shit just right. I grinded into that special spot nice and slow, picking up the pace just a tad.

"Ooh, Shareef. What are you doing to me?" she moaned out breathlessly.

"I'm taming my pussy."

"Oh, shit. Harder," was her response.

I planned to go harder as soon as I felt that juice box pop wide open on my dick.

She held on to me tightly.

"Uh. Uhhh. Fuck me harder, Shareef. Harder."

I deep stroked her pussy like I was an Olympic swimmer.

"Sha.. ree.. Shareef, I gotta peee."

"No you don't. Let that shit go, Ma," I replied through clenched teeth.

Her pussy detonated with just those few words and gushed all on my dick like a running faucet of water on full blast. Her walls put my piece in a choke hold and released it only to put it back in a choke hold, only to loosen it again. The feeling of her walls contracting around my member caused my dick to explode in response. I slowed my pumps, relishing in the feeling of her womanhood *hugging my steel. Our lips connected as if sealing the deal that she now belonged to me.*

## Nicole

Boy those were the good ole days. I made a beeline to the shower so I could hurry up and get fresh and dressed before my girls Latisha, Redd, and Nik Nik showed up and started rushing me. I was always running behind, it never failed.

We were going to a hotel for a convention for black owned businesses and entrepreneurs. I owned my own publishing company named Royal Honey Publications. I had a building set up where everything took place from publishing, editing, shipping, etc. It sort of reminded me of how record companies set up their establishments. I ran my company like a pimp ran his hoes. My shit was tighter than a woman trying to squeeze her big ass feet in a pair of size six stilettos.

Me and my girls weren't just there for the convention, though. We were also there to celebrate my birthday, and as Kevin Hart would say, *turn up*!

I already knew what I had planned to wear. However, where we were going tonight was a mystery to me. The girls kept telling me it was a surprise. That had me nervous because my girls could get a little wild. But whatever it was, I planned to have fun.

After washing up and lathering my silky, caramel skin in lotion, I went to the closet and picked out the suit I'd be wearing. I chose a black pants suit partnered with some red bottoms. My curves filed the suit as if it had been painted on my body. I turned to the side in the mirror to admire my plump ass. Damn, my momma sure gave me a lot to shake. I played with my swoop just a little to get it feathered just like I liked it. I used my fingers to rake through my shoulder length curls then swung them side to side to make sure they bounced just like I liked them to. I was just about to apply my makeup when I heard a knock at my hotel room door.

"Damn." I cursed under my breath. I swear these heffas don't ever run late.

I could hear Tish and Nik Nik going back and forth about some damn milk. They were already cacklin' like a bunch of hyenas early in the morning. I never understood them. One minute they were at each other's throats, then they were right back laughing and joking with each other. Can you say *weird*?

"Hey, bitch," Tish said as I let her and my girls in.

"Hey, hoe," I responded back to her and then reached out to give her a hug. I spoke to Redd and Nik NIk and embraced them as they entered the room as well.

"You know what you wearing tonight?" Nik Nik asked.

"Yea, the short, black dress with the black and gold waist belt I bought when we all went to the mall yesterday, along with my red bottom stilettos," I said.

"Ouch, Mama. Who dick you tyrna get inside you tonight?" Redd questioned.

I swear my girl always said some crazy off-the-wall shit to say and that's exactly why I loved her. I smirked at her comment.

"No one in particular," I said, hoping they wouldn't catch on to the bullshit I had just let slip through my lips. They knew just like I did, that Shareef would be at the convention. Nine times out of ten, we would bump into him tonight while we were out partying later.

"Girl, bye. Who you think you fooling, us or your coochie-coo? You know Shareef gone be all up in that pussy before the night is over," Redd responded.

"Redd! Damn do you not have a filter?"

"Hell no, I'm grown. What the fuck I need a filter fo?"

"Umm, 'scuse me. Did you not hear the shit that just came out ya mouth? And anyways, who says Shareef getting a taste of my cookie even if I do bump into him?"

"Ssshhh. Y'all hear that?" Tish asked.

"Hear what?" I questioned.

"It sound like water running from a faucet," Tish responded.

"Tish, I don't hear no damn water running."

"Oh, my bad that's yo pussy runnin' like a muhfuckin' kitchen faucet after hearing Shareef's name."

Nik Nik and Redd burst out in laughter. I too had to join in on the fun. Only Tish's ass would say something so damn retarded.

"Fuck you," I responded in between giggles.

"Bitch, my name ain't Shareef," spat Tish, turning her nose up.

We all started cracking back up.

As we rode to the place the convention was being held, my mind drifted off to a time when I used to look out of the bus window on my way home from my classes at Central Piedmont Community College.

\*\*\*

*Damn, I wish this lady would shut the fuck up, I thought to myself.*

## Cum For Me

*All I wanted to do was ride home in some peace and quiet. I had just gotten out of my most hated class and had made it just in time to get on the number 9. I was tired and beyond aggravated because I had to run to catch the damn bus.*

"I remember when I was in school. Oohh, those were the good ole days back then. That's when we use to host something called nickel parties. Boy, how I missed those days." Miss-won't-shut-the-hell-up said.

She was about to continue on but I'd be damned if I was going to keep letting her beat my ears like a bass drum.

"Excuse me, Miss. I'm not trying to be rude or anything, but I had a long day and I'm tired. I just want to ride home in peace and quiet. I would be tremendously happy if you would oblige."

"Not a problem, dear. I have had days like those too. You go on and rest, chile."

"Thank you," I replied.

She nodded her head and proceeded to look out of the window, probably still reminiscing about back when. Ten minutes later, I was finally getting off of the bus. It was hotter than the devil's asshole. I pulled the hem of my shorts down since they had risen up while I was sitting on the bus, and began my journey to my apartment.

I was almost to my apartment when I ran into him. I already knew what he was going to say before he even said anything.

"Can I get your number today?" he asked.

"No, Shareef. You know I'm in a relationship with LJ. On second thought, here, take my number and hit me up when you need your hair braided."

"A'ight, Ma, I'ma get at cha," he responded as he walked off.

I smiled to myself as I trotted up to my breezeway and upstairs to my apartment.

I dropped my bag off at the door and went straight to the fridge to grab a soda then went in my room and sat on my bed. As soon as I'd gotten good and comfortable in my bed, I heard the ringtone to my IPhone going off. I reached over and grabbed a hold of my cell. A crease formed in between my arched eyebrows when I didn't recognize the number.

"Hello"

"What's up, gorgeous?"

"Damn, Shareef you ain't even had my number a hot hour and you calling me already?" I huffed when I recognized the caller by his up north accent.

"You said to call you when I needed my hair braided, so I'm calling you to let you know I need my hair braided."

"Your hair is already braided. I meant call me when they start looking ratchet."

"They were looking ratchet, woman. That's why I took them out. Can you do my hair for me tomorrow?"

"Them joints looked mad fresh, but if you want to waste your money then that's you. What time you want them done?"

"Can you meet me at my spot around 3:30?"

"Yea, you better be happy I don't have class on Fridays or your ass would be waiting."

"Well, lucky for me you don't, huh?"

"Uh huh"

"Shareef, I don't want no drama with your baby moms?"

"You ain't even gotta worry about that. She out of town with her peeps and the kids."

"Okay, I hear you."

"Well, that's what it do, Ma. I'ma get at you tomorrow."

"A'ight," I replied as I disconnected the call.

The next day I knocked on Shareef's door, ready to get down to business. I planned to braid his hair and get the fuck on.

He opened the door clad in a black wife beater, some black and red shorts and some black footies, with his fro and all his tatts out.

*Damn, why the fuck he gotta be so fine?* I thought to myself.

"Hey, Shareef, ready to get your hair braided?"

"Yea, come on in, Ma," he said as he stepped aside from the door so I could come inside.

"You want something to drink or eat?"

"Nah, I'm good. Have you already washed your hair?"

"Yea," he responded.

"Cool, where you want me to braid it at?" I questioned.

"Sit on the couch, and I'll sit on the floor. The game on so I get to watch the Heat play."

"Sounds like a plan," I responded as I sat down on the couch.

I started to question why they chose a damn red suede couch but decided that was none of my business, and I really didn't care.

*Shareef handed me a comb and ponytail holder as he sat down in between my legs. I parted his hair and began braiding. My designs were the mofo truth and I knew it. I had swirls and crossovers all throughout his braids. I was platting the end of Shareef's last braid when I felt his hand rubbing up and down my bare legs. Damn, I forgot I was wearing shorts, I thought as I tried to ignore his touch.*

*I finished the plat and was about to jump up when his voice boomed through the quaint living room space. "Stay, stay right there." He reached inside his pocket and pulled a knot of cash out then peeled off a hundred dollar bill. He turned halfway so he was semi facing me and handed me the bill. "Here, thanks for hooking my hair up, Ma."*

*"Shareef, you only owe me twenty."*

*"Well, look at the rest as a big ass tip," he said with a smirk.*

*I smiled as well. My smile faded as he began to stare at me as though I was foreign or something.*

*"I think I should go," I said above a whisper, but for some reason my limbs wouldn't cooperate with what my brain was telling it to do. I was stuck in place.*

*Shareef turned around fully and stood up to his feet before he leaned his lean body into my spread legs. I could feel his hard-on through his basketball shorts. He leaned in closer to my face, softly kissed my lips then pulled back slightly. Then, he leaned back in for another kiss. This time the kiss was soft but not as soft as before. He eased his tongue in between my full lips. Our tongues began to dance in a dance as old as time. As our kiss deepened, I could feel him begin to grind his hips in between my legs. My twat jumped at the feeling. I was dripping wet with need and was praying for some form of relief.*

## Cum For Me

*Shareef unbuttoned my shorts and eased his hands down the band of my panties. His fingers brushed up and down my slit then up over my pearl. My body felt like it was tingling and going numb at the same time. I swear it felt like I was having an outer body experience. I felt his index and middle finger slide inside of my wetness. My hips thrust forward. I started riding his fingers in a slow motion. He leaned closer to my ear.*

*"I want to taste you," he mumbled in a quiet voice.*

*"Shareef," I moaned out.*

*"Can I taste you, Nicole?"*

*My head was too gone to even respond. The next thing I knew my shorts and panties were being pulled off. Shareef stared down at my treasure before sticking his tongue out to taste my juices. He used his fingers and pulled the lid to my pearl apart and flicked the tip of his tongue against it before sucking it in between his warm lips. He flicked his tongue in a fast motion against my clit while he kept his lips closed around it. My hips shot up off of the couch.*

*"Sha .Shareef, sto—stop." My words fell on deaf ears.*

*He gripped my thighs and feasted on my pussy like a starved man.*

*When I left his house that day, I was sure of two things. One, I was addicted to Shareef's tongue game and two, if I didn't get right, he was going to finally get what he wanted, which was to fuck me. But I was determined to hold on to the little relationship I had with LJ.*

I checked out of memory lane just as we approached the hotel where the convention was being held. The itinerary they had set up for the day zoomed by in the blink of an eye.

The highlight of my day was when Shareef got up on stage to speak about his booming bail's bondsman company. Everywhere I went, I would hear about his company. I was happy he'd been able to achieve his dreams.

I had noticed him, however, he had yet to see me, and I was determined to keep it that way. At first, I was excited about seeing him after all this time, but my nerves had really gotten the best of me. So, I purposely stayed out of his line of sight until it was time to leave. I was the first one back to the car.

Later on that night, my girls finally revealed that we were going to the world's famous *Magic City* strip club. I was curious about the spot because I had never seen a stripper up close and personal before, but at the same time, strip clubs weren't my kind of scene. I would much rather be at a place where I could meet some fine ass niggas.

Once there, I headed straight for the bar. I sat there nursing my drink while my girls cut a fool. I was about to get up and go talk junk to them when I felt the heat of someone's gaze on me. My heart sped up and my kitty jumped. There was only one man who had that kind of effect on me, Shareef Devionne Smith. *What a coincidence!* I didn't move a muscle. I sat there like my ass was glued to the damn seat. I could feel him as he got closer and closer.

"Hey, gorgeous. I was wondering what a beautiful lady like yourself was doing sitting here all alone?" he whispered in my ear.

I held my breath for a brief second so I could pull myself together. We hadn't spoken in years, actually since we were teens. Well, technically, since I was a teen because when I was eighteen he was already in his twenties. That was six years and no kids ago, but after all of these years, I had finally come into contact with the man who had flowed through my dreams like a stream of running water. All he had to do was showcase those thirty-two pearly whites, and he had my va-jayjay dripping wet.

"Hey you, I see you came out to enjoy the festivities the 'A' has to offer." I smiled. "And to answer your question, I'm not here alone. My girls over there turning up! I can't believe they have me in damn Magic City. You know this is not my get down," I replied, turning around to face him while trying to conceal the huge grin that was spreading across my entire face.

"Well, I tell you what, how about we step outside and talk so we don't have to speak over this loud ass music?"

"Okay cool, sounds like a plan." I rose to my feet, dropped some bills on the bar top and obliged my old flame's request.

Outside we got in his car and drove around aimlessly while catching up on old times. More than an hour had passed before I asked him to drive me back to the hotel. With his fine ass less so close to me, I didn't want to return to the strip club and look at pussy.

I sent Tisha quick text letting her and my girls know the deal. At the hotel Shareef walked me up to my room.

"I guess this is goodnight, huh?" he questioned, looking into my hazel eyes with his chocolate orbs.

"I guess so." My voice trailed off for a split second before continuing my thought, "Well, it was nice chatting with you. Enjoy the rest of your night," I spat rapidly before turning to put my hotel key inside of the key slot so it would grant me access inside. I needed a cold shower ASAP.

  Before I could even get the key card all the way out of the door, I felt a strong hand grab my wrist and my body being swung around. I didn't even have a chance to respond before I felt the crushing assault of his lips on mine. I was gone the minute our lips connected. It felt as if I had taken a dose of heroin or cocaine and was being taken to that magical place in the sky. I felt high. I could feel the door being opened and my body being pushed inside. I should've been protesting but my body refused to stop at the chance to indulge in such pleasure.

  My legs hit the back of my hotel bed causing me to stumble and fall backwards. I gripped his shoulders tighter, causing him to fall along with me. Our kiss intensified. Feeling his two hundred and forty pounds of muscle on top of my body caused my legs to part like the Red Sea. My hips thrust off of the bed when I felt his groin grind into mine. My mini black dress slid up my caramel colored thighs exposing my purple thongs. His lips slowly moved away from mine only to form a path from my neck on down to my golden paradise. His long fingers peeled away the small thin material that blocked him from his next meal. The warmth of his breath on my inner thigh making a trail to my pussy ignited my insides on fire and had my twat dripping wet. He hadn't even put the dick on me yet and already had me ready to squirt like a water gun. A flicker from his tongue on my womanly pearl nearly sent me over the edge.

  "Oh, shit, Shareef," I whisked out between short breaths.

"Wait. Wait. Wait! We can't do this," I said while making a weak attempt to move out of his grasp. I don't know who I was trying to convince more, him or myself.

He wrapped his strong hands around my thick thighs and pulled me as closely as he could to his mouth, simply ignoring the bullshit that had slipped through my lips. His tongue swam deep inside my pussy causing my back to arch off of the bed from the intensity of the feeling. My body was on fire feeling as though it were about to explode.

"Sha—Sha—Shareef," I muttered out between moans.

Stars burst behind my eyes. At least that's what it felt like. My walls started to contract around his tongue. His tongue game was the truth and it was what had gotten me addicted to him as a young girl.

Shareef pulled back and looked me in my eyes. Through the heat of his gaze it felt as though he was communicating feelings for me that had yet to abandon his heart. After all of the years that had passed between us, my heart still belonged to him, and I could tell he knew it.

I pulled my plush bottom lip in between my teeth as I looked his anatomy up and down from head to toe. His girth made my mouth water and my pussy drip with anticipation.

He looked down at the sun kissed, golden paradise before him. The young girl he knew as a teen had finally grown into the full figured woman he had known she would eventually grow into. His dick jumped just peering down at her 38DDD breast and wide baby bearing hips. Yes, I was definitely all-woman now.

Shareef leaned over my luscious body and eased his way between my parted thighs.

"Look at me. I want to be looking into your eyes when I take back what's rightfully mine," he said to me in a low tone.

I looked him deeply in his eyes and it was at that moment he decided to make his way inside of my walls. He eased the head of his dick inside of my tight kitty. He pulled back and pushed in again a little further, then repeated the process trying to open my walls further to accommodate his nine and a half inch sized steel. I opened my legs wider to grant Shareef's rod greater access inside of my body. He slid back and pushed in long and deep until he reached the hilt. Our movement ceased for a brief second as we looked into one another's eyes. Nothing compared to the feeling I felt at that moment.

## Shareef

*Fuck,* I thought to myself as I moved in and out of Nicole's womanhood. Her juice box was so wet, tight, and warm it made it damn near a struggle not to bust off early. I was a determined man and refused to shoot off until she came at least two more times. I had never been a quick pumper, but the way her pussy was massaging my stick for the first time in my life, I might actually cum early. I put my pole on a mission to find that special spot that I knew would send her over the edge fast, her G spot! I knew exactly where to go. My memory never failed me. I could feel her water dripping down my shaft. I pulled out of her and flipped her over, face down, ass up. I eased my manhood back into her tight, dripping, wet honey spot. I let out an explicative.

*Is it possible that her snatch could have went from great to greater since the last time we had sex,* I thought.

Wasn't no way I was gonna be able to hold back if I didn't pull back for a split second. I pulled out again. I leaned over and kissed her beautiful round ass. My lips trailed lower and lower down the crack of her ass. I used my hands to pry her luscious mounds apart. I flicked my tongue out and licked in between before sticking my tongue into her tight virgin hole. I used the tip of my tongue like a mini dick and fucked her asshole like my dick fucked her snatch. Her back arched upward as I used my tongue to make love to her ass.

"Uuuhhh. Uuhh. Shareef!" She screamed out. I loved hearing her scream my name.

My dick was crying to get back in the game. He was ready to put in overtime on dat ass. I lay on my back, pole sticking straight up in the air. Nicole eased my steel back inside of her with her back toward me. She looked at me seductively over her shoulder as she slowly rode my dick. It wasn't long before she was bouncing up and down on my guy like her ass was a basketball and this was her court.

### Nicole

"Fuck me! Fuck me! Harder. Oh, shit! Damn, Daddy fuck this pussy," I moaned out as I bounced up and down reverse cowgirl style on Shareef's beef cake.

"That's right, Ma. Ride this dick," Shareef said as he grabbed my hips with a death grip.

I slid up and down his pole like this was the Player's Club and my name was Diamond. I climbed off of his dick, turned around on my hands and knees and crawled until I was eye to eye with Shareef's member. I used the tip of my tongue to conduct a taste test. Damn, our juices mixed together tasted sweeter than Hershey's chocolate. I licked him from the beginning of his shaft to the very tip of his mushroomed shaped head before suctioning his hard-on into my warm mouth. I used my right hand to jack him while I sucked on his stick and used my left hand to give his family jewels some much needed attention.

"Damn, Ma. That's how you feel?"

"Um, hmm," I moaned out in response around a mouth full of dick.

I could feel him getting ready to burst. Just as he was about to let loose, I hopped back on his dick and rode him like a mad woman using my pussy muscles to do Kegels on his tool. I felt the very essence of him shoot deeply inside of me I swear it touched my soul. His seed shooting in my womb triggered my own release. My walls rained down heavenly on his dick. He was the only man that could ever make me squirt. Others had tried and failed, but with him, it was like it happened with little to no effort.

As the spasms in my body began to calm down, I leaned forward breast to chest, stomach to stomach, heart to heart and felt my heart swell with love. No matter who I was with, my love for him never faded. My heart always remained his. A tear slipped out of the corner of my eye onto his chest. I wondered how much time we had missed out on. My mind traveled down the what-ifs. *What if I had stayed? What if I had never left and moved away? What if I had never listened to what the people in the neighborhood were saying about him being a negative look for me? Would he be the father to the child I have now if I had never left him?*

"I love you, Shareef," I whispered quietly as another tear slipped out of my eye.

Never in a million years did I think I would feel his strong arms embraced around me, let alone around my nude body.

"I love you too, Ashley Nicole."

My head popped up. I couldn't believe my ears. I didn't even know he had heard me because I said it so low. I looked Shareef in his eyes and saw they were glistening with water. Our emotions mirrored one another.

"I never stopped loving you, Ash. Your body may have left me but I knew, or at least had to believe your heart stayed with me like mines had always been with you. These thots out here can throw the pussy at me all day long, but none of them can have my heart, that's something you already stole a long time ago. I will always love you no matter if we're together or apart."

Words couldn't explain how I felt at this exact moment. I leaned forward and kissed him deeply. He flipped me over on my back and was easing his way back in between Miss Kitty's slippery opening.

*Damn, I love this man,* I thought.

The memories of us together finally became more than wet memories. They became my future fantasies and late night ecstasies.

***The End***

## Caught In a Fantasy
### By
# *Latisha Lewinson*

"No thank you, Mr. Jamerson. It was nice doing business with you and your wife. Congrats on the new house." As I hung up the phone, I was happy to have another sale under my belt. This house made it a total of five sold this month. Happy about the sale, I decided to take the rest of the day off to treat myself to an all day spa and just relax.

As I was gathering up my belongings, my office phone rang. "I am going to let the voicemail pick it up," I said aloud. But the caller did not give up, they called back to back. I looked down at the phone. "Damn! Right when I was about to walk out the door." I picked up the phone. "Thank you for calling KL Realty. This is Kimberly speaking. How may I help you?"

"Hello," the caller replied. "My name is Jasmine Harris, and I was interested in your four bedroom, four bath single family home in Culver City."

"Oh, yes. I just put that one on the market three days ago," I said. "What would you like to know?"

"I'd like to know what the asking price is, and when can I see the home?" Jasmine asked.

"Mmmm, can I put you on hold, so I can pull up the files for this property? I was just leaving for the day, so please bear with me," I said.

"Yes, take your time and thank you so much," Jasmine replied.

"Okay give me one second to pull up the information for you, Mrs. Harris," I said, placing her on hold while I waited for my computer to boot up. I sat back down in my chair and got comfortable, hoping that I would have another sale under my belt.

"Hello, Mrs. Harris, I'm back," I said. "Okay I have the information for the home that you are inquiring about. The price I am asking for the Culver City home is $1,345.00 a month. This is a stately, traditional, well-appointed and spacious home. It's positioned in a desirable, tucked away Culver City neighborhood close to shopping, entertainment, and great schools. It was renovated from top to bottom. As you know, it has four bedrooms and four baths. That includes an enormous master bedroom suite, formal living room, dining room, eat-in kitchen and den area with French doors."

As I continued my spiel, she interrupted, "Can I see it today?"

"Yes, that won't be a problem. It's on my way home."

"It will be my husband and I. What time should we meet you there?"

"Its 1:30 now. Let's say by 3:15."

"Yes, that will be great." I heard the echoes of Jasmine's clap through the phone.

"Okay, I'll see you then. I hung up the phone and grabbed my keys and the property keys and walked out of the door.

Once I stepped outside I put my sunglasses on and took in the summer breeze. I decided that it was a nice enough day to drop the top of my new 2014 red two door SLK 250 Mercedes Benz that I just copped from selling my last two houses. I walked over to my pride and joy and jumped in. I turned my music on and K'LA was blasting through my Bose speakers.

*So many people are sleeping on my girl,* I thought.

I pulled into Chase bank and grabbed my bank bag to deposit money into my business account.

*If I could get six houses sold this month, I could hire a leasing agent to help me around the office*, I thought.

At the age of thirty-two, I was doing the damn thing. Now all I needed to do was find me a good man.

Once I was done in the bank, I made my way outside as a man carelessly ran into me.

"Oh, excuse me." He humbly apologized as he bent down to help me pick up what I dropped out of my hands.

"Thank you," I said, glancing at his face briefly as I proceeded to walk to my car.

*That man looks so familiar,* I thought.

As I was about to cross the street, the man called out my name and I looked back.

"Kimberly?" He looked at me with curious wonder. "Is that you, shawdy?"

I stopped in my tracks and turned around. "Yes, and who are you?" I tried to figure out if I knew this man.

"It's me, Malik, from college." He walked up to me and looked me right in my eyes. "Wow, that's crazy, you haven't changed at all," he said, smiling and showing off his perfectly straight, white teeth.

"Oh, my gosh, Malik. How are you doing?" I exclaimed. I gave him a hug and it felt good being in a man's arms. "I thought you moved to the ATL."

"Yea, I had. But I moved back here to Cali three months ago. I'm actually looking for a house to buy right now." He shyly smiled as he talked.

A customer was trying to get to their car, so I moved to the left. "Excuse me," I said as they walked by.

"Well, today is your lucky day. I'm a realtor and I'm on my way to see a client right now." I went into my wallet and pulled out a business card. "This is my cell. Call me sometime, so we can catch up. But also call my office tomorrow, so I can show you some properties."

Malik took the card and licked his lips. "I will do that. You have a wonderful day, beautiful." He gave me a hug that could make a bitch nut on herself. The strength of his hold alone was intoxicating.

I had to let go. I didn't want a moan to escape my lips. I smiled and backed away. "You have a nice day, too."

I walked to my car without looking back. I assumed he was watching me as I did because I had it going on. I had the looks of twenty year old. A body that women all of all ages would die for. I stood at five feet nine inches and weighed one hundred and eighty pounds. I had a small waist, so most of my thickness was in my thighs and ass. And the icing on my cake was the smooth chocolate coating God blessed me with.

Twenty minutes later, I was pulling into the circle driveway of the home I was scheduled to show Mrs. Harris. I cut my engine and looked around. I didn't see any cars parked in the front, so I guessed I'd made it there before them. I grabbed my folder and the keys to the house and proceeded to unlock the premises and wait for them inside.

I took myself on a tour of the home to familiarize myself with the floor plan. I went upstairs to the master bedroom and I fell in love with the house myself. I walked into the bathroom and noted that the tub was easily big enough for two.

My pussy became wet just thinking about Malik being that plus one and fucking me in there. I leaned against the wall and slid my hand down between my legs, moving my panties to the side from beneath my skirt and started rubbing my pussy as I thought of him. Lord, it had been too long since I'd had something long, hard, and black deep inside of me.

I pushed two fingers inside of my pussy and moved them in and out. My pussy got wetter. I bit down on my bottom lip, finger fucking my pussy as if it was Malik's dick. I began to stroke my fingers harder over my pussy. I felt my orgasm approaching. "Yes! Yes! Yes!"

But then I was interrupted by Mrs. Harris calling my damn name. *Shit!* I was irritated at the fact that I could not get my orgasm. It has been a while since she had maintenance done, but money had to come first.

"Hello? Is anybody here? It's me, Mrs. Harris"

"Dammit!" I quickly washed my hands. I didn't need her smelling my sweet essence during our handshake. "Yes, I'm here. I was tending to some other business," I informed her once she was in earshot. Hurriedly, I met her at the bottom of the stairwell.

*Damn! She looked good.*

She was short in stature with a caramel complexion and a body like K. Michelle. She had long hair down her back and she looked like she was mixed with some Latina.

*If I was into women, she would be my type.*

"Hello, Mrs. Harris." I held out my hand in greeting. "Nice to meet you."

She shook my hand and smiled. "You can call me Jasmine, and thank you for seeing me. I know it was spur of the moment, but I had to see this house. My husband and I saw it online and wanted to see it for ourselves."

"Oh? Is your husband with you?" I looked around.

"Oh, no," she replied. "He had an emergency at the office that he needed to take care of but—" She was cut off by a call coming in on her phone. "Excuse me." She stepped off to the side for privacy.

"Hello, babe." Jasmine greeted. "Okay, I just got here. That's cool, see you in few." She pressed end on her phone and put it back into her purse.

"I'm sorry, that was my husband. He will be here shortly. He's not that far away."

"Okay, that's great. Shall we wait?" I questioned.

"No. I'm anxious. Let's begin." Her smile was gorgeous. I hoped my eyes didn't give away my opinion of her.

I extended my hand, leading her in the direction she was to go. "This way," I instructed.

I gave her the statistics on the house. What year it was built. The history. The ins and the outs, but what was really on my mind wasn't the demographics. Lawd! I was in need of—well, *you know*.

"Wow. This house is so beautiful. I have to have it." She spun in a circle, marveling at the view and lost her balance, bumping right into me. I grabbed her to keep her from falling. She held onto me and pulled herself to her feet. We stood face to face and our eyes locked. A sudden sexual electricity caused the temperature in my panties to rise, but I forced it back down. Sensing my quelled desire, she leaned in without saying a word and kissed me on the lips.

"Mrs. Harris?" I gasped, and jumped back. It wasn't that her lips weren't soft as cotton. She'd just caught me by surprise. One minute I was imagining what her lips felt like and the next I was finding out.

She walked toward me with a careful stride. With a little sugar in her voice that wasn't present before, she said, "I'm sorry, but I thought you wanted me. I mean, the way you've been looking at me."

"Excuse me?" I was embarrassed because she was correct. "I think you misread my look. Since when is a friendly look confused with a flirting one?" Right as she was about to respond, the doorbell rang. "Excuse me. I have to answer that."

I adjusted my pinstripe suit as I walked to the door and opened it. To my surprise, Malik was standing on the other side.

*Damn this is a small ass world.*

"Oh, my gosh. Now, this is crazy." I was shocked to see him of all people.

"Damn, Kim. Two times in one day? That must be a sign of something." He winked his eye and licked his lips seductively before stepping inside.

*What is up with this couple?*

I didn't acknowledge what Malik was making me feel. I simply pointed through the house. "Your *wife* is this way."

I walked in front of him to lead the way and I heard him clearly mumble, *Goddamn! All that ass.*

I had to admit that did something for me, so I put a little more sway into my walk since I knew he was watching it.

Once I joined them together, I offered them free range of the house. "I'll give you two some time to look around. If you have any questions, please don't hesitate to ask. I'll be right over here in the living room." I walked off wondering if they both were watching. *Ooooh,* that kind of turned me on.

As I waited, I went online to check my emails, Facebook, and Twitter accounts. I used all of those social medias to advertise my business.

## Cum For Me

Twenty minutes had passed and although I wasn't rushing them, I hadn't seen or heard them. I became curious. I got up and made my way around the house. There was no sign of them downstairs, so I went upstairs in search of my clients. I looked in three of the rooms and they weren't in either.

Entering the master bedroom through the double doors, I could see Mrs. Harris on her knees. "Well, damn," I uttered softly as I backed out. A few seconds later, my sexual wonder had me crack the door and inconspicuously watch on.

Her soft, juicy lips were wrapped around his dick and all I could hear coming from out of the room were moans, groans, oohs and ahhs.

I peered inside a little closer. Her eyes expanded the more she attempted to deep throat, it looked as if his dick was growing in her mouth. I could not believe what was happening right in front of my eyes. My pussy started getting wet because of it. I crossed my legs and squeezed them tightly, but that was working against me.

*I want to taste his dick, too,* I whined in pleasure agony. I stepped back to where they could not see me, but a spot where I could still see them. I started to play with myself.

My pussy was on fire! I hadn't had sex in so long I was easy to stimulate. An innocent brush against my body or a kiss the right way would have gotten my juices flowing. So, needless to say watching them had me on my level.

All I wanted was to feel Malik inside of me just like he was inside of her, one time. As I put my hand under my skirt making it come up over my ass, I went to look back in to continue my fantasy, but I was busted. Malik eyes met mine.

I jumped back. "Dammit!" I spoke in a soft, low tone.

It was obvious he didn't mind me looking because he smiled and started fucking her mouth like it was her pussy. Then, he began talking nasty.

"Spit on this dick, bitch. Mmmm. Yeah, suck this dick the way I like. Open up wider." He shoved his dick down her throat. Gagging sounds mixed with a lot of moaning traveled throughout the room.

*I want to join in on the sex show. I want him to treat me like that and call me all kind of hoes and bitches.*

As I looked at him, he blew me a kiss. I smiled and started to play with my pussy even more. The intensity stirring between my legs became too much to satisfy on my own. I must have been feeling myself because I walked into the room before I could stop my feet from moving. Coming out my heels and getting on my knees, I moved her hair and started kissing her neck. She was quite receptive.

Malik motioned for her to stop his oral pleasure and tantalize my awaiting mouth. She then danced her tongue across mine. I tasted his flavor through her kiss. It made me that much hornier.

As we were kissing, Malik stepped back, spit on his right hand and rubbed it on the tip of his dick while jerking it back and forth.

Looking from the corner of my eye, I could see that we were turning him on. I pushed her shoulders back, laid her flat on the carpet and spread her legs open. I had never done this before but I was in the moment, so I went with it.

I brought my tongue down on the tip of her pussy, gently licking it while looking at Malik. Her pussy was so wet it turned on *my* faucet. I began to suck on her clit as I eased my fingers inside of her hot pussy.

"Lick this pussy, bitch," Jasmine moaned as she moved her hips in a circular motion. I fucked her pussy with my two fingers the same way I had seen Pinky, the porn star, do Jada Fire one night when I was watching videos.

Malik walked up behind me, got on his knees, and rubbed the head of his dick on my wet, fat pussy. Taking my lips off Jasmine's lower ones and looking back, I licked my mouth. "Take this pussy." I commanded her husband.

Malik slid the head of his dick into my streaming center. He moaned and grabbed my ass firmly, pushing into me deeply. I arched my back and inhaled at the size of his dick against my walls. He moaned as he attacked my pussy as if it was his last time while I resumed eating the shit out of Jasmine's delicious cookie. I ate her so good her head lashed side to side as she cried out in ecstasy.

Breathing heavily, Jasmine sat up and slowly stuck her tongue into my mouth, giving me long, passionate kisses. "I love the way my pussy tastes on your tongue," she muttered.

After she tickled my tongue with hers, she got on all fours, crawled over to Malik, and started kissing him as he continued to fuck my pussy.

There was a symphony of moaning and groaning going on between us. The sounds of his pelvis thrusting against my ass heightened my sexuality.

He then pulled his dick out, and Jasmine started to suck my juices off the head of it. Once she was done lapping my nectar off of his pole, she laid on her back and told me to sit on her face as Malik started to fuck her. I never got my pussy ate like this. My legs were shaking, but she locked onto them, "I'ma suck on your clit like this is my last day on earth," she whispered. I rode her face so hard I thought I might suffocate. But she kept talking that slick shit. "Let it out, baby. Let it out."

I thought I was about to pee on myself. The feeling taking over me was abnormal, but hella good at the same time. I tried to raise up. "I gotta pee." I couldn't control my breathing as I spoke.

Malik chuckled as he continued teasing Jasmine's sweet pussy with his dick. "Naw, baby girl, let that shit out right on her face."

As I let go of my cum waterfalls, Jasmine closed her eyes and opened her mouth wider. I squirted all over the place and she loved it. I then rolled off of her and collapsed onto the floor.

Malik reached his climax and came in his wife's pussy. He lay sprawled on top of her, kissing her. "I love you, Jasmine." He expressed himself as if I wasn't in the room and we didn't just happen.

I was at a loss for words hearing him mention love after we all just fucked. But I couldn't say shit. My back was facing them, so they couldn't see how uncomfortable I was now. I jumped up and ran into the restroom, locked the door and sat on the toilet.

Fifteen minutes later, there was a knock at the door. "Open up," Malik whispered.

I got off of the toilet and made my way to the door. I put my hand on the knob, scared to open it. Taking a deep breath and letting it out smoothly, I opened the door and stood butt ass naked in front of him. I looked down at his dick. I slowly looked back up and past him, seeing Jasmine passed out on floor.

I looked at Malik. "I'm sorry." I started to address the situation but before I could finish, Malik put his tongue down my throat, backed me up and closed the bathroom's door.

All I could do was moan. The way his tongue felt inside of my mouth and the way he was holding me had me gone.

Malik stepped back to take a good look at my body. "Damn! How did you get all that ass? Good god almighty, shawdy." He shook his head.

His dick jumped up and down letting me know that he was turned on. He started to rub on my perfectly sized B cup breasts. The one with a tattooed bleeding heart and a hummingbird on it.

Turning me around and bending me over the counter, he slowly worked his way into my wet pussy.

"Mmmm, damn this pussy is so tight." He whispered into my ear as he took a long deep stroke into my creamy center. He picked up speed and all I could hear was my ass and his pelvis going at it.

I looked back at him. "Choke me, baby. Ohhh, Mmmm," I moaned.

Taking his right hand, he grabbed me around my neck, gripped it, and squeezed it tightly while he pounded into my peach.

I started talking mad nasty to him. "Yeah take this pussy, baby. Fuck me harder."

With the green light, he fucked me so hard my body started to shake. He let my neck go and grabbed my ass. I could feel his dick getting harder in my pussy and I knew right then he was about to cum.

Malik was breathing hard and kicking up a sweat. "Yeah you like this dick? Tell me you like this dick, bitch."

"Yesssss! I like this dick, baby. Mmmm, yes, I like this dick," I moaned. I held onto the sink because my legs felt like they were going to give out on me. This was the best feeling I ever had in my life.

"Mmmm, yes, take this dick." He pounded inside of me until I cried out his name and my juices coated his shaft. I felt him pull out and shoot his hot nut all over my ass.

I didn't care about nothing right then. All I knew was that Malik Harris had some dope dick and I was going to get a weekly repeat of that shit.

Looking at him in the mirror, I saw that he had tattoos covering his chest and stomach like they were a painted on a portrait. He stood about five feet eight inches with a low cut fade and his body was toned like a man fresh out of jail.

Malik just stared and smiled at me without saying one word. I was so lost in my thoughts all I could do was smile back.

Malik walked to the door and swung it open. To our surprise Jasmine was standing right outside with a puzzled look on her face. "What the fuck you are doing, Malik?" She was pissed.

"What the fuck do you mean what the fuck am I doing? I'm doing the same thing I was doing in the bedroom. Fucking." Malik clarified with a straight face.

"So, you're just going to come in the bathroom and fuck her without me, huh?" She seemed genuinely angered by this.

"Pretty much," Malik spoke bluntly.

"Look," I interrupted, "I don't know what the fuck is really going on, but what's done is done. I'm sorry for what went down. All of this caught me by surprise and it will never happen again."

Walking past them, I went into the bedroom and put on my clothes. Once I was done, I walked out of the room and made my way downstairs to the dining room. While I waited for them to come out I was feeling mixed emotions. I never would have thought that I would get down in a menage trois. I shook my head and smiled. *Damn, it was good, though.*

They walked into the dining room. "I'm sorry. But I have to get back to business. Are you all still interested in this property?"

Jasmine was about to say something but was cut off by Malik. "Yes we are," he replied, turning his head and looking at her.

"Yes. We will take it." She mirrored his answer.

Jasmine was standing there in obvious deep thought. It was written all over her face.

"Okay. I'll give you both a call tomorrow so you two can sign the paperwork." Grabbing my belongings and waiting for them to walk out first, I locked up the house, jumped into my car, and pulled off.

After making it home in thirty minutes, I walked into my three-bedroom house and put my keys down on the table. I made my way into the kitchen to pour myself a glass of wine.

*Shit I'ma need the whole bottle.*

I grabbed it at the neck and walked down my long hallway to my bedroom. I kicked off my heels and walked into the bathroom to turn on the water for my much needed bubble bath.

Stepping out of my clothes, I rubbed my fingers over my clit to find out that I was still wetter than ever. All I could do was think about Malik.

*Damn what a woman gotta do to get a man like that?*

I checked the water temperature before stepping in slowly. The heat of the water was making me horny. I needed him, shit I wanted him bad.

I took a drink of my wine and relaxed in the tub for a little while. Once I was done, all I wanted to do was go to sleep. My pussy was sore and I felt a headache coming on. I went into the medicine cabinet and grabbed my bottle of pain pills. I popped two into my mouth and used my hand to drink some water. After walking into my room and getting lotioned up, I put on an oversized tee shirt and jumped in bed.

The next morning I made it to the office around 10:00AM to work on Malik and Jasmine's paperwork.

Once I was done with their forms, I called their house phone. As the phone rang, I hoped Malik would answer because after that look his wife gave me yesterday, I didn't think she was my biggest fan anymore.

"Hello." A deep voice answered and I smiled.

I kept it professional although my thoughts were pornographic. "Mr. Harris, this is Kimberly, the realtor. I wanted to call you and let you and your wife know that we can schedule a Monday appointment to finalize everything."

"Stop calling me by my last name and call me Mal like you used to when I used to tickle your fancy." Malik laughed.

# Cum For Me

"Whatever, Malik. I don't think you have that kind of time."

"Let's see about that. Meet me at Westfield Culver City Mall at BJ's in an hour at the bar."

I was smiling from ear to ear. *Damn. I know I'm wrong but it feels so right.* "Okay, I'll be there." I hung up my phone, doing a happy dance in my seat. I jumped out my chair and walked into the bathroom so I could freshen up. Once I was done, I grabbed my purse and car keys, and walked out the door.

Making it there on time, I pulled up in VIP parking and gave the valet person my keys as he handed me a clip with a number on it.

I walked into the restaurant and spotted Malik at the bar looking at the game on the screen. I stood beside him. "Hey you," I purred.

"What's up, Kim?" He stood up to give me a hug that made me moan in his ear. I felt his dick jump at the sound of my voice.

"I saw you walking in. You look good, baby girl." He rubbed his hand down the sides of my arm. Malik leaned into me. "You look so good that I want to suck on your pussy until you beg me to stop".

"Oh, really," I replied, trying to hide the smile on my face.

"Yes and I want you to feel this dick inside that pussy the way you was thinking about it last night." Malik proposed.

"Who said I was thinking about you?" Who was I kidding? He was the reason I went to sleep so soundly. But I was still curious for his response.

"I was thinking about you," he cooly responded.

My pussy was calling for him to fuck me. I wanted him badly, and I had to have him. I was through with fronting. "There's a hotel down the street from here. Put your mouth where it needs to go." He didn't respond. "I see my cat already got your tongue." I laughed and asked the bartender for a Long Island ice-tea.

Malik laughed, "Shawdy, I'm about to punish that pussy. When I'm done with your little ass you will know who runs shit," he said, shaking his head and laughing some more.

Fifteen minutes later, we pulled into Marriott. Once inside, I waited in the lobby for Malik to pay for the room. He stepped my way and gave me a key with the room number.

"I'll be right back. Go upstairs and get ready to eat your words, shawdy. I want you on the bed with nothing on, playing in that pussy, getting it wet and hot for me."

I watched him walk out of the hotel as he jumped into his all black Tahoe truck and pulled off.

Once I was in the room, I went into the bathroom and took a shower to get freshened up. Then all these thoughts popped into my mind.

*Damn, you are so wrong for this in so many ways. He's married.* Then I thought *Girl, please his wife wasn't saying shit when you was eating her pussy, so why would she care today? Shit he shouldn't have such good dick then she wouldn't have to worry about sharing.*

Jumping out the shower and drying myself off, I walked into the bedroom and turned on the TV to see what was on while I lay in bed naked waiting on Malik to come back. About fifteen minutes later, Malik came walking in the room with a backpack in his hand.

## Cum For Me

He stood in front of the TV just looking at me. "Lay on your back," he commanded. Putting the backpack down, he got on his knees and opened my legs slowly as he nibbled at my inner thigh. Working his way up to my pussy, Malik dove in and I could not hold out if I tried.

I draped my legs over his shoulders and all I could do was moan. "Ahhhhhh, Uhhhhhhh, uhhhhhh, ooooooooooh, Malik, oooh, uhhhhh." He lifted my ass up off the bed and started to massage my ass cheeks while he sucked the shit out my pussy.

He stopped abruptly and stood up. "Malik," I panted. "Baby, stop playing."

"Oh, baby. I'm not done with you yet." Flashing a smile at me while stripping down out of his clothes, he picked me up and sat me on top of him. I slid down, wrapped my lips around his dick and went in. I played with the tip of his dick as he gently rubbed my shoulders. My body was heating up and his dick was getting harder. I pushed my head all the way down onto his dick using my tongue to lick his balls at the same time. Coming back up, I started bobbing on his dick and using my hands like a salt and pepper grinder. Looking in on this show, somebody would have thought I was trying to suck milk from his dick.

"Ummmm," Malik grabbed the back of my head while I was performing surgery on his dick. He released his nut in my mouth. And I swallowed every bit of it while looking up at him. He pulled me onto the bed, flipped me on my stomach and pushed his dick all the way into my pussy. It felt like I could not breathe, he was fucking me that hard. "Ooohhh, baby, fuck me! Yes, fuck this pussy! Punish this pussy, baby!" I called out.

"Shut the fuck up, bitch and take this dick or I'ma fuck you in your ass."

I wouldn't stop moaning for him to pulverize my pussy, so he quickly pulled his dick from my ever thumping punani.

"Now I want that ass. Tell me you want me to fuck you in your ass." He growled.

"Ohh, yes! Fuck me in my ass," I begged.

Pulling out, he punched it into my asshole. He fucked my ass so good all I could do was moan out how good it was. "Yes, baby, just like that."

"Who do you belong to now?" Malik asked as he pounded my ass and played with my pussy.

"I belong to you Malik!" His constant toying with my clit as he showed my back door no mercy sent me over the edge. "Yes, baby! I'm about to cum. Ooohhh, baby I can't take it no more I'm cumming!"

"Ooooohhh, yeah, baby. Cum for Daddy. Cum for Daddy."

I could feel his dick getting harder. I knew right then he was about to cum and he did right in my ass. All we could do was lay there. In no time we both were asleep like babies.

Not hearing the door being open, I felt like somebody was standing over me. I slowly opened my eyes and looked up to see Jasmine pointing a gun at us. I jumped and screamed, startling Malik awake to the same murderous image.

"What the fuck are you doing?" Malik was just as fearful as I.

"I told you I wasn't going to lose you again!" You left me once before behind since side pussy you couldn't leave alone. It's not happening again!" She yelled.

"Baby, put the damn gun down before you do something crazy." Malik slowly got up to ease the weapon from her shaking hands.

"Oh, you want to see crazy, motherfucker? I will show your ass crazy!" She screamed as she shifted the gun at both our heads.

I put my head down and said a silent prayer as the gun went off.

*Boc! Boc!*

## ***The End***

**Craving His Touch**
**By**
# *J Peach*

## Chapter 1

India sat on the bed in her hotel room, leaning against the headboard with a wide smile and a tight stomach as she cradled her cellphone between her ear and shoulder.

"You hear me, shawdy?" The deep, low, baritone voice broke through the other line, causing her sex muscles to contract.

Even with this feeling, she rolled her eyes while biting into her lower lip to contain her smile as if the man on the phone could see her.

"I hear you," she replied. She licked the bottom of her top lip, letting the smile seep into her voice.

"You hear me, but is you gon' do what I tell you?"

Again, she rolled her eyes. "Mhmmm," India mumbled to get under his skin.

"Mhmmm? Why you wanna play with me, shawdy? If I was out there, you know I would snatch yo ass up."

"Why, Jay'Shawn? I said I hear you."

"But, is you gon' do what I tell you?"

Looking at the phone, Indy shook her head as she gave in. She knew he wasn't playing and knowing he was coming back home tomorrow, she wasn't willing to test him or ruin the surprise she had for him.

India had met Jay'Shawn a year ago on Facebook. He was a friend of a friend. He had sent her a message trying see what was up with her and right away they clicked hard. Though they lived in two different states for the past two years it hadn't stopped them from talking on the phone or texting day in and day out.

"Yeah, I'mma do what you tell me," she replied with hesitation in her voice.

India hated how he was making her feel at the moment. She was tempted to hang up the phone on him. Even though she disliked the feelings, she knew the only reason she really said it was because they were on the phone. Truth be told, bending over for a man wasn't something she'd ever done in her entire life, but for some reason when it came to Jay'Shawn a part of her really wanted to.

His persistence, possessiveness and that no-bullshit attitude, mixed with his rough baritone voice which seemed to vibrate from the phone's speaker straight to her body made her give in a little.

"See, that wasn't hard. Why you always tryna make shit difficult? If you do as I say, we good," Jay'Shawn said, pulling India from her reverie. Taking her silence as a submissive agreement, he smiled to himself and continued. "You gon' give me some pussy, tonight?" This made her laugh out loudly, and she shook her head at the thought.

"No, Jay'Shawn, I'm not about to play with you tonight. No, No, No." The smile in her voice was evident and he knew he could talk her into it.

"How you gon' tell me *no*? That's my pussy ain't it?"

Her head shook as if he could see her gesture, and she continued to laugh. "Jay'Shawn, stop. Fo'real, I'm not about to go there with you tonight," she said, biting into her

169

lower lip. Her eyes rolled up in her head as she groaned at her contracting sexual muscles.

"You ain't answer my question, though. Ain't that my pussy?"

This is where her battle began. She wanted to say *nigga hell no this my shit,* but the constant throb of her pussy muscles, and the tightening of her lower stomach and pelvis caused her to be at a loss for words for a few seconds. All that could be heard from her end was heavy breathing.

"You hear me?" he asked as he waited for her to answer.

Licking her lips which had suddenly become dry, India cleared her throat as she closed her eyes and replied, "It's yours." She whispered.

Jay'Shawn heard her, but he wanted her to say it again. This time without hesitation. "That's my pussy?"

With a silent groan she complied and answered, "You know this your pussy."

Upon hearing those words, Jay'Shawn's lips formed into a smile. "Then give me *my* pussy."

With that, Indy put the phone on speaker and began scooting down on the bed until she lay flat on her back.

"Wrap yo' arms around my neck, stick yo' tongue out and give me a kiss." She complied with doing everything he'd told her to do.

India's eyes closed as her tongue slid between her slightly parted lips, slowly rubbing the bottom before caressing her lower fuller one.

"Take yo' panties off." He growled.

Once again, she quickly complied. She raised her hips up off of the bed as she pulled her boy-short panties down below her hips and thighs, pulling one leg out and then the other.

"You got 'em off?" His deep voice broke through the speaker.

Instantly, her legs widened, her hips raised slightly higher as her ass tightened from the sound of him.

"Yes," she replied with a whispered moan.

Jay'Shawn didn't hear her answer, but he knew the shaky pants all too well and knew she was ready.

"Close yo' eyes and imagine I'm there strokin' that pussy. Rub that clit, baby. Get that pussy nice and wet for me."

India moaned as her pearl swelled from her touch. She imagined it was Jay'Shawn's touch instead of her own. You like the way I play with that pussy?"

Jay'Shawn groaned out as he stroked his dick. Loving the sounds she made as her voice quivered filled with lust, he began rubbing pre-cum over his leaky mushroom tip. He gave it a slight squeeze as his hand went down and then back up his shaft.

"Yes, I love the way you play with my pussy. Spread yo' legs wide for me while I run my dick over that clit." He groaned into the phone as he pictured himself sliding inside of her throbbing sex. Vividly seeing the image in his mind, his eyes closed tighter as did the grip on his dick. Thrusting his hips in an upward motion, he once again groaned deeply. "Put two fingers in that pussy for me, baby. Yeah, like that. Just like that. I'm 'bout to bust this pussy open."

Moaning right along with him, India thrust two fingers deep inside her soaking sex as she envisioned Jay'Shawn stroking inside of her deep and hard. The images in her head were so vivid they caused her sex muscles to milk her fingers faster. Her chest began to rise and fall harder from her heavy panting.

"Mmm, Jaaay. Ooh, shit, baby. Just like that," India said, rolling her hips. She began grinding her pussy into her palm, causing the flat surface to rub against her clit. Ssss—.harder—harder."

At that very moment, their thoughts became one and both were feeling and seeing the same thing.

Jay'Shawn's strokes became harder as he placed India's legs on his shoulder, giving her deep strokes. Their pants, moans and groans mingled together on the phone as they both continued pleasing themselves.

India imagined digging her nails into the skin of his lower back while pulling him closer and even deeper inside of her. She could see her hands locked around his body as she grinded herself into him, craving to make them one.

"Ooooh, Jay'Shawn, ooooh, baby, like that. Oh, my God!" She cried out in sheer bliss. Biting into her full bottom lip, she imagined her sex muscles gripping around his dick.

He too imagined feeling the contraction of her pussy on him. Jay'Shawn then slowed his thrusting hips. He wasn't yet ready to lose his nut. "Turn around and push that ass up for me."

She rolled over and grabbed a pillow to press her forehead into. She spread her legs wide, dipped her back low and raised her ass high.

"You know I'm 'bout to tear this ass up don't you?" All India could do was moan in reply, unable to find her voice, as anticipation set deeply in her core. "Push them fingers in deep, knuckle deep."

India's fingers slid in and out of her pussy getting them wetter.

## Cum For Me

Jay'Shawn's vivid imagination allowed him to see her clearly, and he couldn't help but groan at the sight before him. Her light brown ass pushed up in the air gave a clear view of both her fat pussy and asshole. Though his hand strokes became faster, in his mind it wasn't the hand that was wrapped tightly around his dick causing it to pulse. It was the tightness of her womb trying to force his nut to come all too soon.

"Ah, shit! Work that pussy, Indy. Give Daddy his pussy." Jay'Shawn's demanding voice shook India to the core while taking her to her peak.

"Ooh, Jaay. Daddy I'm cummin'." India moaned loudly as her fingers moved in and out of her heated sex, feverishly hitting that sweet spot. Her hips shook and rolled as she rode out her orgasm. "Ooh, ooh, baby. Oh, my God!" Her shaky moans left her mouth and her lower body continued to jerk.

Hearing her hard moans, Jay'Shawn got even more excited. He squeezed his mushroom tip then stroked up and down his dick, reaching his own mind boggling orgasm.

"Ah, shit, mmm." A long moan started deep in his throat as he released all over his hand.

She too was feeling satiated. India lay panting, catching her breath from their steamy phone sex.

But with the images of India's glistening core embedded in his head from the constant Skyping they'd been doing, he knew exactly how that pussy was looking. And he was ready for another round. Those thoughts caused him to become erect once again. This time, he wanted to taste her sweet nectar. The urge was so bad that his mouth ached as his throat became dry. With his eyes closed tightly, his mind and body fell deeper.

He could see himself licking and feasting from her swollen pearl, down her slit to the opening of her vagina. With his face pressed against her sex swollen lips, as his tongue would thrust deeply inside of her pussy. He would let his tongue swirl around and around, stroking her still sensitive core.

He was so turned up, she had to join him for another one. "Get those fingers drippin' wet, baby." Jay'Shawn instructed in a deep but low-spoken masculine voice.

Still on fire, she didn't hesitate. "Okay, baby." India's panting voice spoke through the line.

"Rub that asshole for me, baby. Get it wet," he directed. The groan from the other end brought a smile to his face. "Nuh, uh, baby. Don't go doing all that. You know I'm 'bout to be all in that ass tonight. Now, gone get that ass wet for me."

Doing as she was told, India groaned out loud once again. She didn't know how much longer she could take it without erupting like a lava filled volcano.

Without a doubt, she loved their playtime, but she was ready for him to be with her, in her. That's precisely why she flew out from Chicago and down to Memphis. She wanted to surprise him and make their talks reality.

She wanted him flesh to flesh because playtime was becoming almost painful. But there would be no more waiting, they were only days away from his release.

The mere thought of being able to finally touch him made her body ache more, making her want to cum even harder. With her ass still in the air, coating two fingers with her juices, India brought her now dripping fingers to her anus, getting the little hole wet.

The sound from her mouth told Jay'Shawn that she wasn't comfortable.

## Cum For Me

"N'all, baby girl. You gotta relax. You can't be doing all that," Jay'Shawn chimed in, stopping her movement.

India looked up only to stare at an empty room which caused her brows to furrow. *How the hell did he know?* She mentally questioned herself and received an answer to her unasked question.

"Yo' breathing and all that shit changed. I ain't gotta be around to know what the fuck you doin'. I done already told you, shawdy, we been doin' this too damn long for me not to pick up on shit like that. Now gone relax, I got you." Instinctively, her body relaxed and she bit into her lower lip loving the sound of his voice "Now, gon' get that ass wet for me."

As if he could see her, she nodded while rubbing her hot spot. Once her fingers were good and wet, they found their way back to her anus.

"Push two fingers inside yo' ass,"

India's eyes closed and she moaned as she inserted two fingers inside of her ass. From there, their anal play started.

India's fingers moved in and out of her ass, fast and hard. Her fingers opened and closed, causing her anus to stretch beyond its natural width. She was doing everything Jay'Shawn commanded of her through the phone while her other hand played with her clit. She pinched, rubbed and spanked the swollen pearl until her ass and pussy muscles began tightening. Her body shook violently as she reached her peak with a loud pleasurable moan. "Ah, shit! Ahhhh, shit!"

Jay'Shawn's deep, long grunt came from the speaker soon after. His nuts tightened and his toes curled as he reached that high, feeling himself climax. Sperm squirted from his pee hole and landed onto his stomach.

"Mmm, Oh, my God," India continued to moan lowly as she lay flat on the bed from exhaustion.

Hearing the lustful moan caused Jay'Shawn to laugh out. He knew he had once again taken her to the point of no return. "I know damn well yo' ass ain't 'bout to fall to asleep."

She nestled herself even more in the comfort of the bed. Now, fully relaxed, she still managed to sound out a light moan before fully replying, "Shut up. I'm not sleep."

Jay'Shawn laughed as he got up with his phone, headed to the sink area clean himself up. "Yo' lying ass, I could hear yo' ass snoring."

Laughing, India sat up in the bed. She could hear the water running in his background.

"I wasn't even sleep, so how could you hear me snoring? Man, whatever. Shut the fuck up," she said, making her way into her own bathroom. She laid a towel on the floor then stood on it before turning the water on in the sink. She proceeded to clean up as well. Even after releasing just minutes ago, her pussy was still pulsating and her body still slightly trembled.

*Damn!* she moaned.

## Chapter 2

**D**ays later, Jay'Shawn had been released from a prison out in Memphis, Tennessee after having served a two year sentence for a parole violation. But being locked up for those twenty-four months did nothing to knock his hustler's mentality because the moment he touched down, he and a friend drove out to Cali to meet up with a drug connect.

India felt put off when she learned of his trip. Although he didn't know she was in town waiting on him there She felt as though he could've made the drive to come to her hometown in Chicago like they discussed instead of risking more trouble.

Although she was angry about his decision, she kept her feelings to herself to prevent starting an argument with him. "When am I gonna see you now?" She hoped that he would say a day or so which would prevent her trip there being done in vain.

Running a hand over his head, he dreaded having to be honest. His initial plan was to head to Chi-Town to get his shawdy, but some other shit had fallen into his lap a few days before his release that he couldn't bypass.

His boy, Benny, had the hook up to cop some work out in Cali. It was supposed to be an in and out deal to put guap in both of their pockets. Jay'Shawn would get paid and then make it out to India, on boss status.

But the day they hit the state and called for the meet, the nigga they were supposed to link up with had gotten his spot hit. After learning this, Jay'Shawn was ready to head back home. He had a bad feeling in the pit of his stomach and wanted out of the shit, period. But somehow he let Benny talk him into staying until he found another connect.

The fact that Jay'Shawn really didn't want to go back empty handed was reason enough for him to stay until he was straight.

"To be honest, shawdy, I don't even know." With a long drawn out sigh, he decided to come clean and tell India the truth regarding his stay, and the shit that had happened. He explained to her exactly how he was feeling and held nothing back. He told her everything.

Once he was done talking, India had a gut feeling that something wasn't right. *If the connect got busted they were shit outta luck, but why would Benny even suggest finding someone else?*

"How long Benny been knowing these cats? I mean, does he normally deal with folks out there?" She was still pissed that he kited to the West coast without stopping in the Midwest, but she was overall concerned for him.

"From my understanding n'all, he don't know nobody out here like that. Shitt, he met dude through another nigga."

India's face formed into a snare at his words. "Jay, are you serious right now? So, he's in a city where he knows no one and he's talkin' about finding someone else to deal with? Hell no, Jay'Shawn! Bae, get outta there. Please, listen to me. I don't like the sound of this. It just don't seem right. I'm not tryna say yo' boy on some bullshit, but baby, I don't trust this shit at all. Not at all. Jay'Shawn, get the hell out of that state now," India said, grabbing her laptop and pulling up a web page for plane tickets out of the LAX.

As she was doing her thing on the computer, Jay'Shawn took heed to her warning. In fact, he had actually had the same bad feeling. He just kept it to himself. Subconsciously, he grabbed his twin 9mm and checked the magazines. He took the safety off of both guns and put one in each chamber.

"Bae, if you can make it to the airport within a half hour you can catch the 12:30AM flight back to Memphis or there's one leaving at 2:45AM."

Jay'Shawn's heart did a double beat in his chest from the concern in Indy's voice. He had to admit that getting to know her better over the past year on a deeper level made him feel as though she had his ass wrapped around her finger. He felt as though India was the balance he needed to keep him from losing himself fully to the streets. He had someone to come home to, and a woman he could see himself falling in love with. Hell, sometimes he could possibly see himself marrying her. He was already feeling the love and hadn't even psychically touched her ass yet.

"N'all, baby, I can't catch no damn flight. I'ma have to drive out this bitch. I wasn't even supposed to leave the state."

Hearing him say what she already knew pissed India off, and she didn't hesitate in agreeing with him. "That's exactly what I was thinking, Jay. That was dumb as hell on your part anyways. I mean to fuckin' leave knowing you not supposed to, then for this shit to happen on top of that. You staying down there is fuckin' stupid, period."

"Aye, who the fuck yo' ass think you talkin' to, Indy? You better lower your fuckin' voice. Yellin' like you done lost yo' goddamn mind! I know what the fuck I'm doing." Jay snapped.

India rolled her eyes up in her head. "Obviously not." Her attitude didn't go unnoticed.

Jay'Shawn looked at the phone and his brows raised in aggravated frustration. "Shawdy, don't make me leave here just to come to Chi-Town and yank yo' lil' ass up! Cool that shit, real talk, baby girl. You hear me?"

India knew the way she was coming at him wasn't cool, but she really couldn't hide her attitude. Just the simple fact of him knowing he shouldn't have taken his dumb ass down there in the first place without first getting some background on them niggas was enough to make her livid.

"Whatever, Jay'shawn, I'm not 'bout to argue with you. The point is, you need to get yo' black ass back to Memphis." Letting out a heavy breath, she got out of bed in search of some clothes. "Or I can catch a flight—"

"What the fuck you gon' catch a flight out here fah?" Jay'Shawn angrily cut her off.

India couldn't understand why he was getting mad at her when all she wanted to do was help him out by getting his stupid ass out of a state he had no business being in to begin with.

"I was planning on flying out to yo' simple ass and helping you drive back, but whatever, Jay. You obviously got this. So you figure this bullshit out." She was ready to leave Memphis and head back home.

"When I see yo' ass just know, I'ma slap the fuck outta you." His threat rolled off his tongue with deep promise.

It didn't seem to faze India, though. It was nothing more than bullshit, phone talk to her. "Fuck you, Jay'Shawn! Nigga, you can try it if you want to. Get the fuck off my phone, stupid ass." She pressed the end button without giving him a chance to reply. After ending the call, she tossed her phone on the bed then threw her body across the bed.

## Cum For Me

It wasn't long afterwards when she heard Trey Songz' jam *Foreign* playing from the speakers as the phone rang. Looking at the phone seeing Jay'Shawn's name, India rolled her eyes. She was not in the mood to argue with him more than she had. Instead, she chose to ignore his call, get comfortable in bed and push his fucked up attitude to the back of her mind.

She tried to fall asleep, but it wasn't coming easily. Worry began to root its wicked self in the pit of her stomach. So, she silently prayed for him to be okay and make it out of that city in one piece.

## Chapter 3

It was one o'clock in the morning and he had no idea where he would go, but he knew he couldn't stay in the room pissed off. With India not answering his phone calls, sitting alone was only going to make his blood boil even more.

India only spoke what he already knew, but it pissed him off that it took her to spit game at him in order for him to get up and actually make a move. Even though he hated to believe or even think Benny was on some foul shit, it was starting to look that way.

Jay'Shawn decided he'd walk three doors down to Benny's room. His hand raised up, ready to rap on the door, but he caught himself as he heard voices mumbling from the other side.

He made out his mans' talking to a female. Figuring Benny had found a shorty to smash, Jay'Shawn was about to head back to his room when the voices became louder. Instinctively, he stood there and listened.

"Ben, I don't know why the fuck you wanna wait. The more time we spend waiting gives him more time to think shit ain't right. We shoulda done this the first night y'all got here." The girl said.

"Kristy, if you don't lower yo' fuckin' voice, I'll break yo' fuckin' neck." Benny snapped at the female he'd met at a club in Hollywood over two years ago.

Kristy was Cali born and bred. Ever since that night they had become tight. Thick as thieves, even. The stayed hitting licks together. Their biggest hit would've been Tremaine, the connect Benny and Jay'Shawn were supposed to meet the night they arrived in town.

## Cum For Me

The plan was to kill him and set Jay'Shawn up for the rap. But with Tremaine's spot getting hit by the police it set them back. Now they had to wait until the heat of the hit cooled down before they made their move.

Benny could tell Jay'Shawn was starting to get antsy about being down in Cali too long, especially with him just being released, and now this shit. He knew he had to make his move and quickly. The one thing he knew for sure was he couldn't let Jay'Shawn go back to Memphis alive. While Jay'Shawn was on lock, Benny had been running shit, not by his self though.

Jay was still the nigga calling shots from behind bars and he didn't like that at all. He'd gotten a small taste of what being a boss was like. Having niggas at yo' beck and call, willing to die or kill a nigga with the quickness for you. He wanted that, to feel that power for himself and by himself.

A part of him knew the only reason niggas showed him respect was because he was Jay'Shawn's boy. But greed consumed Benny's soul, he needed the money, power, and respect off of his own merit. Not Jay'Shawn!

"Don't tell me you 'bout to *bitch out* on me now, Kris baby?" Benny asked as he stood walking toward her.

"No, I'm not. I'd never do that, but bae if he's smart like you say he is, why give him time to figure shit out? You already told him you didn't know anybody out here. Benny, if you don't know anyone, how the hell do you expect to find another connect? At least introduce me to him so he can think I'm the one introducing you to the people out here," explained Kristy. She took ahold of his face, slowly kissing his lips.

Once their lips touched she had to hold back from gagging, but the urge quickly went away and a sinister smile covered her face as she imagined emptying the clip of her baby .380 in his face.

They had been cool up until that point. The moment Kristy learned of Benny's plan to kill his best friend, Jay'Shawn, someone he had known since the third grade, she set one of her own plans in motion because she couldn't respect or trust a nigga who would cross his mans. She knew it was only a matter of time before he would be plotting against her as well.

"I'll introduce you to him in the morning, after that we'll try to get up with Tremaine. I'm tryna have this shit done by tomorrow night," Benny concluded.

"Okay," she replied. She was ready to make moves as well. With a wide smile, she thought about the money she was about to inherit.

On the other side of the door, the man they planned to rob was formulating his counter plan.

## Chapter 4

Having overheard everything that had been said, Jay'Shawn knew Benny was on some bullshit. It fucked him up because they had been boys since playground days. Now, in his eyes Benny was just like every other nigga, not to be trusted.

Turning around Jay'Shawn headed for the stairs. Quickly bouncing down them two at a time, he headed out on foot to the nearest gas station.

Arriving at a Shell Station, he grabbed a bottle of bleach, latex gloves and trash bags. With his items in his hand, he checked out trying his hardest to avoid the cameras. Once he was done, he quickly made his way back to his motel room.

He went inside and put on a pair of latex gloves, then he stripped the bed of its comforter, sheets and pillow cases. Then, he proceeded to stuff them inside one of the large trash bags. He walked in the bathroom and pulled out two face towels, placing them in the bag as well. When he had everything inside the trash bag, he tied it tightly, then sat it off to the side before he cleaned the bathroom, the toilet, the sink and the tub.

Leaving out of the bathroom, he went into the main room wiping off everything he'd touched, including the TV, remote, light switch, door knob, lamp and the table.

It was 3:15AM By the time Jay'Shawn was done, but the room was white glove ready. After taking his luggage and garbage bags to the truck, he threw them in the back and went to Benny's room.

***

The moans from the room let him know they were still awake. Jay'Shawn gave the door three hard rips. The knocks caused both Kristy and Benny to jump hard.

"Who the fuck is it," Benny snapped, pushing Kristy off of him as her eyes rolled up in her head. She could feel an attitude forming deeply inside her core.

"Nigga, it's me. Open the goddamn door!" Jay'Shawn's deep baritone voice replied.

Not thinking anything of it Benny quickly snatched the door open.

"Shawn?" replied Benny's confused voice as he opened the door. "What the fuck you doing out here? Nigga, do you know what time it is?" he questioned, not even noticing the look on his boy's face.

Turning his back on Jay'Shawn, he went to the other side of the room to slip on his boxers. It wasn't until he didn't get a reply that he took his mans in. "You good Shawn? What's goin' on man?" he questioned, tilting his head sideways.

Jay'Shawn mimicked his move. "I don't know G, you tell me. What's up?"

Benny moved to sit on the bed, but Jay'Shawn grabbed his Nines with the silencers and pointed one at him, and the other at Kristy. "Nuh, uh bitch, don't even think about it," he spat out menacingly. A bullet had already been put inside the chamber, so all he had to do was squeeze the trigga and let the bitch rip into both of their heads and faces.

"Jay'Shawn, man, what the fuck you doin'? Chill with that bullshit—" Benny stopped talking in mid-sentence when Jay'Shawn took steps toward him. His brows furrowed. He was trying to understand what was going on. He knew Jay'Shawn didn't know shit, so why the fuck was he suddenly bugging out?

"Fuck you, B! I knew shit wasn't right when we got to this bitch." Jay'Shawn spat.

"But you was my nigga." Benny shook his head with his hands raised.

Thinking Benny now had Jay'Shawn's full attention, Kristy slowly scooted to the edge of the bed, waiting on the right moment to grab her gun from the drawer.

Benny continued, "What the fuck you talkin' 'bout, folk? Look, I know you on edge about being out here with everything that happened, but I found this other cat out in Oakland who got some work," explained Benny.

When Jay stopped and looked as if he was listening, Benny thought he had his hooks once again embedded deeply inside Jay'Shawn.

"So you ain't on no shady shit?" Jay asked with a raised brow, locking eyes with Benny.

"Hell n'all! Especially not with you, man. We been boys all our lives, man. Hell n'all!" exclaimed Benny, shaking his head as if the mere idea of it was downright stupid.

"Put it on all you love if you ain't on no bullshit," said Jay'Shawn.

"I put it on all I love," vowed Benny.

Jay'Shawn chuckled, silently dismissing that nigga's vow. He pointed his gun at Kristy and pumped three shots into her head.

*Boc! Boc! Boc!*

Her head exploded in a burst of red and her body slumped down to the floor.

"Jay? What the fuck nigga?" Benny screamed out as he ran to Kristy's limp body. "Man, I ain't on no bullshit!"

"Fuck you, G. You a pussy ass nigga!" On that note, he put four hollow points in Benny's head. Once he slumped over, Jay'Shawn didn't hang around.

## Chapter 5
One Month Later

India met up with her best friend at the mall. After some shopping, they ended up in the food court. Aria was interested in catching up on her love life.

"What's going on with you and Jay'Shawn? I haven't heard you talking about him as much?" India's best friend Aria asked.

"There's nothing to really tell. I mean, that nigga crazy, and I just can't. He sometimes says and does dumb shit not thinking about the after effects of his words."

After the argument she and Jay'Shawn had when he was in Cali, India decided fell back a little. She was still really feeling him but sometimes he would be hard to deal with.

"I get it kinda, but from the way you two talked I thought it was serious, but I guess not. He seemed hella cool, though," Aria mentioned.

"Bitch, how the fuck you sound? He seemed hella cool? Yo' ass never talked to him, so how the fuck would you know?" India asked, laughing.

Aria simply rolled her eyes. "Bitch, I did talk to him once on the phone. I actually talked to him the other day while you were playing," Aria said, faking an attitude.

Hearing her say she talked to Jay'Shawn made India suspicious. She knew her girl would never be on no shiesty shit, but what did they have to talk about?

Catching her girl's attitude, she couldn't help but rub it in. "He sounded hella good too. Nigga had a bitch dripping from the words *what's up?* Shittt, I was a few seconds away from asking if he wanted my phone virginity.

You know I ain't never had phone sex before but a bitch was ready to have her cherry popped."

Though India wanted to be mad she couldn't help but laugh at her friend's silly personality. "You play too much. I hope you didn't tell him nothin' about me 'cause I'm not talkin' to him right now," India confessed. From the furrow of Aria's brows and the slight width she added to her eyes, India knew her ass had done something. "You did, didn't you?"

Aria's phone vibrated which it had been doing for the past half hour. "No, I haven't. Look, I gotta go to the bathroom I'll be back."

"No the fuck you don't. Aria, what did you do?" India asked with seriousness in her tone.

All Aria could do was open and close her mouth like a fish. She didn't want to spoil the surprise. Once again her mouth opened then closed before a relieved breath left her parted lips. "Nothing. Damn, yo' ass need to chill. I was just messing with you. Well, I did talk to him only because he was with Martell. He just asked about you is all. I told him you was good. That's it. Now can I go to the bathroom, please?"

Though India only halfway believed her, she let her go. "That's all yo' ass better had said too," she commented with a roll of her neck and eyes.

"That shit ain't cute, yo' fuckin' eyes gonna get stuck."

India's head couldn't have turned around fast enough from the deep voice she knew all too well. Hell, the voice she had masturbated to so many times over the past year.

"Jay'Shawn?" India managed to get out before she was pulled up from her seat.

## Cum For Me

"So, you avoiding me now, Indy? A nigga can't get no conversation no more, huh? It's just fuck me now, huh?"

Aria let out a loud laugh as she watched her best friend become speechless. India always had a mouth piece on her so seeing her like this was comical. She could also see her girl was glad to see Jay'Shawn. A man couldn't be soft or weak messing with her friend, and Aria could tell he was neither.

"Well, I'm gon' leave now. It was nice meeting you Jay'Shawn."

Finally, looking at Aria, he gave a head nod. "You too, shawdy. Good looking." He thanked her.

Giving him a little smile, Aria waved bye to them both before she left and headed home.

"So, you don't know how to answer the phone, Indy?" he asked. Getting herself together she tried to shrug his hands off of her only to have them tighten on her forearm.

"Let me go, Jay'Shawn. You should've told me you was coming instead of trying to piss me off all the time." India snapped. She was happy he was there, but at the same time mad because he hadn't told her he was coming.

"Who the fuck is you talkin' to?"

Rolling her eyes she bit into her lower lip as she glanced up at him. Not able to contain her excitement any longer, she threw her arms around his neck and held him tightly. Happy to be actually holding him, she smiled from ear to ear but leave it to Jay'Shawn to fuck with her good mood.

"Hell n'all. Get the fuck off me. Shittt, don't get excited now. When just a week ago yo' ass wasn't tryna give a nigga no fuckin' play. I came down here just to fuck you up. Real shit, shawdy. Don't ever do no bullshit like that, you hear me."

Not really listening or caring for his choice of words, she nodded her head. All she wanted to do was hold him. She still couldn't believe he was standing in front of her.

"Don't act like that. You know you're just as excited to see me as I am to see you, so stop playin' and give me a kiss." Standing on her tip toes, India puckered up her full sized lips while wrapping her arms around his neck.

Pissed and all, Jay'shawn couldn't deny the fact he was just as excited to be seeing her. He decided he was gonna let her ignoring his calls slide for right now, but she was gonna definitely pay for the shit later.

Right now, he just wanted to talk, to see if their chemistry was just as strong in person as it had been over the phone.

# Cum For Me

## Chapter 6

Two hours after Jay'Shawn's arrival, the pair found themselves in a dimly lit Chinese Restaurant, sitting in the far back enjoying each-other's company. They talked about any and everything as they laughed and even argued about the smallest things. All in all, they were having a good time.

"How long are you staying here?" India asked. Pushing her plate away, she leaned forward with her elbows on the table. She intertwined her fingers and stared at Jay'Shawn while he answered.

"Damn, you tryna get rid of me already, huh? A nigga just touched down and you ready for my ass to leave? Let me find out you got a nigga 'round here somewhere. I'ma fuck the both of y'all up," Jay'Shawn threatened, making her laugh as she rolled her eyes. "Roll 'em again I'ma pop 'em out." He smirked.

Just to mess with him, she did it again but harder and this time a bit longer. He quickly, but playfully hopped out of his seat.

"Okay, okay. I quit fo' real. We not 'bout to play in here. Gon' now. Sit down somewhere."

Ignoring India's protest, he slipped in the booth beside her. Using his feet, he moved the table over a bit. India rolled her eyes as she watched him get comfortable while scooting down in the seat.

"So, you think it's cool to avoid me? You feel just because you mad and feeling some type of way you don't gotta answer the fuckin' phone?" The question caught India off guard because she thought they had moved passed that.

"Yeah, you pissed me off and I thought you was just making excuses for not wanting to see me, so I didn't wanna talk to you for a minute. I was just gon' fall back and let you do what you wanted to do. It's as simple as that," India told him truthfully. If he wasn't going to try and make an effort, she was just going to let him go and keep their relationship as a friendship-only thing.

She had been thinking on it for the past week and if he hadn't showed up, then their fate would have been sealed as just friends indefinitely.

"You gon make me knock the shit out yo' ass. You ever do some shit like that again, I'ma fuck you up. Real shit, shawdy." A promising threat was thick in his voice. It was one that told her she better not say shit else smart because he was still hot about her actions. But being the stubborn, smart mouth woman she was, she had to reply.

"Whatever, man. Next time don't be playin' so damn much because I was 'bout to say fuck this whole thing. I swear I was. My body was already goin' through detox."

"Why the fuck you wanna test me? All yo' ass had to say was *okay Jay'Shawn* and be done with it. Yo' ass gotta make shit difficult tho'. That's a'ight, I'ma have that ass in line in no time."

India's lips twisted to the side still not believing what he was saying. There had been guys before him who tried to put her in check but India was simply too hot-headed for all that. Most niggas just didn't have the patience to deal with her. To India, they were simply too weak to handle a strong minded chick such as herself. If it was one thing she couldn't deal with, it was a nigga who was softer than her. She was hot tempered and needed someone who could deal with her, not run, whine or cry about the shit she did. India wanted a man to stand up to her, not bail out of an argument before she did.

## Cum For Me

With Jay'Shawn, she felt like he could be that anchor that kept her in check, but at the same time she really didn't know. So, she was going to push his buttons. Her intentions were to let shit slide today because this was their first encounter and she really didn't want to ruin it.

"I don't need to be in line. I'm fine." The slight glare coming from his face caused her to end her sentence with a laugh before turning the conversation in a different direction. "No, seriously though, I'm glad you came down here."

Grabbing his hand, she gave it a slight squeeze as she stared at him. Catching eye contact with Jay'Shawn, India looked down with twisted lips, trying to keep the smile from spreading across her lips. A laugh escaped her throat before spilling from her mouth.

"You knew I was coming down here. Yo' ass just had to act the fuck up to get me here faster."

*If I knew avoiding him was gonan have his ass here in a week I would've done this shit while he was still incarcerated,* she thought. *Maybe that would've brought his dumbass here instead of Cali.* Staring at him, she said nothing in reply.

India just gazed at him trying to figure out why him? How someone she'd met online had her feeling as if they had known each other for years. She'd have this giddy feeling form in the pit of her stomach. The feeling had her lower abdomen so tight it caused her pelvis to shiver. These feelings had India thinking this could be a forever type thing.

Even so the thought of him not being able to deal with her stubbornness was still in question. Was Jay'Shawn man enough to really deal with a hot-headed, short tempered India?

Jay'Shawn stared at India with the same thoughts in mind. He didn't know if she could really handle him or his life style. A hood nigga was all he was, all he knew how to be. The hood mentality was embedded deeply in his soul, and he didn't know if India was emotionally strong enough to deal with that. His selfish side said it didn't matter if she was or not.

India was the first female he'd ever clicked with on a personal level and allowed his feelings to get involved. Shit had to be serious if he took a fuckin' eight hour drive to her just because she wouldn't answer the damn phone. He had every intention on coming there to beat her ass for that bullshit, but that plan failed once he saw her.

"Come here." His head jerked to the side slightly as he motioned for her to come to him.

Scooting closer to him, Indian leaned forward ready to kiss him, thinking that's what he wanted and it was, but it wasn't the only thing.

"What the hell are you doing? Let me go." Before their lips could touch, India was being pulled into his lap in a straddling position.

"Shut up. Why you gotta be loud? Ain't nobody thinkin' 'bout us. Now, gimme a kiss."

Looking around, she saw no one paying them any attention. Plus, they were in the far back of the restaurant with little light, barely noticeable. Turning her gaze back toward him, she laughed lightly.

"You play too much. I could've kissed you from my seat."

Even though she'd made the statement, her lips puckered up in a playful manner. Jay'Shawn couldn't help but laugh at her silliness as he too leaned forward, pressing his lips to hers. The contact of their lips quickly erased the feelings of playfulness with feelings of lust and love. India pecked his lips once then twice, letting her mouth linger on his for a few seconds longer before she made a move to pull back. Once she did, Jay'Shawn caught her bottom lip between his teeth as his hand found the nape of her neck, pulling her back down to him.

Sucking on her top then bottom lip, India's mouth opened allowing his tongue entrance. Their tongues soon started their own intimate dance, causing low moans to sound in the back of India's throat, as well as her hips to start a slow grind on him.

Jay'Shawn's hand moved down her back, landing on her ass. Lifting her up slightly, he began messing with his jeans. India tried pulling herself out of her lustful state, but found it hard to do. Truth be told, it had been a long time coming and she wanted him. Her desire to feel him was so strong her body had made her mind up for her.

Even though she wanted him in the worst way, she still felt the need to protest. Grabbing his wrists, she broke their kiss, only pulling back slightly so her tongue could play with his lips. "Jay, we can't." The words came out just above a whisper against his mouth.

Jay'Shawn's head leaned forward trying to catch her lips once more, but she pulled out of his reach just as he released himself from his jeans.

Feeling the head of him pressing against her covered sex had India lowering herself back down him. "Shawn, not in here." The pressure from his erect dick added to her swollen clit, had India biting at his bottom lip and her hips moving a bit faster. She had him gripped tightly around his wrists.

"How the fuck you gon' say not here and you doin' this bullshit?" Jay'Shawn questioned as serious as hell. She had him fucked up if she thought fuckin' with him like that and then saying *not here* was gonna stop him. She seriously didn't know the nigga she was with and he was about to show her just that. You couldn't play with a man like him then cry wolf. If he had thought for a minute she was serious, yeah he'd stop, but the fact that her hips were still rolling and the tip of her tongue continued to play with his lips said otherwise.

    India couldn't respond to what he was saying because her voice alone would've given away her intentions. She knew what her body wanted just as much as Jay'Shawn did. There was no point in trying to continue denying them both a quickie. It was all their bodies needed.

    Jay'Shawn's finger hooked the crouch of her panties, pulling them to the side. Once he did that, India handled his dick, stroking it from the base to the leaky tip, giving it a slight squeeze. India locked their lips, as she ran the mushroom head along her slit a few times before placing it at her opening.

    Gripping her hips, holding them tightly, his hips pushed up at the same time hers came down. The action had India breaking the kiss and her mouth parting as she breathed him in, taking the breath he'd exhale from the feel of her.

    "Fuck!" Jay'Shawn groaned out from the tight grip her pussy held on his dick. He watched as India's head rolled lazily to the side, her mouth still parted, hips rolling slowly before grinding hard on him.

    Leaning back against the table, her hand came out in front of her and gripped the front of his shirt, grabbing his skin as she did so.

"Ooh." India lowly moaned as Jay'Shawn rocked her hips faster on him, trying to bring them both to that orgasmic high.

The table rocked noticeably as Jay'Shawn's hips thrust in an upward motion, causing India's ass to hit it. The sound of their bodies coming together grew louder as did India's moans with every hit he made to her sweet spot.

"Ah, shit," Jay'Shawn groaned out. His forearms slipped underneath her thighs and he began raising India up and bringing her back down on his dick even faster. For a minute he'd forgotten where they were and was ready to lay her on top of the table until India wrapped her arms around his neck bringing her mouth to his ears.

"Ah, ah, yes! Yea. Mmm. Sssss. Ooh you feel so good." She gasped and moaned in his ear before biting at his lobe then moving to his neck sucking, biting, panting and moaning as her fingernails dug deeply in the top back of his head.

Her moans had him picking up the pace, but the way her pussy gripped and squeezed around his dick had him damn near losing his mind as he felt his nut coming closer. India worked her inner sex muscles, clenching and unclenching, milking his dick. Her body soon tightened, causing her lower half to shake as her pussy contracted faster.

"Oh, God." India's lips pressed into his neck to muffle her scream of pleasure as she rode out her orgasm. With the shaking of her body, the tightening of her inner walls, Jay'Shawn's nails dug into her thigh. His hips jerked upwards, sending India's body bouncing three more times as he released his nut inside of her with a long low groan.

Panting heavily, neither moved as they held onto each other trying to regain their breaths. India soon let out a faint whine. What they had just done and where they had done it began breaking through the lustful haze she was in. Feeling embarrassed about their public display, her face tucked deeper into his neck, not wanting to get up just in case anyone had saw them.

From the constant low whines India kept letting out, he quickly caught on to her embarrassment. Laughing, he slapped her on the ass hard. That caused her to sit up straight and punch him in the chest.

"Stop, stupid ass, That shit hurt!" She snapped, kinda pissed from the unexpected hit.

"Shut the fuck up. You know you like that shit." Staring at him hard, she ended up laughing from the serious look on his face.

"N'all, shawdy, you gotta be still or you gonna wake him back up fully and I'ma have yo' ass folded on this fuckin table."

Biting the bottom of her lips, she tightened her pussy muscles on him as she leaned forward, letting her tongue flicker over his top lip before pulling the bottom lip inside her mouth. Feeling him twitch inside her, India's hand slid between their bodies. Raising her hips, she pulled his stiffening dick from her pussy, stroking him then giving the head a slight squeeze.

"This how you gonna play it?" Jay'Shawn asked with a nod of his head, not caring for her reply.

"I'm not playing. I was just about to get up and didn't want your business all out," was India's explanation though he didn't believe shit she was saying.

Without a word he got up from his seat, pulling money from his pocket. Throwing a few bills on the table, he grabbed India's hand, pulled her from the booth and began dragging her out of the restaurant.

"Jay, stop pullin' me."

Ignoring her, he continued to make his was out of the restaurant.

"For real?"

Again, she didn't get a reply as they made it outside. Jay'Shawn looked around for a few seconds before locating his truck. Once he spotted the Lincoln Navigator, his steps became more determined until they reached it. Hitting the alarm and unlocking the door, he snatched the back door open.

"Get in." Without giving her a chance to get in, he pushed her in the backseat.

Once they both were inside, he reached in the front, started the truck and turned on the air before settling back.

He wasted no time pulling her shirt and bra off before pushing India on her back. Gripping her skirt and panties, he pulled them down her hips and then off. Tossing them to the side, he pulled off his shirt then unbuckled his jeans.

This had most definitely been a long time coming. He wanted to go slow but now that he'd gotten a feel of how she felt on him, slow wasn't an opinion at this moment.

India had no complaints toward his eagerness, and her mind was in tune with his.

She then sat on her knees and leaned forward, grabbing his dick. She stroked it from the base to the mushroom shaped head. Covering the tip with her palm, she smeared pre-cum over his tip before taking her hand back down his base while bringing her mouth to his head. Kissing the tip once then twice, her tongue shot out flicking over the leaky hole, getting a taste of him. She moaned at the salty flavored liquid seeped out. After licking around his rim, her mouth opened and engulfed his head as she cupped his balls. India teased his dick, sucking on the head as if it was a sucker, licking over it trying to savor the flavor before taking him inch by inch inside her mouth. She took him so deep, her lips kissed his pelvis and his tip touched the back of her throat.

"Ah, fuck!" Jay'Shawn groaned out, grabbing a handful of India's hair. His grip tightened as her jaws sunk in and her head began to bob back and forth. India's wet mouth caused her slurping to sound louder before she released him with a pop. Spitting on his dick her hands stroked him as her mouth found its way to his sack. Taking his balls inside of her mouth, she sucked and moaned at the same time her hands squeezed around the rim of his dick.

"Ooh, shit!" Jay knew if he didn't stop her soon he'd be cummin' again. Even so, the shit felt amazingly good. From the way she tongued his dick then swallowed his shit, it had him wanting to release his nut down her throat. The way her warm mouth wrapped around his sack had his balls tightening along with the way his legs locked up and his toes curled. Jay'Shawn was about to lose his mind.

The grip on her hair tightened as he pulled her off his dick, quickly turning her around and grabbing the back of her neck. He pushed her forehead into the seat as he positioned himself behind her. Spreading her ass cheeks, he slid his dick between the crack of her ass. Doing this had India pushing into him even more while rolling her hips and simultaneously shaking her ass against him. Glancing over her shoulder, she gave him a seductive smile behind heavy eye lids. A moan left her mouth from the anticipation of what was about to happen again. The feeling had India's stomach tight and her pussy throbbing.

## Cum For Me

Jay'Shawn began stroking himself while slapping India's ass, causing it to jiggle even more. When he made his way to her opening, he pushed deeply inside of her sexual walls. At the same time, his hand came back down on her ass, causing her pussy muscles to squeeze tightly around his dick. Pulling out once more, he thrust back inside her fast and hard starting with deep, short strokes.

India didn't miss a beat as she threw her ass back on him going stroke for bounce. She ground hard against him while gripping his hips, trying to pull him as deeply inside of her as possible.

Jay's hand snaked around her neck pulling her up as he gripped her chin. He turned her face sideways, bringing their lips together. India continued her bounce as he played with her breasts. Not once did his hips stop their brutal thrust. If anything they became harder, making it impossible for her to kiss him back. The pleasurable moans spilled from her mouth.

"Ah, ah, ah, ah, ooh, ooh!" India's pants grew louder once Jay'Shawn's hand moved to her sexual treasure box. His fingers played with her pearl. Her body immediately started to tighten as her pussy muscles milked his dick faster. Her ass muscle tightened causing her body to shake as her orgasm ripped through her body. Jay held onto her tighter, his thrusts becoming frantic. With three powerful thrusts, he too released his seeds deeply inside India once again.

"Fuck, shawdy. You gon' have a nigga draggin' yo' ass down south," he stated, falling back on the seat before pulling India on top of him.

Cuddling into his chest, India straddled his hips as her fingers caressed his collar bone to his shoulder. After kissing his chest, she glanced up at him laughing as his words sank in.

"Hmm, is that so?" she asked, stretching her neck up to bite at his chin.

"Hell yeah! I'm serious as fuck yo'. Shitt, you shoulda been thinkin' 'bout it too. I told yo' ass that when I was locked up before I even got out." He refreshed her memory while massaging her ass with both his hands.

"Honestly, I thought that was all talk. You know how niggas do."

"No the fuck I don't. I only know what the fuck I do, and I don't say shit I don't mean, period. Don't come comparing me to those fuck-ass niggas you used to dealin' with. Bullshit, I don't do, baby girl, you gon learn that," explained Jay'Shawn in a serious tone.

Moving to Memphis was something India had never thought about. Honesty, she didn't know how this thing with them would play out. Talking to him and catching feelings for him wasn't planned. Now that the subject of moving had been brought up, she didn't know what to say as many different scenarios started to play in her head.

*What if I move out there and he flips on me and becomes this entirely different person?* She thought.

She didn't know how this thing was going to go but moving was something she couldn't rush to do. Though she thought it, she didn't voice it.

Her only reply was a simple, "We'll talk about it later, okay? This isn't really the place to have that talk, don't you think?" Moving her finger in a circular motion around the truck had the both of them laughing.

Staring down at India, Jay'Shawn licked his lips with a slight nod of his head. To him everything was already set because she was moving to Memphis whether

her mind was set on the idea or not. He'd give her a month tops, to square shit away and say her goodbyes to her people before he brought her home with him where she belonged.

"We'll most definitely talk about it later." The seriousness in his voice didn't go unnoticed.

It actually made her smile that he wanted her to move with him. Staring up at him, once again their eyes locked. India's lips pursed together as her neck stretched up, kissing his lips. Jay'Shawn's head titled sideways as his mouth opened, deepening the kiss. His hand tightened on her ass and his dick became hard once more.

Lifting her ass up slightly, India's hand reached behind her, taking hold of his dick, stroking him to his full length then lining him up with her opening. Their lips broke apart as she eased down on him, breathing him in as he filled her completely.

Kissing down to India's neck, Jay'Shawn sucked and bit at the skin, leaving a trail of passion marks along his way from her collarbone to her chest. Their hips moved in sync. His upward thrust matched her bounce.

India's head went back as her hips started a back and forth grind, causing Jay'shawn's nails to dig into them. Leaning forward to her bouncing breasts, he took her right nipple inside his mouth, sucking while his tongue swirled around the little nub.

Their movement became faster, desperate as the pleasurable feeling built stronger once again. His balls tightened as India's pussy muscle began throbbing faster on his dick from the repeated hit to her sweet spot.

The locking of their lower bodies had India shaking as her nails dug in his chest. Her head tilted back as a loud

205

and long moan left her mouth from the strong orgasm that ripped through her body.

Jay's frantic thrusts soon turned into jerking as he too came long and hard with a long groan sounding in the back of his throat.

Neither said a thing as they lay limp on the backseat of the Navigator.

It wasn't long after India's breathing evened out and light snores could be heard from her very satisfied mouth.

Jay could do nothing but laugh. But he was just as tired and moving right now wasn't an option for him either. Shawdy laid that shit down without a doubt.

He was thankful she had fallen asleep before he did. Ain't no babe ever put him to sleep after a few nuts.

*Yeah I gotta gon' and cuff shawdy real fast,* he thought.

With that thought in mind, he too fell asleep, dick limp, balls aching and buried deep inside India's still pulsing sex.

# Chapter 7

"Indy, hurry yo slow ass up!" Jay'Shawn rushed, making India eyes roll up in her head as usual.

"I'm coming! Just give me one second," came her slow reply as she put on a light coat of eyeliner. Once she finished, she traced the pencil over the rim of her lips, then added some clear gloss. Rubbing her lips together, she popped them twice.

Moving to the full length mirror she took in her appearance, smoothing out the knee length silver dress, turning sideways. Taking herself in and liking what she saw, a smile formed on her lips.

"Bring yo ass on!" Jay yelled once again from the living room.

Grabbing her jacket, cellphone and black clutch bag, she was ready to go. Leaving out of the room going into the living room were Jay'Shawn was, she walked around the couch and stood in front of him just as his mouth opened to yell again.

"Fo' real?" She placed her hands on her hips.

"Hell yeah, wit' yo' slow ass." His eyes roamed for a few seconds before they jumped to the watch on his wrists. Looking back at her, he licked his lips.

"Nope, let's go," she said, holding her hands out for him to take. She already knew what he was thinking.

"What you noping about? I'm just saying you look good, is all."

India lips pursed together at the lie coming out of his mouth. She didn't doubt he wasn't serious about her looking good, but that wasn't all.

For the past two days since Jay'Shawn had been there, India had picked up on a lot of his traits. From his sex looks to his just wanna chill demeanor. His sex look and voice she'd learned quickly. She had to admit the low but deep tone with the added slanted eyes always had her pussy contracting.. But no matter how sexy he sounded, she wasn't about to have sex with him right now. Her poor kitty needed a break from the beast known as Jay'Shawn.

    The past couple of days they had been locked in her apartment jumping each other like rabbits. He really fucked her up last night as he brought up her avoiding his calls. He fucked her so hard and as he spanked her ass repeatedly. Though it was just last night, her ass cheeks still stung and her pussy was sensitive. She was a few seconds away from taking off the silky boy-short panties. But she was hella satisfied from the rough sexual punishment he gave her.

    Even though the sex was amazing the conversation was even better. Jay'Shawn kept India laughing with the crazy stories he'd tell her. Truthful or not, she didn't care. The shit was still crazy in a funny kind of way. But it also let her know he was a man not to be played with when it came to certain shit.

    India knew he was heavy in the streets but not brutally mixed in it. He never told her what happened out in Cali until last night before they had sex. Learning they had been best friends, she looked for any signs of regret for killing him, but she found none. He was neutral about the whole thing and talked as if it was nothing but a run in a park. He didn't go into details about what happened, simply said he did what needed to be done. She didn't know how to feel about that part of him, honestly.

    What India did know was that she was attached to him and was willing to deal with his life style if it meant being with him. Explaining this was something she couldn't do for the life of her, but she wanted Jay, so looking past his flaws was nothing. He was the first man she had ever clicked with on a friend type level before it became something sexual and even then it started with phone sex.

She was a big girl who could take care of herself, and if this was a mistake it was one she'd learn from, but so far it didn't feel like it.

Learning how cruel he could be, India had no doubt that she was gonna push the hell out of his buttons. She continued to promise him they were going to stay into it because of their strong personalities, neither ever willing to back out until the other had the last word. That alone, was going to be the ultimate challenge for the both of them.

"Stop, you play too much. Let's go," she said as he touched her breast.

"I didn't know you were putting this on, and hit my hand again I'mma choke yo' ass."

Rolling her eyes she stared at him while biting the inside of her lip. With his eyes locked with hers, his hand went to her breast again playing with the nipple causing it to stand out erect. His other hand moved down her stomach, going to the hem of her dress, then slipping underneath it. India's hand once again shot out, slapping his shoulder then pushing him away from her.

"Didn't I just tell you not to hit—"

"Yo' hand. You said don't hit your hand which I didn't. Now come on. I'm not about to play with you, Jay'Shawn. Come on now. You was just rushing me to leave," India whined as he grabbed her around the waist pulling her body to his.

"We can stay in, watch a movie and order some food in. What you think?"

From the look on his face and in his eyes, she knew he was serious. He was just trying to get some good-good. India knew it and she didn't mind being locked in the apartment with him, especially since he would be leaving in a few days to go back home.

"We can do that but we not having sex."

Jay's face scrunched up at her declaration.

"Well, shit, we might as well go out then."

Laughing, India pushed him down on the couch and then climbed into his lap. "Man shut the fuck up. I don't feel like going out now."

"Who the hell you tellin' to shut up?" He raised a brow. He was ready for her ass to say *you* so he could drop her on the damn floor.

"Nobody. You wanna help me take off my dress?" India asked not about to fall into whatever trap he was trying to set her up for.

"Mmm hmmm," he replied as his mind played the different positions he was about to have her in once he took her dress off.

"Bet, yo' ass do!" She got off of his lap, leaned down and pecked his lips. "I'll be right back." She left out of the living room.

Jay sat there stuck for a few seconds before he laughed it off. He had to admit it to himself they had been going at it nonstop since he had been there. For that reason alone, he was gonna give his shawdy a break, but come 12AM her ass was fair game.

"Indy, what you wanna eat?" He walked into the bedroom and flopped on the bed, and watched as she undressed.

"It don't matter. We could call in something or I can whip some taco's up if you gotta a taste for it." She volunteered as she pulled on a yellow beater then a pair of black shorts.

"Yeah, you can gone hook that up." He pulled her onto him and then rolled on top of her.

"You gonna help?" India asked before puckering up her lips.

Staring at her for the longest time, he shook his head. He was never the lovey-dovey type but with India he didn't mind it, and he honestly didn't know how to feel about it, or the new found feelings he was having for her. Yeah, she most definitely had her hooks deep in him.

## Chapter 8
### Two Months Later

"Mmmm, Jay'Shawn, ooh baby." India moaned out as she gripped the nape of his neck, grinding her pussy against his mouth and fingers. He sucked on her pearl as his fingers moved deeply inside her, stroking her sweet spot before rubbing her pelvis bone and pressing down.

The action had India feeling like she was actually getting fucked. Her hips were raised up off of the bed and her thighs began shaking as she began to squirt. Jay'Shawn's fingers moved faster and his mouth sucked harder, causing India's pleasurable cries to bounce off the bedroom walls. Her body gyrated violently just like he wanted it to. Removing his finger and mouth from her pussy, he quickly sat up.

Placing his erect dick at her opening, he thrust deep inside her pulsing body. Loving the feel of her pussy gripping and sucking him in deeper. Rolling India on her side, holding her right leg up, his pelvis slapped against her ass as he continued his pleasurable assault on her body. He kissed her calf and while holding her thigh he slid his down to her sex going to her sensitive clit. His fingers pressed against the little pearl rubbing.

"Ah, ah, ooh, sssss, noo. Oh, My God! Oh, My God, Oh! My God! Ooh, ooh, sssss, mmmm." Biting into the sheets, India once again let out a string of muffled moans. Spitting out the sheet her forehead pressed into the mattress as she grabbed her hair. "Ooh, shit. Jay, ah, baby." India was about to lose her damn mind from the constant pleasure gyrating through her body. Her pussy milked his dick faster as she once again came hard.

## Cum For Me

India didn't know what the hell Jay'Shawn was taking, but his sex game had been on a new high as of lately.

"Ooh," India moaned out as he rolled her body over once more.

Grabbing her hips, he raised her ass up in the air. Spreading her cheeks, he spit on her anus as he slapped his dick against her ass and smeared his spit over her hole. Spitting again, he stroked his dick a few times before lining it up with her anus. Feeling him there, India instinctively squeezed her ass tightly together.

"Nuh, uh, shawdy. You gotta relax. I got you, baby girl. Gon' relax." Jay'Shawn's voice was calm but lustful as his fingers dug into her ass and lower back, massaging deeply. Doing so had India relaxing almost instantly, causing low moans to leave her mouth from the work of his fingers. Feeling her muscles loosen up, he leaned forward kissing her lower back before biting her left butt cheek.

India once again moaned while pushing her ass back. Smiling, he sat up, slapping her right cheek. Bringing his dick back to her anus and lining the tip with her hole. He fed her ass inch by inch until his pelvis was pressed flat against her ass. Pulling out, he repeated his movement until India started rolling her hips giving him the go. That was all he needed.

Jay'Shawn's hips thrust into India's ass as his nails dug into her skin, causing a friction of both pleasure and pain. The hard thrusts of his pelvis caused India to wanna meet him half way while shaking her ass, throwing it back on him. But Jay wasn't having it tonight. His hips rotated, moving in a circular motion. Grabbing a handful of India's hair, he pulled her up. Tilting her head back, his mouth went to her neck, sucking and biting at the skin as his hand went to her breasts, squeezing, pinching and pulling at her nipple.

India's head lay back on his shoulder, her mouth parted as he bounced her on his dick. Her chest heaved up and down. Cry after cry left her mouth from his assault on her body.

Jay'Shawn was loving every bit of it as he pumped to get her off as well as himself. Spreading her legs he thrusts two fingers inside her pussy trying to find her sweet spot. It didn't take him long to find it. Once his fingers hit it, India's body jerked a bit harder and she gripped his wrist.

"No, no, no, ooh, ooh, Shawn, ooh." Feeling the contraction of her pussy on his fingers, he picked up his pace, making India's cries become louder as her body started to shake.

His pace became frantic, his hips jerking, pushing his dick harder inside her.

Once India's ass muscles squeezed tighter around his dick, he lost his nut deep inside her ass at the same time she released her juices, coating his fingers.

Leaning forward on India, his lips pressed against her shoulder twice before he rolled over on his side bringing her with him. His hand began drawing invisible circles along her sweaty skin as his lips pressed against her sweat drenched neck and shoulder.

He wasn't gonna let India fuck him like she had when they first met. Nope, he couldn't. India's ass had become too cocky after a while and he had to put her in her place and let her know who was running shit. As of lately, he'd been doing a helluva a job. He felt kinda bad for doing his baby girl like that, but he had to admit their sex was mind boggling.

## Cum For Me

India's body was hot. She couldn't move as she lay there panting heavily. He was most definitely laying pipe like no other. He simply couldn't be out done.

India began to hate her cocky demeanor also, but at the same time she loved it for the simple fact she was never unsatisfied when it came to sex with him.

For the past two months after moving down to Memphis, Tenseness, their sex lives and everything in their personal lives was simply amazing. Everything felt as if it was moving way too fast then at the same time not fast enough. It was like they were in a honeymoon state, one that India didn't want to ever end.

India rolled over to face him, throwing her leg over his. Neither said a word. Both speechless, they just stared at one another, still panting heavily.

Slowly their breathing started to even out, becoming in sync as they continued to stare at the other minutes longer.

"I love you," both said at the same time. Thinking it coincidence, they laughed it off as nothing.

"I love you too," again the pair spoke at the same time. Again they laughed.

Jay'Shawn being the first to get the feeling back in his body rolled on top of India. Staring down at her, he couldn't think of any other woman to have in his life. He fell for India raw and hard and there was no going back for him. He wanted her, and the thought of someone else having her sent a string of violent thoughts to his head. Yeah, he had to lock shawdy down, and fast just in case she came to the realization this wasn't what she wanted.

"Marry me—" As soon as those words left his mouth, India pushed him off of her, hopped off the bed and ran into the bathroom. Her reaction fucked him up and he became pissed until he heard her getting sick. Worried, he quickly jumped out of the bed and ran into the bathroom, thinking she might be sick from her body being dehydrated from their rough play.

"Indy, baby, you good?" The worry in voice was evident.

India wasn't good. She'd been keeping a secret for the past two days, afraid to tell him because it was still earlier in their relationship. She was also scared he'd flip out and throw out false accusations. She'd seen it done so many times with niggas who was in his line of work. She was scared his reaction would ruin the honeymoon state they were in.

"Come on, baby girl, you good." Jay'Shawn wiped her mouth with tissue before pressing the bathroom cup filled with water to her lips.

After she finished the cup of water, he pulled her up from the floor and sat her on the counter and then went to run the bath water.

"Shawn." She paused once she got his attention. Her mouth opened then closed again. Not knowing how to tell him, she figured now was the best time if any. "Jay'Shawn." He once again he looked up at her. "Shawn, I'm pregnant."" She felt so relieved getting it off her chest.

India hadn't been feeling well for a few weeks and she'd gone to the health clinic and learned she was two and a half months pregnant. She'd gotten pregnant on their first meeting.

Jay'Shawn turned off the bath water while turning to face India. His brow raised as his head tilted sideways. "What?" He asked in a confused tone.

"I said I'm pregnant…"

Cum For Me

***The End***

## A Long Time Cumming
### By
# *Ca$h*

Sonja sat on the sofa in her living room, sipping on a glass of iced tea and listening to the old Mary J. Blige and Method Man's classic *All I Need.* That song always took her back down memory lane to 1994 when she was a twenty-one year old hottie and so in love with a nigga named Reasun. That young, handsome, thug had come from New York to Fort Worth, Texas and put the game in a headlock. During his brief rule in the streets, muthafuckas had to get down or lay down.

  Niggas learned quickly that Reasun would push a fool's cap back without hesitation. Every time someone mentioned his name or told a tale of how he had left another rival's body bullet-riddled and slumped, Sonja's panties would get sticky wet. There was something, back then, about a killah that put fear in other killahs that turned her the fuck on.

  Sonja recalled longingly how Reasun's name was on the tongue of every girl in the hood, but she was the one he had chosen. Every single time that big, black hunk of a man called her *Ma,* his deep baritone sent a surge of sexual energy coursing through her body. Her nipples would harden at the mere touch of his hand. When he wrapped her in his powerful arms and kissed her, Sonja's clit would jump out of its delicate hood and go crazy inside of her panties. And when he entered her with all of that manhood that he packed, her pussy squirted cream all over his thick, hard shaft.

Strongly reminiscing, she had to squeeze her thighs together tightly to keep her coochie quiet.

*Lawd, that man knew how to make me scream his name.*

Sonja inhaled deeply then let her breath out slowly. Their love had been a six month whirlwind of dangerous excitement and endless days of counting money, whipping up product, and sucking and fucking until the sun came up, then they would fall asleep, spooned together and satiated just to repeat the process the next day and the next.

The sex was absolutely intoxicating, but the one thing that stood out most in her memory was that Reasun had been a one woman man. She never had to worry about him disrespecting her with the next bitch or slinging dick all over Forth Worth. In return, Sonja had been his ride or die long before the title became cliché. Back then, a bitch had to earn wifey status, good pussy and a sick head game wasn't enough. She had held money, drugs, and secrets of his that could've sent her to prison for a very long time. But the way he had held *her* made it so very worth the risks.

*Damn, baby, it's been twenty years and I still miss you.*

She wrapped both hands around the glass and closed her eyes as bittersweet memories of her one and only love brought a smile to her face and tears to her eyes. Enemies had ambushed him up on the hill on Wellesley Ave. and left him with his brains splattered on the windshield of his Benz. The day Reasun died, a part of her soul had perished along with him. Many said she hadn't smiled since. One thing for certain, she definitely hadn't loved again and she doubted that she ever would.

Sonja swallowed her pain as Mary sang beautifully.

*Like sweet morning dew*
*I took one look at you*
*And it was plain to see*
*You were my destiny*
*With you I'll spend my time*
*I'll dedicate my life, I'll sacrifice for you*
*Dedicate my life for you*

    Sonja sang right along with Mary. And when Method Man started rapping, she matched him word for word. She recalled her and Reasun at Como Lake, sitting on the hood of his ride bumping that song.
    Every ho' that walked past cut their eyes at her enviously. The dudes nodded their heads at Reasun in salute. Sonja had loved basking in the glow of his immense street reputation. Her nigga was a hood celebrity and everybody recognized her as his girl. Then, in the snap of a finger it was all snatched away and she was shipping his body back to New York.
    Sonja still wondered which one of those bitch ass niggas ultimately betrayed her man. She had never found out. But neither would she ever give up her search for the identities of his killers, although it seemed as fruitless as her search for a love that would help her not miss him so much.
    There had been others since the day her soul died, but none of them had ever been able to measure up to her boo. In fact, in comparison to him their hustles were petty and their glow was dim. In bed, those nigga's dick games was trash. Besides, if a man's aura didn't get her juices flowing long before they hit the sheets the thrill just wouldn't be there. And the way men were built these days, they wanted her and every other rwoman with a big ass.

The fuck if she was going to be a muthafucka's side piece. Reasun had shown her that she deserved to be the one and only.

Five years ago, Sonja had decided that until she met a man that could measure up to him, she would be celibate and please herself. She had a cachè of toys upstairs in her bedroom to help her along.

*And I'm about to use one of those bad boys tonight,* she thought as she sat her iced tea on a coaster on the end table and rose up from the couch with her pussy already throbbing in anticipation.

Sonja's supple ass jiggled as she went to close and lock the front door, which she had left ajar to let a little fresh air in. Standing behind the locked screen door looking out onto the streets, she saw the familiar movements up and down the block where she resided on the hill in Como, a neighborhood on the Westside of Fort Worth. Stylish trucks and cars drove by bumping an array of rap music and young boys hung out on the block, hustling incognito. And at any moment the clap of gunshots could erupt and disturb the tenuous peace.

Sonja had lived in this hood her entire life, so the ever-present danger that lurked all around her didn't faze her one bit. Besides, she had a baby nine-millimeter sitting close by and if any drama came to her front door, she was going to stamp that shit *return to sender*.

A smile crept on Sonja's face. At forty-one years old she was still gangsta. She brought her hand up to shield her eyes against the intense rays of the June sun. Looking across the street she saw two men who she recognized, standing nose to nose, apparently engaged in a dispute. One of them was KeyShawn, a twenty-eight year old D-boy that reminded her of Reasun in many ways. He was well over six feet, muscular, and as black as Texas tea. KeyShawn had a few trap houses in Como and he was known to rule over them with an AK-47 that he didn't hesitate to let spit.

KeyShawn's arms moved animatedly and his voice boomed, "Bruh, if you don't go get my cheddar—every last dollar of it—I'ma make the coroner call your family with some sad news. Test my muthafuckin' get down if you want to!" He grabbed ahold of the man's collar and shoved a ratchet in his face.

A few seconds later, Sonja watched as KeyShawn led the man named Bo inside a house. She shook her head, wondering why Bo would test a nigga like KeyShawn's gangsta.

*Doesn't he know he's messing with a beast?* Sonja felt her pussy tingle. Ten or fifteen years ago she would've cuffed KeyShawn and helped him refine some on that goon shit. With her at his side he could lock the game down.

Closing the door and heading upstairs, Sonja couldn't help carrying images of KeyShawn's young butt with her. She wondered if he had a thorough chick on his team or if the wrong lil' bitch was going to be his downfall. She hoped like hell he wouldn't let the latter happen. KeyShawn was a real nigga and deserved much better.

Sonja knew that because one day, almost a year ago, *One time*—as they referred to the police—was all over the block looking for him in connection with a shooting. Sonja had hid KeyShawn in her house for nearly forty-eight hours until the block cooled down and the cops dispersed. During those two days, they had spent a lot of time talking about the game and sharing their ideas on life in general. Sonja was left with the impression that KeyShawn was a serious young man with strong street principles and his seasoned swag was a definite turn on. Often, Sonja chided herself for even thinking about that young boy in that way.

She walked to her window, parted the blinds, and looked up the street just in time to see KeyShawn headed to his car clutching a shoe bag. She hadn't heard any gunshots, so she concluded that Bo must've wised up and paid what he owed. *Good*, she thought as she allowed the part in the blinds to close.

An hour later, the sun had retreated and the sky darkened. Sonja was enjoying a relaxing bubble bath. Vanilla scented candles burned and the soft blue lighting in the bathroom jibed well with the sounds of Maxwell that played from the iPod in her bedroom.

Imagining her ideal man singing the lyrics softly in her ear, Sonja leaned her head back and caressed her nipples. They instantly became taut and ached to be sucked. She lifted one of her 40DD's up to her mouth and ran her tongue around the nipple.

"Ummmm," Sonja moaned.

She parted her thighs, sunk her hand down into the bath water and let it slowly creep up her thick, red, luscious thighs to her pulsating pussy. Her lower lips swelled as she sensuously parted them and delicately ran her finger up and down the length of her opening. Heat rose up her body and caused her lips to quiver as she moaned loudly. Her honeypot was on fire.

Sonja dipped a finger inside of her steaming vagina and her ass rose up to meet her probing digit. "Sssssss." She imagined that her finger was Reasun's skilled tongue. "Baby, baby, baby," she cried out.

Sonja's legs opened wider and her finger sank deeper inside of her buttery cup. Her tight pussy gripped and massaged it like it was nine inches of male beef. As her passion built up, she removed her sticky finger from her kitty and ran it tenderly up her split until it came in contact with her excited clitoris.

The moment she touched that sensitive little bud, lights exploded inside of her head. She circled her pearl familiarly until her hips rocked back and forth with her manipulations. Her mouth opened and she let out a long wail. Damn, she needed something black, thick and long inside of her.

Sonja continued to rub her clit until it throbbed. The faster she rubbed, the harder it grew. She used her thumb to tantalize the slippery bud while inserting two fingers from the same hand inside of her hot canal. She knew exactly where her weak spot was and her fingers went straight to that small spongy area. Oh, how she wanted to explode!

"Eat me," she uttered, trying to summon up memories of Reasun pushing her legs over her head and sucking her pussy like it was a sweet, delicious peach. Usually, that was all it took and Sonja would erupt like a volcano. But this time she was unable to picture his face. To her surprise a different but very familiar face appeared in her imagery. When that young, dark chocolate, thug covered her pussy with his thick lips, she sucked in her breath and her head felt dizzy. "Oh, my God! Don't stop!" she cried out.

Sonja squeezed her eyes tighter and tried to freeze his image in her mind, but somehow it disappeared completely. "Noooooooo!" she groaned in frustration. She tried to will his thuggishly handsome face to reappear. Her thumb rubbed rapidly and her two fingers delved deeper into her gooey G-spot. But with no image in her mind she could not reach a climax.

# Cum For Me

Thoroughly unsated, and with her V on fire, Sonja got out of the tub, dried off, and hurried to her room to retrieve her toys.
*Fuck that shit.*
Tonight, she was going to use her Mandingo dildo. That muthafucka would fill her up very nicely and hopefully give her the body-shaking climax that she needed.
As she brought the long, thick, black instrument out of the top drawer of her nightstand and unwrapped it from its protective cloth, she lifted it to her mouth and licked the bulbous head.
"Daddy, I want you to punish mama's pussy tonight. You hear me?" She spoke to the dildo in a low, seductive tone as if it was the thugged out nigga that she still craved.
Giddy and hot with a wet pussy that was in bad need of relief, Sonja made her way to the bed. She laid on her back and placed a pillow under her bodacious ass, tilting it up for a good self-fuck. Just as she brought the tip of the dildo to her pearl tongue, the intrusive sound of her doorbell interrupted her stimulation.
"Mannnn, what the fuck!" she yelled. "Ugh!"
Sonja laid still and prayed that whoever was at the door would get the hell on somewhere and let a bitch get a nut. But the fuck if they did. The untimely visitor laid on the doorbell, intent on getting her to answer. "Jesus muthafuckin' Christ," she growled.
Reluctantly, she hopped out of bed, threw on a short robe, and stomped downstairs. Without checking the peephole, she snatched the door open and stood there with her hands on her wide hips and a scowl on her pretty red face.

"Don't shoot me," he said. His deep, manly voice melted her frown instantaneously. She stood looking up into the face of that nigga who had just visited her imagination. After a full minute he said, "You gon' stand there all night or you gon' invite me in?" The little smile on his face underscored the lightness of his tone. And that gorgeously black muthafucka had the nerve to have a deep dimple in his right cheek. It was her first time noticing that.

Sonja could hardly talk, her pussy was having a fit and the breeze of the night air caused her nipples to poke out of the sheer material of her robe. She let out a slow breath and stepped aside without saying a word.

KeyShawn's long dreads hung down his back as he walked inside with a backpack slung over his broad shoulders. As he took a seat on her couch, he could hear music coming from upstairs. "Oh, my bad. Did I interrupt anything?" He rose up off of the couch, ready to leave without stating his purpose for stopping by.

Sonja almost tackled him. "Not at all. I'm here alone as always," she emphasized. A hand on his sculpted chest encouraged him to sit back down. She took a seat in an overstuffed chair across from him, wondering why she had felt the need to stress she was always alone. "Uh—" she stuttered "what can I do for you? Do you need a place to hide out again? I mean, if the police are—"

He put a large hand up to cut her off. "Nah, it's nothin' like that. Not really."

Sonja watched his lips move and the tingle between her thighs made her squirm around in her seat. She studied those long fingers of KeyShawn's and imagined them going in and out of her excited pussy.

*Damn, I'm acting like a cougar. Calm down,* she chastised herself.

# Cum For Me

"You okay?" he asked, picking up on her discomfort but unaware of what was causing it.

All Sonja could do was nod her head up and down. She was afraid to open her mouth or a primal cry might have escaped. KeyShawn licked his lips. "Well, I know this is going to catch you off guard but just hear me out." He sat the backpack on the floor between his feet and scooted up to the edge of the sofa. Leaning forward and taking both of her hands in his, he spoke with the confidence of one who was used to getting what he wanted. "Tomorrow I have to turn myself into the feds to begin serving a five year bid. I came to make you my woman before I go away."

At first Sonja was speechless—that had surely came out of left field. Then she regained her cool. "Just like that, huh?" she asked.

"Nah, there's a little more to it," he replied.

"You mind sharing?"

"Not at all, baby." He stroked her palms with his fingers sending sexual electricity straight to her moistening center. "Like I said, I gotta go do a bid. I don't have a soul out here I can trust. I got a baby mama, but I don't fuck with her like that. I take care of my seed but that's it. Every dollar that I've saved up is inside this bag." He patted the backpack on the floor. "I've shed and spread blood for those old dead white men in there and there's no way I'm leaving it with any of the thirsty muthafuckas I know. I wanna leave it with you because I know your story and I know you're real. I don't think you would fuck over me," he said and looked into her eyes for confirmation.

Sonja gave it to him unfettered. "I wouldn't," she assured. "But baby, you don't have to make me your woman to protect your money. I would never do you dirty."

"I know that. Trust me, that's not why I wanna make you my woman. Ever since we spent those two nights talking and sharing our stories, I've thought about you constantly. I kept trying to wait until I built my weight up on the streets, then I was going to step to you. But life didn't play out like that. So I'm here now, asking you to be my mine. With a woman like you by my side, when I return to the streets I'll go straight to the top."

Sonja pondered what he had just said. She couldn't deny that his young ass was worth the risk. If he was serious, she would have herself a real boss in the making. With her wisdom at his disposal they could truly prosper. Five years was a long time, but the way her loyalty was set up, she could do that shit without blinking an eye. But what if she dedicated herself to him and he came home five years later on the bullshit? Or maybe he was already running game, she considered.

"KeyShawn, if you just want to fuck tonight, we can do that. I'm on my grown woman. And to be honest, I was just thinking about you. It's been a long time since I've had sex and I'm dying for some good dick. Just promise me a nut and we're good," she said, unabashed.

KeyShawn flashed a little smile and stroked his chin. "Baby, this ain't about a nut. Let's keep it one hundred. I could get that anywhere. I'm trying to make you mine." He gazed into her eyes with his pretty, light browns, reiterating his genuineness. The words that followed came from a place in his heart that had remained untapped until now. The more he talked, the more Sonja could hear the sincerity in his voice, but she had to be absolutely certain.

She got up and sat beside him, pressing her exposed thigh against his leg. Staring into his beautiful orbs, she didn't sugarcoat her response. "KeyShawn, I'm in my forties. I don't have time to play games. If you really want a rider, I'm that bitch. I'll hold you down while you're doing your bid, but I don't go for any fuckery. You get one chance to betray my trust and I drop you like it's hot."

"I already know," he smirked. "But you ain't talking 'bout nothin'. Now, close your eyes."

Sonja complied. She felt him take her hand and slip a ring on her finger. Then he kissed her lips and told her to open her eyes. The single carat diamond ring sparkled. "My promise to you," he explained with his dimpled smile.

Sonja looked down at the promise ring and felt twenty-one years old all over again. She was blushing so hard, her face turned red. Her arms went around his neck and she pulled him into a passionate kiss. With their tongues interlocked, she could taste the trace of weed on his buds. A thug wasn't a thug if he didn't smoke that *killa*. Sonja sucked KeyShawn's tongue with pent up hunger.

Breaking the lip lock, she said, "That's my promise to *you*, baby."

KeyShawn explained some particulars regarding his surrender tomorrow and what he expected from her, then he stood up to leave. Sonja stood up too. They hugged for a long time before they broke the embrace. KeyShawn kissed her again then started for the door. Sonja reached out and grabbed his arm. He turned around and looked down at her from his 6'3 height.

Sonja said nothing. She reached up with a delicate hand and pushed her robe off of her shoulders, allowing it to fall to the floor. Her body wasn't as flawless as it had been in her twenties but she had kept herself up well. She was not ashamed to give him an eyeful of what now belonged to him.

KeyShawn's mouth fell open when he took in her sexy nakedness. Her big titties were an aphrodisiac by themselves with their perfectly round areolas circling her long, taut nipples. His eyes then traveled down her body to a 32-inch waistline that flared out to wide, gunslinger hips. Her fat, bald mound stuck up like a ripe cantaloupe begging for him to taste its sweet nectar. He lifted his eyes back to hers and saw a burning desire in her gaze.

Sonja's words echoed her look. "Nigga, you're not going away for five years without giving me some dick before you leave. Don't make a bitch act up on Day 1," she threatened, half seriously.

KeyShawn replied by swooping her up into his arms and carrying her upstairs. Sonja wrapped her arms around his neck and directed him to the master bedroom. Maxwell was still crooning as they entered the room. The lighting further set the mood for the sexual escapades that lay ahead. KeyShawn gently laid her on the bed and began taking off his clothes. Sonja brushed the dildo onto the floor and savored the show. His body was beautiful. He had the long chiseled frame of an athlete, with no visible fat at all. When he removed his boxers, what swung between that nigga's legs should have been against the law. Now it was Sonja's mouth that hit the floor.

"Don't get scared now," he teased, shaking what looked like a mule's dick at her. "I'ma need you to get back on your grown woman and handle this python I'm about to introduce you to."

Wasn't any punk in Sonja. She had gone without it too long to run from the challenge. "Bring that muthafucka here," she replied, sitting up and motioning with a finger.

## Cum For Me

KeyShawn didn't have to be asked twice. His eyes was focused on that plumpness between Sonja's legs as he stepped toward her.

Sonja took ahold all of that dick and brought it up to her mouth. *I'm about to show this young boy what he'll have waiting for him when he comes home.*

She couldn't quite wrap her hands around his entire girth, and even both hands didn't cover the length, but her stroke made his rod swell rapidly. She slowly ran her tongue around the glistening head, stopping to taste the precum that seeped out.

"Umm, Daddy," she moaned. "I'm about to suck the hell out of this dick."

"Do that shit."

Sonja ran her tongue all the way down his lengthy pipe. It grew longer and stiffened like lead. She took him into her, hot, wet mouth and slurped loudly as both hands stroked in unison. She let her spit run down from the corners of her mouth, coating his rod completely and then she cleaned it off expertly. Looking up at him with sexy eyes, she licked the head like it was the tip of an ice cream cone.

KeyShawn rose up on his toes and grabbed a handful of her hair. "Spit on this dick. Wet that muthafucka up real good," he said in a guttural tone.

Sonja stepped her head game up, one thousand. She took the dick deep into her mouth and worked her jaw and throat muscles in such harmony, KeyShawn's knees wobbled. "You like this head, baby?" she mumbled around a mouthful of thick, hard meat.

"Fuckin' right, I do."

Sonja swallowed his dick so far down her throat, she began gagging. But that didn't slow her down one bit.

It had been so long since she'd tasted real beef, she didn't ever want to spit it out.

KeyShawn was close to bustin' a fat ass nut, but he didn't want that. Hell no! That first one was going inside that juicy pussy of hers. He drew his hips back, pulling his dick from inside of Sonja's slick, warm cavern. She gripped it in protest, not wanting to release that mammoth slab of steel.

"Noooo," she pouted.

"Don't worry, I'ma give it back to you," he promised. "Lay down and spread your pussy open for your nigga. Let me see that sweet pinkness, so I can suck it and coat my tongue with your juices." He stroked himself as she followed his command.

Sonja wiggled her ass into position and theatrically opened her legs, throwing one up on her shoulder. She reached down with one hand and parted both of her moist nether lips. Delectable pink goodness winked at KeyShawn as she made her womb breath in and out.

He licked his lips and dove in head first. His lips were soft and patient. His tongue and fingers probed artfully. In seconds, KeyShawn had her clutching the sheets and cursing the heavens for creating a muthafucka with head so goddamn fiyah. Sonja thought that she was going to die.

"Ooh, Daddy. Sssssss. Do that shit." She bit down on her lip to stop herself from screaming.

The tip of KeyShawn's tongue traced small circles around her swollen clit and sent a bolt of lightning shooting from her pussy to her brain. Sonja cried out his name. When she felt him ease a thumb in her asshole, she went crazy.

## Cum For Me

"Yes, nigga, do that. Drive a bitch out of her goddamn mind." Her plea mirrored his intentions.

KeyShawn knew that after tonight he wouldn't be getting any pussy for sixty months, so he decided to put work in on that ass. He sucked her flower gently until it stood up in full bloom. Her rose bud hardened with every flick of his tongue. In her heightening passion, Sonja released the sheets and wrapped her hands in his dreads, pulling his whole face into her wide open kitty.

"Eat this pussy, baby. Eat it like it's your last muthafuckin' mean," she panted.

He licked her candy from the very top down to the bottom. Then he did something that blew Sonja's mind. He pushed both of her legs over her head and started eating her brown eye. Sonja was gone! That shit felt freaky good. She absolutely loved a man who wasn't afraid to be nasty in bed.

"Oh, yeah, Daddy, put that tongue all the way inside my ass. Hell, yeah, you nasty muthafucka, eat this good booty hole."

KeyShawn tilted her ass up higher and devoured her brownie. As he ate her booty, he fucked her sopping wet pussy with two, long fingers. "Oh, God. Oh, God. Oh, goddamn God. I'm 'bout to cummmmm," she wailed in ecstasy. "I'm cumminggggg."

KeyShawn kept sucking that crinkly hole and punishing that cootie with his fingers until Sonja released her sweet juices all over his face. "Gimme some more," he said, continuing to take her higher and higher into bliss.

Sonja came all over his face a second time, but she was not done yet. Now she was greedy for a third orgasm and she wanted to feel that steel inside of her throbbing coochie.

233

"Fuck me, baby. I need that dick in my tight pussy. I want you to beat this pussy until I can't walk."

Rising up and stroking himself to a maximum erection, KeyShawn ordered, "Face down, ass up."

Eagerly, Sonja assumed the position. Her big, red, round ass welcomed anything he had in mind. KeyShawn positioned himself behind her. He spat in his hand then lubricated that python for easier entrance. Gently, he ran the head up and down her saturated love canal, coating it with her natural moisture.

Sonja sucked in her breath when she felt that bulb-like head part her petals. Her pussy slowly received his push and then it gripped him with virgin-like tightness. Her shit was so hot, KeyShawn had to grit his teeth and close his eyes to hold back the nut that desperately wanted to spray from his hose. He gripped her hips and held her still until he was back in control of himself.

The dick sunk deeper, all up inside of Sonja's slippery walls. "Give me that dick, nigga. I want you to pop the elastic inside this bitch," she said in a gravelly tone, filled with burgeoning desire to be manhandled.

"Hush. This is where I talk all the shit and you just moan and try to run." He thrust his hips forward, filling her with all ten inches as he began to pound that pussy vigorously. It sucked his dick like her mouth had done earlier. But now KeyShawn was in control and when he hit the bottom of her sweet box, she tried to crawl forward and escape the pain that came with the pleasure. "Who's *that* nigga?" He pulled her back onto the dick and slapped her ass.

"You are, KeyShawn!"
*Whack! Whack!*

## Cum For Me

"Where are you trying to go? Don't run, take this dick like a big girl."

Sonja couldn't escape so she bossed up and threw that punanny back at him with zest. "Get it, baby. Beat it." The fuck sounds emanating from the smacking of their bodies and the intense sexual energy between them was loud and squishy. KeyShawn had her hot box talking to him.

Sonja backed that ass up on him and made her cheeks clap as he drove in and out of her with no restraint. Her walls stretched to accommodate his humongous size and the friction inside of her pussy caused her love to come down in a torrent of cries. All she could do was scream out his name as she creamed all up and down his powerful shaft.

Beads of sweat covered KeyShawn's chest and his face contorted as his sacs filled with semen. His blood engorged phallus became a weapon of destruction. He forced her thighs further apart and long stroked in and out of her sticky goo. That pussy felt like a full pardon.

"Nut in me, Daddy. Nut inside your woman," she beckoned.

This time KeyShawn couldn't hold out. He leaned forward, wrapped both arms around her waist, and put a hunch in his back. Pounding her like a jackhammer, he exploded with an animalistic growl that shook the bedroom walls. Sonja tightened her muscles and massaged every last seed out of his loins that he had to give.

Later, they lay in each other's arms perfectly satiated and feeling as if they were bonded together. They talked well into the night before falling peacefully asleep. When morning came, they made slow, passionate love. Sonja was glutinous and she wanted him to dream about her every day he was away. She climbed up on his dick and taught his young ass a thing or two as the sounds of Keyshia Cole's *Complete Me* played from her iPod.

When the time came for KeyShawn to turn himself in, she drove him to where he was scheduled to surrender. In the parking lot of the building, they hugged like longtime lovers.

"Hold me down, baby," he said needlessly. Sonja was a true rider.

"I will, Daddy," she vowed. "I'm going to show you how a real bitch gets down for her man. By the time you come home, that $150,000.00 will be a half million. Watch your girl boss up."

KeyShawn had no doubt that she would do everything she promised. He kissed her one last time then headed inside. Sonja kept waving goodbye until he disappeared from sight. When she got back in the car and pulled off, her pussy jumped as she replayed the past twelve hours in her mind. She squeezed her legs together tightly. Yep, the pussy was officially on lock until her young boss came home.

*The End.*

Cum For Me

Ca$h & Company

## Coming Soon From Lock Down Publications

LOVE KNOWS NO BOUNDARIES **II**

By **Coffee**

THE KING CARTEL

By **Frank Gresham**

BONDS OF DECEPTION

By **Lady Stiletto**

THE DEVIL WEARS TIMBS **II**

By **Tranay Adams**

DON'T FU#K WITH MY HEART **II**

By **Linnea**

BOSS'N UP **II**

By **Royal Nicole**

## Available Now

LOVE KNOWS NO BOUNDARIES

By **Coffee**

SLEEPING IN HEAVEN, WAKING IN HELL **I & II**

By **Forever Redd**

THE DEVIL WEARS TIMBS

By **Tranay Adams**

DON'T FU#K WITH MY HEART

Cum For Me

By **Linnea**

BOSS'N UP

By **Royal Nicole**

A DANGEROUS LOVE

By **J Peach**

Ca$h & Company

## BOOKS BY LDP'S CEO, CA$H

TRUST NO MAN

TRUST NO MAN 2

TRUST NO MAN 3

BONDED BY BLOOD

SHORTY GOT A THUG

A DIRTY SOUTH LOVE

THUGS CRY

THUGS CRY 2

TRUST NO BITCH

TRUST NO BITCH 2

TRUST NO BITCH 3

TIL MY CASKET DROPS

**Coming Soon**

TRUST NO BITCH (EYEZ' STORY)

THUGS CRY 3

BONDED BY BLOOD 2

Cum For Me

CPSIA information can be obtained
at www.ICGtesting.com
Printed in the USA
LVHW080849310519
619719LV00016B/286/P